SHAKESPEARE'S

TRAGEDY OF HAMLET.

WITH

INTRODUCTION, AND NOTES EXPLANATORY AND CRITICAL.

FOR USE IN SCHOOLS AND CLASSES.

BY THE

REV. HENRY N. HUDSON, LL.D.

———•———

BOSTON, U.S.A.:

GINN & COMPANY, PUBLISHERS.

1903

TYPOGRAPHY BY J. S. CUSHING & CO., BOSTON, U.S.A.

PRESSWORK BY GINN & CO., BOSTON, U.S.A.

PREFACE.

SINCE the first volume of my *School Shakespeare* made its appearance, which was about nine years ago, very considerable advances have been made in the way of furniture and preparation needful or desirable for such a work. This is especially the case with the play here presented in a new dress. And my own long and constant occupation in teaching classes in Shakespeare has, I would fain hope, now brought me a somewhat larger and riper fitness for doing what is requisite in this particular field. Moreover the stereotype plates of this play, as also of some others, have been so much and so often used for the pamphlet sections of the volume, that they have become not a little worn and defaced. These are the principal reasons for setting forth the present edition.

I still adhere to my old plan of foot-notes, instead of massing the annotation all together at the end of the play. This is because ample experience has assured me, beyond all peradventure, that whatever of explanation young students need of Shakespeare's text — and they certainly need a good deal — is much better every way when placed directly under the eye, so that they can hardly miss it ; and because at least nineteen in twenty of such pupils will pass over an obscure word or phrase without understanding it, rather than stay to look up the explanation in another part of the volume. In this instance, however, I have meant to exclude from the foot-notes all matter but what appeared fairly needful or useful for a proper understanding of the Poet's language and mean-ing. As will readily be seen from some of the foot-notes, I am indebted to Mr. JOSEPH CROSBY, of Zanesville, O., for most valuable aid towards this part of my task. The matter so used has been communicated to me in a private corre-spondence with that gentleman, running through several years, and extending over the whole field of Shakespeare, and throwing more light on dark and difficult passages than I have received from any other living commentator on the Poet.

Another advantage of the method of foot-notes is, that it operates as a wholesome restraint against overdoing the work of annotation. And surely, if we may judge from what has been done, it is so much easier to multiply superfluous notes than to keep within the bounds of what is fairly need-ful in this kind, that some such restraint seems eminently desirable. Shakespeare, it scarce need be said, has suffered a great deal from this sort of exegetical incontinence. And perhaps the tendency is stronger now then ever before to smother his workmanship beneath a mass of needless and even obstructive annotation. An inordinate fecundity of explanation is quite too much the order of the day. There have been divers instances, of late, where we find the gloss, I cannot say out-weighing, but certainly far out-bulking, the text. Surely it is better to leave students a little unhelped than thus to encumber them with superfluous help. These burdens of unnecessary comment are really a "weariness of the flesh"; and even hungry minds may well be repelled from a feast so overlaid with quenchers of the appetite. Nor have the Poet's editors yet got their minds untied from the old vice of leaving many of his darkest things unexplained, and of explaining a multitude of things that were better left to take care of themselves. For pupils ought not to be put to studying Shakespeare at all, until they have grown to such a measure of intelligence, that they may be safely presumed to know several things without being told.

Such being the case, or at least my view of the case, I am not without apprehension, that some excess may be justly charged upon what is here done. Self-restrained and sparing as I have meant to be, still there is a considerable addition to the number of notes given in my former edition. But, in the matter of annotation, it is not easy to strike just the right medium between too much and too little. Here, again, I have been mainly guided by the results of my own experience in teaching; aiming to give such and so many notes as I have found needful or conducive to a fair understanding of the Poet's thought.

In the present stage of Shakespearian study, I suppose it would hardly do, even in a book designed for school use, to leave the matter of textual comment and textual correction altogether untouched. Accordingly there will be found, at the end of the play, a body of CRITICAL NOTES, wherein I have drawn together whatever seemed necessary or desirable to be said in the way of textual criticism, and of comment on such particulars of textual correction as are here admitted. In doing this, I have almost unavoidably been led to note a few instances of different readings.

These few cases excepted, I have purposely, and with full deliberation, abstained from every thing in the line of variorum comment and citation. For, indeed, such matter, however right and good in its place, can hardly be of any use or interest save to those who are making or intending to make a specialty of Shakespearian lore. But, of the pupils and even the teachers in our schools and colleges, probably not one in five hundred has, or ought to have, any thought of becoming a specialist in Shakespeare, or a linguistic antiquary in any department of study. To such students, a minute discussion or presentation of various readings must needs be a stark impertinence; and its effect, if it have any, can hardly be other than to confuse and perplex their thoughts. In this, as in other walks of human service, the processes of elaborate study are of very limited use, and may well be confined to a few; while the last results of such study are or may be highly useful to all. I hold, indeed, that Shakespeare ought to be made much more of than he is in our higher education: not, however, with the view of fitting people to be editors and critics; but that they may have their minds and hearts rightly attuned to the delectations of his poetry and eloquence and wisdom; and that they may carry from the study some fair preparation of liberal thought and culture and taste into the common pursuits and interests of life. The world is getting prodigiously overstocked with authors; so many are aspiring to gain a living by their wits, that the thing is becoming a dreadful nuisance: and it really seems full time that we should begin to take more thought how a condition of "plain living" may be sanctified with the grace of "high thinking"; and how even the humbler and more drudging forms of labour may be sweetened by the pure and ennobling felicities of unambitious intelligence.

A question has lately been raised, and is still pending, as to the comparative value of verbal and of what is called æsthetic criticism; and some have spoken disparagingly, not to say contemptuously, of the latter, as a mere irrelevancy, which they would fain be rid of altogether. Verbal criticism certainly has its place, and in its place is not to be dispensed with; and it has at least this advantage over the other, that it is strictly necessary in the study of such authors as Shakespeare, who abounds in words and phrases which, to common readers, are quite unintelligible without such help. This, however, may easily be overdone, and in fact sometimes has been hugely overdone, insomuch as to become little better than a sheer incumbrance ; nevertheless, on the whole, it has been of incalculable service. But the other, I must think, has done good service too, and has fairly justified its claims to a high estimate in Shakespearian lore : albeit I have to confess that some discredit has of late come upon it, from the fact that, in divers cases, it has taken to very odd and eccentric courses, and has displayed an ill-starred propensity to speculate and subtilize the Poet's workmanship clean out of its natural propriety. Transcendental metaphysics, whether applied to science, to philosophy, to art, or to whatsoever else, of course loves to "reason high, and finds no end, in wandering mazes lost." Whatever it takes in hand, it can easily discover any meaning it wants, and as easily argue away any meaning not in accordance with its idealistic predilections ; so using its alchemy as to "extract sunbeams from cucumbers," or to resolve gold into vapour, just as it happens to list. But these abuses may very well be struck off without casting away the thing itself. And the æsthetic criticism of Coleridge, Schlegel, Charles Lamb, Hazlitt, and Mrs. Jameson, has probably done more to diffuse and promote the study of Shakespeare, than all the verbal criticism in the world put together.

The *Introduction* here given, as also some of the foot-notes, is mainly occupied with matter in this line ; the aim being, to aid such students as may care to be aided, towards what may be termed the *interior* study of Shakespeare's characters. Ordinarily, in books designed for such use as the

present, I deem it better to reproduce extracts from ap·
proved masters in critical discourse than to obtrude any
judgments of my own.   But my views of Hamlet are so
different from those commonly put forth, that in this case I
judged it best to set them aside, and to occupy the limited
space at my disposal with a presentation of my own thoughts.
In this part of the work, I have derived much furtherance
from Professor Karl V. erder's able essay on Hamlet, portions
of which, very choicely translated, are given in Mr. H. H.
Furness's great and admirable work, the variorum edition of
the play.   My own views were indeed substantially the same
long before I had any knowledge of the German Professor,
and even before his essay was written ; but I would not if I
could, and certainly could not if I would, disguise that I am
indebted to him for much aid, and more encouragement,
towards a full statement and expression of them.

The occasion moves me to protest, with all possible earn-
estness, against the course now too commonly pursued in
our studying and teaching of English literature.   We seem
indeed to have got stuck fast in the strange notion, that children are never learning any thing unless they are *conscious*
of it : and so we are sparing no pains to force in them a
premature and most unhealthy consciousness of learning.
Nothing is left to the free and spontaneous vitalities of
Nature.   Things have come to such a pass with us. that a
pupil must live,

> Knowing that he grows wiser every day,
> Or else not live at all, and seeing too
> Each little drop of wisdom as it falls
> Into the dimpling cistern of his heart.

Hence our education is kept at a restless fever-heat of am·

bition and emulation; and this naturally involves an incessant urging of high-pressure methods. We have no faith in any sowing, save where the seeds "forthwith spring up, because they have no deepness of earth." So eager and impatient are we for immediate results, that the conditions and processes of inward growth are, as far as possible, worked off and got rid of. But the results attained by this straining and forcing are necessarily false and delusive; and presently wither away, because they have no root.

Thus in our hot haste to make the young precociously intellectual, we are just burning real health and vigour of intelligence out of them; or, at all events, the best that can be gained by such a course is but what Wordsworth justly deprecates as "knowledge purchased with the loss of power." For, in truth, when people, of whatever age, see themselves growing from day to day, they are not really growing at all, but merely bloating;—a puffing-up, not a building-up. And we shall assuredly find, in due time, nay, we are already finding, that those who get ripe before they are out of their teens begin to rot before passing their twenties. For such a forced and premature action of the mind can only proceed by overtaxing and exhausting other parts of the system; and must needs be followed by a collapse of the mind itself equally premature. In other words, where the brain is built up at the expense of the stomach, the brain itself must soon break down. And, as "the child is father of the man," so of course the smart boys of our educational hot-beds can only blossom out into grown-up intellectual manikins.

Now, in opposition to all this, be it said, again and again, that the work of education is necessarily secret and unconscious just in proportion as it is deep and generative. For

the mind is naturally conscious only of what touches its surface, rustles in its fringes, or roars in its outskirts; while
that which works at its vital springs, and feeds its native
vigour, is as silent as the growing of the grass, as unconscious
as the assimilation of the food and the vitalizing of the
blood. When its springs of life are touched to their finest
issues, then it is that we are least sensible of the process
So it is rightly said, "the gods approve the depth and not
the tumult of the soul." Only the dyspeptic are conscious
of their gastric operations: the eupeptic never think of
their stomachs, are not even aware that they have any.

One would suppose that a little reflection on the workings
of the infant mind might teach us all this. For children,
during their first five years, before they can tell any thing
about it, or make any show of it in set recitations, and while
they are utterly unconscious of it, do a vast amount of studying and learning; probably storing up more of real intelligence than from any subsequent ten years of formal schooling. And such schooling is no doubt best and wisest when
it continues and copies, as far as may be, those instinctive
methods of Nature. But the pity of it is, that our education, as if "sick of self-love," appears to spurn the old wisdom of Nature, preferring to take its rules and measures
from a proud and arrogant intellectualism.

In the mental and moral world, as in the physical, the
best planting is always slow of fruitage: generally speaking,
the longer the fruit is in coming, the sounder and sweeter
when it comes; an interval of several years, perhaps of ten,
or even twenty, being little time enough for its full and perfect advent. For growth is a thing that cannot be extempo-
rized; and, if you go about to extemporize it, you will be
sure to cheat or be cheated with a worthless surface imita-

tion : that it is to say, in place of a growth, which is slow
and silent, but full of juice and taste withal, will be substituted a swift, loud, vapid manufacture.

What a teacher, therefore, most especially needs (and
parents need it too) is the faith that knows how to work
and wait ; — to work diligently, carefully, earnestly ; to wait
calmly, patiently, hopefully ; — that faith which, having its
eye on the far-off future, does not thirst for present rewards,

> Nor with impatience from the season ask
> More than its timely produce.

For Nature, the honest old Mother, is far better, stronger,
richer, than our busy and meddlesome intellectualists, who
are straining so hard to get ahead of her, have the heart to
conceive.   Human wisdom may indeed aid and further her
processes ; but it is stark folly to think of superseding them.
And the forcing system now so much in vogue is essentially
a levelling system ; though, to be sure, it can only level
downwards : perhaps, indeed, the circumstance of its looking to a compelled equality is what makes it so popular ; —
a thing sure to issue in a manifold spuriousness ! For its
estimate of things is, for the most part, literally preposterous.
Minds of a light and superficial cast it over-stimulates into a
morbid quickness and volubility, wherein a certain liveliness
and fluency of memory, going by rote, parrot-like, enables
them to win flashy and vainglorious triumphs by a sort of
cheap and ineffectual phosphorescence ; thus making them,
as Professor Huxley says, " conceited all the forenoon of
their life, and stupid all its afternoon " : while, upon minds
of a more robust and solid make, which are growing too
much inwardly to do any shining outwardly, it has a dis-
heartening and depressing effect.   Thus the system operates

to quench the deeper natures, while kindling false fires in the shallower.

Hence, no doubt, the feeling, which can hardly be new to any thoughtful teacher or parent, that "strongest minds are often those of whom the noisy *school* hears least." For, under the system in question, modest vigour is naturally eclipsed by pert and forward imbecility,— the proper characteristic of minds that have not strength enough to keep still. But minds thus heated into untimely efflorescence can hardly ripen into any thing but sterility and barrenness : before the season of fruitage, the sap is all dried out of them. To quote Professor Huxley again : "The vigour and freshness, which should have been stored up for the hard struggle for existence in practical life, have been washed out of them by precocious mental debauchery,— by book-gluttony and lesson-bibbing : their faculties are worn out by the strain upon their callow brains, and they are demoralized by worthless, childish triumphs before the real work of life begins." Of those who are so incessantly driving on this bad system, we may well ask, with Wordsworth,—

> When will their presumption learn,
> That in th' unreasoning progress of the world
> A wiser spirit is at work for us,
> A better eye than theirs, most prodigal
> Of blessings, and most studious of our good,
> Even in what seem our most unfruitful hours ?

Now, Shakespeare, above all other authors, should be allowed to teach as Nature teaches, else he ought not to be used as a text-book at all. And here, I suspect, the great danger is, that teachers, having too little faith in the spontaneous powers of Nature, will undertake to do too much, will keep thrusting themselves, their specialties and artificial preparations, between the pupil and the author. With average pupils, if of sufficient age, Shakespeare will make his way, slowly and silently indeed, but effectively, provided his proper efficacy be not strangled and defeated by an excess of learned verbalism. For his great superiority lies very much in this, that he writes close to facts as they are : no cloud of words, nothing, stands between his vision and the object. Hence with him, pre-eminently, language is used as a transparent, invisible vehicle of thought and matter ; so that the mind, if rightly put in communication with him, thinks not of his expression at all, but loses sight of it, in the force and vividness of what is expressed. Beautiful his speech is indeed ; but its beauty lies in this very thing, that it is the crystal shrine, itself unseen, of the speaking soul within. The less, therefore, the attention of students is diverted from his matter to his language by external calls, the quicker and stronger will be their interest in him ; — an interest free, natural, and unconscious indeed, but all the better for that : so that the teacher will best further it by letting it alone ; will most effectively help it by leaving it unhelped. For the learning of words is a noisy process ; whereas the virtue of things steals into the mind with noiseless step, and is ever working in us most when we perceive it least. And so, when Shakespeare is fairly studied in the manner here proposed, the pupil will naturally be drawn to forget himself ; all thought of the show he is to make will be cheated into healthful sleep ; unless, ay, unless —

> Some intermeddler still is on the watch
> To drive him back, and pound him, like a stray,
> Within the pinfold of his own conceit.

Not, however, but that something of special heed should

be given to the Poet's language, and his use of words; for
many of these are either unfamiliar or used in unfamiliar
senses: but this part of the study should be kept strictly
subordinate to the understanding of his thought and meaning, and should be pushed no further than is fairly needful
to that end.   But I have ample cause for saying, that in many
cases, if not in most, altogether too much time and strength
are spent in mere word-mongering and lingual dissection; a
vice as old indeed as Cicero's time, who pointedly ridicules
it in describing one as "a chanter of formulas, a bird-catcher
of syllables."   In fact, as we are now chiefly intent on edu-
cating people into talkers, not workers, so the drift of our
whole education is, to make language an ultimate object of
study, instead of using it as a medium for converse with
things: for we all know, or ought to know, that the readiest
and longest talkers are commonly those who have little or
nothing to say.   On every side, teachers are to be found
attending very disproportionately, not to say exclusively, to
questions of grammar, etymology, rhetoric, and the mere
technicalities of speech; thus sticking for ever in the husk
of language, instead of getting through into the kernel of
matter and thought.

Now, as before implied, Shakespeare, least of all, ought to
be taught or studied after this fashion.   A constant dissecting
of his words and syllables just chokes off all passage of his
blood into the pupil's mind.   Our supreme master in the
knowledge of human nature, it is little less than downright
sacrilege to be thus using him as the raw material of philo-
logical exercitations.   In the degree that it is important
people should acquire a taste for him and learn to love him,
just in that degree is it a sin to use him so; for such use
can hardly fail to breed a distaste for him and an aversion to

him. Doubtless there is a time for parsing, as there is for other things ; but people cannot parse themselves or be parsed into a relish for Shakespeare's workmanship, or into a fruitful converse with his treasures of wisdom and power.

And with the young, especially, the study of vernacular authors should be prosecuted in entire subservience to the knowledge of things : if turned into a word-mongering process, it touches no free and natural springs of interest, and so becomes tedious and dull, — just the thing to defeat all that pleasure which is the pulse of mental life. For the proper business, as also the healthy instinct of young minds is, to accumulate and lay in stores of matter : the analytic and discriminative processes naturally belong to a later period ; and to anticipate the proper time of them is a very bad mistake. But the knowledge of things proceeds too slowly and too silently for the ends of school-room show. Boys in school and college shine chiefly by the knowledge of words, for this is the mere work of memory ; but, in practical life, men are useful and successful in proportion to their knowledge of things : which knowledge proceeds, to be sure, by the measures of *growth*, and therefore is far less available for competitive examinations and exhibitory purposes. And so, forsooth, our children must be continually drilled in a sort of microscopic verbalism, as if we had nothing so much at heart as to make them learned in words, ignorant of things. Hence, too, instead of learning how to *do* some one thing, or some few things, they must learn how to smatter of all things : instead, for example, of being taught to sing, they must be taught to prate scientifically about music.

Thus our educational methods are all converging to the one sole purpose of generating a depurated and conceited intellectualism ; which is just about the shallowest, barrenest, windiest thing in the whole compass of man's intellectual globe. But, what is strangest of all, so becharmed are we with our supposed progress in this matter, as not to see, what is nevertheless as plain as the Sun at midday, that we are taking just the right course to stunt and thwart the intellect itself. For the several parts of the mind must grow in proportion, keeping touch and time together in the unity of a common sap and circulation, else growth itself is but decay in disguise. And when the intellectual man, through pride of self-sufficingness, sequesters itself from its natural commerce and reciprocation with the moral, emotional, and imaginative man, the intellect must needs go into a dry-rot.

I was convinced long ago, and further experience has but strengthened that conviction, that in the study of English authors the method of recitations is radically at fault, and ought seldom if ever to be used. For that method naturally invites, and indeed almost compels, the pupil to spend all his force on those points only which are, or may be made, available for immediate recitational effect. But, if the author be really worth studying, all, or nearly all, that is best in him escapes through the fingers of this process, and is left behind ; the pupil having no occasion for attending to it, nor any strength of attention to spare for it. He does nothing but skip lightly over the surface of what is before him, picking up such small items as the tongue and memory can handle ; but remaining quite innocent of all its deeper efficacies, which would indeed be rather an incumbrance than a help in reference to what he has in view. For the best thing that the best authors can do is to quicken and inspire the student's mind : but quickening and inspiration are nowise things to be recited ; their natural effect is to prevent glibness of memory and tongue : and, while the pupil is intent only on what he can recite, the author's quickening and inspiring power has no chance to work ; and he just runs or slides over it without being touched by it, or catching any virtue from it. It is just the difference of mere acquirement and culture : for what the mind gains in the way of acquirement merely, is lost almost as quickly as it is got ; but whatever of culture is gained abides as an inseparable part of the mind itself. Thus the same rule holds here as in so many other things, that, when pupils are studying merely or mainly for effect, all the best effect of the study is inevitably missed.

For these reasons, I have never had and never will have any thing but simple exercises ; the pupils reading the author under the teacher's direction, correction, and explanation ; the teacher not even requiring, though usually advising, them to read over the matter in advance. Thus it is a joint communing of teacher and pupils with the author for the time being ; just that, and nothing more. Nor, assuredly, can such communion, in so far as it is genial and free, be without substantial and lasting good ; far better indeed than any possible cramming of mouth and memory for recitation. The one thing needful here is, that the pupils rightly understand and feel what they read : this secured, all the rest will take care of itself ; because, when this is gained, the work is, not indeed done, but fairly and effectively begun ; and what is once so begun, will be ever after in course of doing, never done. For people cannot dwell, intelligently and with open minds, in the presence of "sweetness and light," or within the sound of wisdom and eloquence, without being enriched, —enriched secretly, it may be, but permanently ; for the enrichment is in the shape of germs, which have in them the virtue of perennial growth. And when I find the pupils taking pleasure in what they are about, entering into it with the zest and spirit of honest delight, then I know full well that they are drinking in the author's soul-power, and that what they are drinking in is going to the right spot. For, to find joy and sweetness in the taste of what is pure and good, is the strongest pledge that things are going well. And such a communing of youthful minds with genius and mellow wisdom has something of mystery and almost of magic in it. Rather say, it is a holy sacrament of the mind. As beautiful too as it is beneficent : in this naughty-lovely, or this lovely-naughty, world of ours, I hardly know of a lovelier sight. There is, be assured there is, regeneration in it

INTRODUCTION.

History of the Play.

"THE Revenge of Hamlet, Prince of Denmark, as it was lately acted by the Lord Chamberlain's Servants," was registered at the Stationers' on the 26th of July, 1602. This entry undoubtedly refers to Shakespeare's tragedy, and is the first we hear of it. The tragedy was printed in 1603. It was published again in 1604; and in the title-page of that issue we have the words, "enlarged to almost as much again as it was." This latter edition was reprinted in 1605, and again in 1611; besides an undated quarto, which is commonly referred to 1607, as it was entered at the Stationers' in the Fall of that year. These are all the issues known to have been made before the play reappeared in the folio of 1623. The quartos, all but the first, have a number of highly important passages that are not in the folio; while, on the other hand, the folio has a few, less important, that are wanting in the quartos.

It is generally agreed that the first issue was piratical. It gives the play but about half as long as the later quartos, and carries in its face abundant evidence of having been greatly marred and disfigured in the making-up. Mr. Dyce says, "It seems certain that in the quarto of 1603 we have Shakespeare's first conception of the play, though with a text mangled and corrupted throughout, and perhaps formed on the notes of some short-hand writer, who had imperfectly taken it down during representation." Nevertheless it is evident that the play was very different then from what it afterwards became. Polonius is there called Corambis, and his man Reynaldo is called Montano. Divers scenes and passages, some of them such as a reporter would be least likely to omit, are wanting altogether. The Queen is represented as concerting and actively co-operating with Hamlet against the King's life; and she has an interview of considerable length with Horatio, who informs her of Hamlet's escape from the ship bound for England, and of his safe return to Denmark; of which scene the later issues have no traces whatever. All this fully ascertains the play to have undergone a thorough recasting from what it was when the copy of 1603 was taken.

A good deal of question has been made as to the time when the tragedy was first written. It is all but certain that the subject was done into a play some years before Shakespeare took it in hand, as we have notices to that effect reaching as far back as 1589. That play, however, is lost; and our notices of it give no clue to the authorship. On the other hand, there appears no good reason for believing that any form of Shakespeare's *Hamlet* was in being long before we hear of it as entered at the Stationers', in 1602.

Source of the Plot.

Whether, or how far, Shakespeare may have borrowed his materials from any pre-existing play on the subject, we have no means of knowing. The tragedy was partly founded on a work by Saxo Grammaticus, a Danish historian, written as early as 1204, but not printed till 1514. The incidents, as related by him, were borrowed by Belleforest, through whose

French version, probably, the tale found its way to the English stage. It was called *The History of Hamblet.* As there told, the story is, both in matter and style, uncouth and barbarous in the last degree ; a savage, shocking tale of lust and murder, unredeemed by a single touch of art or fancy in the narrator. The scene of the incidents is laid before the introduction of Christianity into Denmark, and when the Danish power held sway in England : further than this the time is not specified. A close sketch of such parts of the tale as were specially drawn upon for the play is all I have room for.

Roderick, King of Denmark, divided his kingdom into provinces, and placed governors in them. Among these were two warlike brothers, Horvendile and Fengon. The greatest honour that men of noble birth could at that time win was by piracy, wherein Horvendile surpassed all others. Collere, King of Norway, was so moved by his fame that he challenged him to fight, body to body ; and the challenge was accepted, the victor to have all the riches that were in the other's ship. Collere was slain ; and Horvendile returned home with much treasure, most of which he sent to King Roderick, who thereupon gave him his daughter Geruth in marriage. Of this marriage sprang Hamblet, the hero of the tale.

Fengon became so envious of his brother, that he resolved to kill him. Before doing this, he corrupted his wife, whom he afterwards married. Young Hamblet, thinking he was likely to fare no better than his father, went to feigning himself mad. One of Fengon's friends suspected his madness to be feigned, and counselled Fengon to use some crafty means for discovering his purpose. The plot being all laid, the counsellor went into the Queen's chamber, and hid

behind the hangings.   Soon after, the Queen and the Prince
came in ; but the latter, suspecting some treachery, kept up
his counterfeit of madness, and went to beating with his
arms upon the hangings. Feeling something stir under them,
he cried, "A rat, a rat!" and thrust his sword into them ;
which done, he pulled the man out half dead, and made an
end of him.   He then has a long interview with his mother,
which ends in a pledge of mutual confidence between them.
She engages to keep his secret faithfully, and to aid him in
his purpose of revenge ; swearing that she had often prevented his death, and that she had never consented to the
murder of his father.

Fengon's next device was to send the Prince to England,
with secret letters to have him there put to death.   Two of
his Ministers being sent along with him, the Prince, again
suspecting mischief, when they were at sea read their commission while they were asleep, and substituted one requiring the bearers to be hanged.   All this and much more
being done, he returned to Denmark, and there executed
his revenge in a manner horrid enough.

There is, besides, an episodical passage in the tale, from
which the Poet probably took some hints, especially in the
hero's melancholy mood, and his apprehension that "the
spirit he has seen may be the Devil."   I condense a portion
of it : " In those days the northern parts of the world, living
then under Satan's laws, were full of enchanters, so that
there was not any young gentleman that knew not something
therein.   And so Hamblet had been instructed in that
devilish art whereby the wicked spirit abuseth mankind.   It
toucheth not the matter herein to discover the parts of divi-
nation in man, and whether this Prince, by reason of his
over-great melancholy, had received those impressions, divin-

ing that which never any had before declared." The " impressions " here spoken of refer to the means whereby Hamblet found out the secret of his father's murder.

It is hardly needful to add that Shakespeare makes the persons Christians, clothing them with the sentiments and manners of a much later period than they have in the tale ; though he still places the scene at a time when England paid some sort of homage to the Danish crown ; which was before the Norman Conquest. Therewithal the Poet uses very great freedom in regard to time ; transferring to Denmark, in fact, the social and intellectual England of his own day.

General Characteristics of the Play.

We have seen that the *Hamlet* of 1604 was greatly enlarged. The enlargement, however, is mainly in the contemplative and imaginative parts, little being added in the way of action and incident. And in respect of those parts, there is no comparison between the two copies ; the difference is literally immense, and of such a kind as to evince a most astonishing growth of intellectual power and resource. In the earlier text we have little more than a naked though in the main well-ordered and well-knit skeleton, which, in the later, is everywhere replenished and glorified with large, rich volumes of thought and poetry ; where all that is incidental and circumstantial is made subordinate to the living energies of mind and soul.

Accordingly Schlegel well describes this play as " a tragedy of thought." Such is, indeed, its character ; in which respect it stands alone among all the tragedies in being ; and it takes this character from the hero's mind. Hamlet everywhere floods the scene with intellectual wealth, and this in the varied forms of wit, humour, poetry, and high philosophy, with large stores of moral and practical wisdom : affluent with the spoils of learning, of genius, and art, he pours out in inexhaustible variety and profusion, enriching and adorning whatever he touches, and making it fresh, racy, delectable, and instructive. And he does all this without any sign of exertion ; does it with the ease and fluency of a free native impulse, such as to preclude the idea of its being a special purpose with him. For, with all his redundancy of mental treasure, he nowhere betrays the least ostentation of intellect. It is plainly the unlaboured, unaffected issue of a mind so full that it cannot choose but overflow.

But perhaps the leading characteristic of this play lies in its strong resemblance to the Classic Tragedy, in that the action is, in a very peculiar degree, dominated by what the ancients called Fate, but what, in Christian language, is termed Providence. In no other modern drama do we take so deep an impression of a superhuman power presiding over a war of irregular and opposing forces, and calmly working out its own purpose through the baffled, disjointed, and conflicting purposes of human agents. Of course, the Poet's genius is itself the providence of the play. But here, again, his insight is so profound and so just, his workmanship so true to the course of human experience, that all things come to pass just as if ordered by the Divine Providence of the world. And, however the persons go at cross-aims with each other or themselves, they nevertheless still move true to the author's aim : their confused and broken schemes he uses as the elements of a higher order ; and the harshest discords of their plane of thought serve to enrich and deepen the harmonies of his ; their very blunders and failures ministering to his success, their wilfulness to his law, their madness to his reason.

Political Basis of the Action.

The principal personages of the drama stand at or near the head of the State, and thus move in the highest public representative capacity : the whole world of Denmark is most nearly concerned in them as the recognized supreme organs of the national life and law. In the political order of the play, the Danish crown is partly elective, partly hereditary ; that is to say, elective within the circle of a particular family and kindred. Whatever there is of hereditary right belongs to the Queen, who is accordingly described as "the imperial jointress of this warlike State." She was the only child of the former King ; and Hamlet's father was brought within the circle of eligibility by his marriage with her. Of course, when her first husband died, and she married a second, the second became eligible just as the first had done. So that Claudius, the present King, holds the crown by the same legal title and tenure as Hamlet's father had held it.

A horrible crime has been committed, — a crime the meanest, the blackest, the hatefullest that man is capable of. Claudius has murdered his own brother and his King ; stealing upon him in his sleep, and pouring a slow but deadly poison in his ear, which so wrought that he seemed to die of a natural though mysterious disease. The deed was done so secretly and with such consummate craft as to elude and defy all human discovery. It was and could be known only to the author of it, and to God ; even the victim knew nothing of it till after his death. No trace of the crime, not an atom of evidence, nothing even to ground a suspicion upon, exists, save in the conscience of the criminal himself. So that the hideous secret lies buried in the grave of the murdered man ; and no revelation of it is possible on Earth, but

by his coming out of the tomb. Through this act of fratricide and regicide, Claudius has hewed his way to the Danish
throne ; he having beforehand made love to the Queen, and
seduced and corrupted her.

Claudius is essentially a low, coarse, sensual, brutish villain ; without honour and without shame ; treacherous and
cruel in the last degree ; at once hateful, loathsome, and
execrable. At the same time he is mighty shrewd and saga-
cious ; quick and fertile of resource ; inscrutably artful and
cunning ; withal, utterly remorseless and unscrupulous, and
sticking at nothing, however base or wicked, to gain his ends,
cr to secure himself in what he has gained. Thus he stands
forth, "a bold bad man," of a character too vile and too
shocking to be suffered to live, yet exceedingly formidable to
contend with, — formidable from his astuteness, formidable
from his unscrupulousness ; above all, formidable from the
powers and prerogatives with which he is invested as an
absolute king. Such as he is, Hamlet knows him thoroughly ;
understands alike his meanness, his malice, and his cunning ;
takes the full measure both of his badness and his potency.

It appears that the Queen was nowise an accomplice directly in the murder ; that she had, indeed, no knowledge of
it, perhaps no suspicion. But she has incurred guilt enough
in suffering such a wretch to make love to her, when she had
a husband living ; in being seduced by his "wicked wit and
gifts"; and then in rushing, with indecent and shameless haste,
into a marriage held deeply criminal in itself, even though
the forms of decorum had been strictly observed in the time
and manner of it. These doings have fallen with terrible
weight upon her son, oppressing his soul with unutterable
grief and shame, and filling his mind with irrepressible suspicions and divinings of foul play. He knows not how or

why it is, but he feels that the air about him is all tainted with the breath of hypocrisy and lust, of treachery and murder; insomuch that he would gladly escape, even by his own death, from scenes so horrible and so disgusting.

Hamlet's Madness.

The proper action of the play turns upon the circumstance, that the hero meets and converses with the ghost of his murdered father, and thence learns by what means Claudius has reached his present position. He thereupon starts off in a most strange, inexplicable course of behaviour: he seems quite beside himself; acts as if he were crazy.—Shakespeare's persons, generally, affect us just like those in actual life; so that we severally take different impressions and form diverse opinions of them. Especially is it so in the case of Hamlet. Hence it has been variously argued and discussed, whether his madness be real or feigned, or whether it be sometimes the one, sometimes the other. My own judgment is, and long has been, that he is really mad; deranged not indeed in all his faculties, nor in any of them continuously; that is to say, the derangement is partial and occasional: in other words, he is mad in spots and at times; paroxysms of wildness and fury alternating with intervals of serenity and composure. My main reasons for this judgment are as follows:—

1. From the natural structure and working of his mind; from the recent doings in the royal family; from the state of things at the Court; still more from his interview with the Ghost, and the Ghost's appalling disclosures and injunctions, "shaking his disposition with thoughts beyond the reaches of his soul"; above all, from his instant view and grasp of the whole dire situation in which he is now placed;—from all this, he *ought* to be crazy; and it were vastly to his credit,

both morally and mentally, to be so : we might well be amazed at the morbid strength or the natural weakness of his mind, if he were not so. We are told that, against stupidity, the gods themselves are powerless. And, sure enough, there are men with hearts so hard, and with heads so stolid and stockish, that even the gods cannot make them mad ; at least, not, unless through some physical disease. Hamlet, I think, can hardly be a man of that stamp.

2. It is a part of the old ghost-lore, that the being talked with by a ghost either finds a man mad or makes him so. If the ghost be subjective, — that is, a mere spectral illusion born of a diseased or frenzied brain, — then the interview finds him mad, the pre-existing madness causing the illusion : but if, on the other hand, the ghost be really objective, and duly authenticated as such, as it is in the case of Hamlet, then the interview causes the madness. This old notion is referred to by Horatio, when he tries to dissuade Hamlet from following the Ghost, on the ground that the Ghost may depose his " sovereignty of reason, and draw him into madness." At all events, the being thus ghosted was held to be no such trifling matter as we are apt to consider it : it was accounted a very pokerish, soul-harrowing business ; insomuch that a man, after such an experience, could hardly continue the same he was before. And so Hamlet, directly after his conversation with the Ghost, on being rejoined by his friends, flies off into a course of behaviour so strange, so wild, so eccentric, as to throw them into amazement.

3. Hamlet is believed to be really mad by all the other persons in the play, though they are quite in the dark as to the cause ; all, I mean, except the King, whose evil conscience renders him nervously suspicious that the madness is assumed, to cover some hostile design. Of course, this so

general belief arises because he acts precisely as madmen often do ; because his conduct displays the proper symptoms and indications of madness : nor does it make at all against this belief, that his behaviour has many contra-indicants. And, on this point, Hamlet himself, it appears, agrees with the rest : for, in his generous apology, his solemn appeal, to Laertes, near the close, — where I cannot think it just to pronounce him insincere, — he alleges his mental disorder as fairly entitling him to the pardon which he asks for the offence he has given. And, indeed, it seems to be admitted, on the other side, that, if Hamlet were actually mad, he could not enact the madman more perfectly than he does. " If," says Professor Lowell, " Shakespeare himself, without going mad, could so observe and remember all the abnormal symptoms as to be able to reproduce them in Hamlet, why should it be beyond the power of Hamlet to reproduce them in himself?" This means, I take it, that Hamlet counterfeits madness with an imitation so perfect as to be indistinguishable from a genuine case. But, if so, then what ground is there for saying it is not a genuine case?

4. Many distinguished members of the medical profession, deeply learned in the science, and of approved skill in the treatment, of insanity, have, in our time, made a special study of Hamlet's case, as also of Shakespeare's other delineations of madness ; and — without a single exception, so far as I know — have all reached the same conclusion. I cannot but think that here their judgment ought to have much the same weight which it is allowed to have in actual cases. Dr. Conolly of England, referring to Hamlet's first soliloquy, —

O, that this too-too solid flesh would melt, &c., —

has the following : " Of his father's ghost he has at this time

heard nothing.   No thought of feigning melancholy can have
entered his mind; but he is even now most heavily shaken
and discomposed, — indeed, so violently, that his reason,
although not dethroned, is certainly well-nigh deranged."
Dr. Isaac Ray, also, formerly of Providence, in a very able
and well-considered essay on the subject, states it as "a
scientific fact, that Hamlet's mental condition furnishes in
abundance the pathological and psychological symptoms of
insanity in wonderful harmony and consistency."   And Dr.
A. O. Kellogg of Utica fully concurs with Dr. Ray.   "There
are," says he, "cases of melancholic madness, of a delicate
shade, in which the reasoning faculties, the intellect proper,
so far from being overcome, or even disordered, are rendered
more active and vigorous.   Such a case Shakespeare has
given us in the character of Hamlet, with a fidelity to nature
which continues more and more to excite our wonder and
astonishment, as our knowledge of this intricate subject
advances."

It is to be remembered, however, that a mind diseased is
by no means necessarily a mind destroyed; and that it may
be only a mind with some of its faculties whirled into intem-
perate and irregular volubility, while others of them are more
or less palsied.   And Dr. Ray justly observes, in regard to
Hamlet, that madness "is compatible with some of the ripest
and richest manifestations of intellect."

Hamlet himself both affirms and denies his madness; the
one in his moments of calmness, the other when the fit is
strong upon him.   Nor is there any reason but that in both
he may be perfectly sincere.   It is commonly supposed that
insane people are always unconscious of their state; whereas there are many cases in which the patient is more or less
conscious of it.   And the degree of consciousness is apt to

be inversely as that of the disease. So that the being conscious is no sure proof of simulation ; in fact, any one simulating would be almost certain to pretend unconsciousness, and so betray his falsehood by overacting his part. Thus Hamlet, in the first turn of his distemper, when he utters such " wild and whirling words," seems to be at least partly aware of his state, for he speaks of it. Once only (in the scene with his mother) does his paroxysm run to so high a pitch that he loses the consciousness of it entirely, insomuch that he goes to arguing against it. In this case, at least, his mind is completely enthralled to illusions spun out of itself; the ghost which he sees and hears being purely subjective, as is evident in that his mother neither hears nor sees any thing of the kind. Well might she say, " this bodiless creation ecstasy is very cunning in." Yet here his intellectual faculties are kindled to the most overwhelming eloquence, burning both his mother and himself with their preternatural light.

Shakespeare's great, earnest, delicate mind seems to have been specially charmed with those forms of mental disease in which the intellect is kindled into preternatural illumination and expression. We have many instances of this ; as in old Timon's terrible eloquence of invective ; in Macbeth's guilt-inspired raptures of meditation ; in Lear's heart-withering imprecations ; and most of all in Hamlet's profound moralizing, his tempestuous strains of self-reproach, and his over-wrought consciousness of " thoughts that wander through eternity." I have sometimes thought that an instinct of genius may have put the Poet upon these frequent displays of mental exorbitancy, because the normal workings of the human mind did not afford scope enough for the full discharge of his own colossal and " thousand-souled " intellectuality.

My own idea, then, is, that, in order to make this play emphatically a tragedy of thought, the Poet's method was, to conceive a man great, perhaps equally so, in all the elements of character, mental, moral, and practical; and then to place him in such circumstances and bring such influences to work upon him, that all his greatness should be made to take on the form of thought. And with a swift intuitive perception of the laws of mind, which the ripest science can hardly overtake, he seems to have known just what kind and degree of mental disturbance or disease would naturally operate to produce such an irregular and exorbitant grandeur of intellectual manifestation.

To return for a moment to the particular question of Hamlet's madness. Why should he feign to be mad? How can he further, or hope to further, his end by assuming such a part? It does not help him onward at all; it rather hinders him; the natural effect of his conduct being to arouse suspicions in the King's mind, to put him on the alert, and to make him guard himself with redoubled vigilance. Let us see how it is.

The Ghost enjoins upon Hamlet two things; first, " Revenge this foul and most unnatural murder "; second, " Howsoever thou pursuest this act, taint not thy mind." Thus time and manner are left to Hamlet's own judgment; only he must not, he must not corrupt himself with any wicked or dishonourable course of action. He is solemnly warned against pursuing revenge by any methods involving self-defilement; and is to proceed as ever bearing in mind that

> Him, only him the shield of Jove defends,
> Whose means are pure and spotless as his ends.

He might take off Claudius as secretly, and in some such

way, as Claudius has taken off his father; but this would be to stain himself with the most abominable guilt and baseness. Whatsoever he does, he must be ready to avow it in the face of all Denmark, and to stand responsible for it. Come what may, he must, he can, use no arts but manly arts. Observe, then, what a dreadful dilemma he is placed in: he must punish, it is his most sacred duty to punish, a crime which it is not possible for him to prove, and which must not be punished till it has been proved. His strong, clear head instantly takes in the whole truth of his situation; comprehends at a glance the entire case in all its points and bearings. All this may well fill him, as indeed it does, with the most excruciating and inevitable agony; and, while he thus lives in torture, his mighty suffering, even because he is so strong, arouses all his faculties, and permits not a particle of the intellectual man to be lost.

Thus, from the time of his interview with the Ghost, all is changed with Hamlet; all, both without and within: henceforth he lives in quite another world, and is himself quite another man. All his old aims and aspirations are to be sternly renounced and thrust aside: life can have no more joys for him: his whole future must be cast in a new shape. All the duties upon which his thoughts have been hitherto centred are now merged in the one sacred, all-absorbing task enjoined upon him as from Heaven itself.

Now so great, so sudden, so agonizing a change within cannot but work some corresponding change without: it will naturally and even necessarily register itself in his manner and behaviour: while he *is* so different, how is it possible he should appear the same? And he himself evidently foresees that this change will cause him to be regarded as beside himself, as out of his right mind; especially as he cannot disclose the reason of it, and must, by all means, keep the cause of that change, or even any whisper of it, from reaching the King or the Court. A behaviour so strange, so odd, so unaccountable, must needs appear to others to have sprung from a stroke of madness. All this he clearly forecasts, as indeed he well may. And he desires, apparently, that his action may be so construed: he lets his "antic disposition" have free course; and rather studies than otherwise to sustain and strengthen the imputation of madness, by his conduct. If any see fit to call this feigning, so be it: the question is not worth wrangling about. "To this degree," says Professor Werder, "to this degree, which is relatively slight, he makes believe, he *plays* the madman. But, because it is essentially his truth, the effect of his real suffering, of his shattered being, to which his mind gives vent, so far as it can without betraying his secret; because it is *his* torture, his rage, his cry of woe, his agony, thus outwardly expressed; therefore this playing of his is not *merely* feigning, and because not merely, therefore not feigning at all, in the strict sense of the word."

Hamlet's alleged Defect of Will.

Our hero is not indeed master of the situation; but he *understands* the situation, which is just what most of his critics have not done; and he is not master of it, simply because, as things stand, such mastery is quite beyond the power of any man, without help from above. The critics in question insist upon it, that the one thing which Hamlet ought to do, and which he would do, if he had any real backbone of executive energy, is, to strike the avenging blow with instant dispatch, on the first opportunity. Such an opportunity he has, or can make, at almost any time

But to do thus would be both a crime and a blunder, and a blunder even more than a crime. How shall he justify such a deed to the world? how vindicate himself from the very crime which must allege against another? For, as he cannot subpœna the Ghost, the evidence on which he is to act is available only in the court of his own conscience. To serve any good end, the deed must so stand to the public eye as it does to his own; else he will be in effect setting an example of murder, not of justice. And the CROWN will seem to be his real motive, duty but a pretence. Can a man of his "large discourse looking before and after" be expected to act thus?

We, to be sure, long impatiently to have the crowned murderer get his deserts, because the whole truth of his guilt is known to us; but the people of Denmark, Hamlet's social and political world, know nothing of it whatever, and can never be convinced of it, should he proceed in that way. For the Ghost's disclosures were made to his ear alone; nobody else heard a word of them. And is it to be supposed that the Ghost's tale will be received on his sole word? that, too, in behalf of an act by which he has cut away the only obstacle between himself and the throne? The very alleging of such grounds will be regarded as, if possible, a worse crime than that in defence of which they are alleged. To the Danish people Hamlet will needs himself appear to be just what he charges Claudius with being. Claudius is their lawful King; they are his loyal subjects: they will not suffer their chosen ruler to be assassinated with impunity; they will hold themselves bound to wreak upon Hamlet the very vengeance which he claims to have wreaked upon him. Unless he summons the Ghost into court as a witness, every man will set him down either as a raving maniac, to be held in chains, or else as a monstrous liar and villain, who has murdered at once his uncle, his mother's husband, and his King; and then has trumped up a ghost-story in order at the same time to shield himself and to blacken his victim.

Most assuredly, therefore, the deed which the critics in question so loudly call for is the very thing of all others which Hamlet ought *not* to do, which he must not do; which, moreover, he cannot do, for the simple reason that he is armed with such manifold strength; because he is strong in reason, in judgment, in right feeling, in conscience, in circumspection, in prudence, in self-control, as well as in hand, in courage, in passion, in filial reverence, and in a just abhorrence of the King's guilt. That he does not deal the avenging stroke at once, — than which nothing were easier for him, were he not just the strong-willed man that he is; were he a mere roll of explosive, impotent passion, like Laertes; — this the critics aforesaid ascribe, some to constitutional or habitual procrastination, others to an intellectual activity so disproportionate as to quench what little force of will he may have.

Against all this, I make bold to affirm that, if Hamlet has any one attribute in larger measure than another, it is that very power which these critics accuse him of lacking. They, forsooth, see no strength of will in him, because, while he has this, he has also the other parts of manhood equally strong. Now, the main peculiarity, the most distinctive feature of Hamlet's case is, that, from the inevitable, pressing, exigent circumstances of his position, — circumstances quite beyond his mastery, quite beyond all mere human mastery, — his strength of will has, and must have, its highest exercise, its supreme outcome, in self-restraint and self-control; an indwelling power laying the strong hand of law upon him, and causing him to respect the clear, consenting counsels of reason, of prudence, of justice, and conscience, — counsels which his quick, powerful, well-poised intellect perfectly understands. And the act which the critics require of him, so far from evincing strength of will, would do just the reverse ; it would evince nothing but the impotence of a blind, headlong, furious passion, — a transport of rage so violent as to take away all that responsibility which everybody understands to adhere to a truly voluntary act. In other words, it would be an act not so much of executive energy as of destructive fury.

Why Hamlet does not strike the King.

Hamlet, as before observed, is called upon to revenge a crime which is altogether unproved, and which, from the nature of the case, is utterly *unprovable*, except from the criminal's own mouth : apart from this source, he has not, and cannot get, a particle of evidence available for impressing upon the world wherein he lives a judicial or even a moral conviction of the King's guilt. This is just the cardinal point in Hamlet's case. So that, matters standing thus, killing Claudius would be not so much a punishment of the guilty as a murder of the proof. As the only possible evidence is to come from Claudius himself, he must by all means be kept alive, till he can be made his own accuser, and a witness against himself; or rather, till either his conscience shall drive him to " proclaim his malefactions," or else his guilt, to barricade its safety, shall thrust him upon other crimes so monstrous and so evident, that all shall see him as he is, and acknowledge his punishment just. Meanwhile, Hamlet must, above all things, refrain from the avenging stroke ; must strain his utmost powers, if need be, to that

end.   That he does thus hold himself back from the deed to
which his burning passion for justice and his righteous thirst
of vengeance are continually urging him, — in all this I must
still think he displays an almost superhuman degree of that
very thing which he is alleged to be without.

The critics indeed talk just as if it were a matter lying
solely between Hamlet and Claudius ; just as if the people
of Denmark had nothing to say, no rights involved, no concern, in the question.   Hamlet does not see it so ; and he
would discover a pitch of egotism literally inhuman, if he
did.   Every lover of his kind naturally desires, both in life
and in death, the good opinion of his kind.   This is partly
because such opinion is an indispensable condition of his
serving them.   And so Hamlet has a just, a benevolent, and
an honourable concern as to what the world may think of
him : he craves, as every good man must crave, to have his
name sweet in the mouths, his memory fragrant and precious
in the hearts, of his countrymen.   How he feels on this
point, is touchingly shown in his dying moments, when he
wrenches the cup of poison from Horatio's hand, and appeals
at once to his strong love and his great sorrow : —

> O God, Horatio! what a wounded name,
> Things standing thus unknown, shall live behind me!
> If ever thou didst hold me in thy heart,
> Absent thee from felicity awhile,
> And in this harsh world draw thy breath in pain,
> To tell my story.

Thus the hero's hands are inextricably tied, — tied, not
through any defect, nor through any excess, in himself; not
through any infirmity of will or courage or resolution, but
from the insurmountable difficulties of his situation.   It is
not that an intellectual impetuosity, or a redundancy
of thought, cripples or any way retards his powers of

action; but that the utter impossibility of acting, without covering himself, in all human account, with the guilt of parricide and regicide, prodigiously stimulates and quickens his powers of thought, and keeps his splendid intellect in an incessant transport of exercise. And so the very plan of the drama, as I understand it, is to crush all the intellectual fragrance out of him, between a necessity and an impossibility of acting. The tremendous problem, the terrible dilemma which he has to grapple with, is one that Providence alone can solve, as Providence does solve it at the last.

As if on purpose to warn and guard us against imputing Hamlet's delay to the cause alleged, the Poet takes care to provide us with ample means for a different judgment; showing him, again and again, to be abundantly energetic and prompt in action whenever the way is clear before him. So it is in his resolution to meet and address the Ghost; in his breaking away from the hands of friendship when the Ghost beckons him to follow; in his devising and executing the scheme for making the King's "occulted guilt unkennel itself"; and especially in his action on shipboard, when he sends the King's agents to the fate they have prepared for himself. In these cases, as in various others also, he discovers any thing but a defect of active energy : his mental powers range themselves under the leading of a most vigorous and steady will. And his conduct appears, moreover, strictly normal, and not spasmodic or exceptional; I mean, it is clearly the result of character, not of disease.

Why the Poet does not make Hamlet strike.

Thus much for the reasons of Hamlet's course, as these are personal to himself. But the Poet had other reasons of his own, indispensable reasons of art, for not making Hamlet act as the critics would have him. Shakespeare portrays many great criminals, men, and women too, who for a while ride in triumph over virtue wronged, persecuted, crushed. And he always brings them to punishment, so far as this world can punish them. But he never in a single instance does this till their crimes are laid open to the world, so that all about them recognize the justice of their fate, and are righteously glad at what befalls them. In all this Shake-speare is profoundly, religiously true to the essential order and law of all right tragic representation. For our moral nature, as tuned in sympathy with its Source, reaps a deep, solemn, awful joy from such vindications of the Divine law.

Now the very nature and idea of a proper tragic revenge or retribution require that the guilty be not put to death, till their guilt has been proved ; and so proved, that the killing of them shall be manifestly a righteous act, — shall stand to the heart and conscience of mankind as an act of solemn and awful justice. To such a revenge, — the only revenge that Hamlet can execute or ought to execute ; the only re-venge, too, consistent with the genius of the work ;— to such a revenge, punishment is necessary ; to punishment, justice is necessary ; to justice, the vindication of it in the eyes, not merely of the theatre, but of those among whom the action takes place. So that, if Shakespeare had made Hamlet kill Claudius a moment earlier than he does, he would have vio-lated the whole moral law of his art, — that law whose " seat is the bosom of God, her voice the harmony of the world." And in that case the tragic action, instead of being, to the persons concerned, in any proper sense a righteous proceed-ure, instead of appealing to their high and sacred sympathies with justice, would be a mere stroke of brutal violence, or, at the best, an act of low, savage, personal revenge ; such an act as would inevitably array their sympathies with justice *against the avenger of crime,* and enlist them in behalf of the criminal. Thus the proper music of the work would be utterly untuned, and for the terrible of tragic art would be substituted the horrible of untragic bungling. This were to write tragedies for the coarse theatrical sense, for the vulgar apprehension of the crowd before the curtain, and not for the inner courts of the human soul !

Catching the King's Conscience.

All through the first two Acts of the play, and until late in the second scene of the third Act, Hamlet more or less doubts the honesty of the Ghost. The old belief in ghosts held, among other things, that evil spirits sometimes walked abroad, in the likeness of deceased persons, to scare or tempt the living. Hamlet apprehends the possibility of its being so in this case. He therefore craves some direct and decisive confirmation of the Ghost's tale from the King's conscience. When the advent of the Players is announced, he instantly catches at the chance, thus offered, of testing the question, and the possibility, if the Ghost's tale be true, of unmasking Claudius, and of forcing or surprising him into a confession. Nothing could evince more sagacity in planning, or more swiftness in executing, than the action he takes in pursuance of this thought : —

> I've heard
> That guilty creatures sitting at a play
> Have by the very cunning of the scene
> Been struck so to the soul, that presently
> They have proclaim'd their malefactions;
> For murder, though it have no tongue, will speak
> With most miraculous organ. I'll have these players
> Play something like the murder of my father
> Before mine uncle : I'll observe his looks;

I'll tent him to the quick: if he but blench,
I know my course.   The spirit that I have seen
May be the Devil: and the Devil hath power
T' assume a pleasing shape; yea, and perhaps,
Out of my weakness and my melancholy, —
As he is very potent with such spirits, —
Abuses me to damn me.   I'll have grounds
More relative than this: the play's the thing
Wherein I'll catch the conscience of the King.

The scheme, I need not say, succeeds.   The King's behaviour in the interlude fully authenticates to Hamlet, perhaps also to Horatio, the Ghost's tale.   Hamlet now *knows*
that Claudius is indeed guilty.   And Claudius also, as Hamlet well understands, knows that he knows it.   But the evidence thus caught, however assuring to Hamlet, is nowise
available for the ends of social or even dramatic justice.
The Ghost's tale is still just as impossible to be proved to
the mind and heart of Denmark, as it was before.   But this
advantage has been gained, that Claudius must now do one
of two things: he must either repent and confess, or else he
must try to secure himself by further measures: an attitude
merely passive or defensive will no longer do.   If he does
not repent, there is henceforth a mortal duel between him
and Hamlet: one, or the other, or both, of them must go
down.   As Hamlet lives but to avenge the murder, he must
neither die himself nor let the King die, till that work is
done.   Force he has a hand to repel; fraud he has a mind
to scent out, to detect, to defeat; and Claudius must get up
very early, and be very busy when up, to out-craft him.

Hamlet seeing the King at Prayer.

The result of the interlude excites Hamlet to the utter-
most: his faculties, his sensibilities are all wrought up to

their highest tension. All on fire, as he is, he may well say,

> Now could I drink hot blood,
> And do such bitter business as the day
> Would quake to look on.

In this state of mind he comes upon Claudius while in the act of praying. Now he has a fair chance, now, in his white-heat of rage, to deal the avenging blow : the self-convicted fratricide is there, alone, before him, and is completely at his mercy. All through his frame the blood is boiling : still his reason tells him that such a hit will be a fatal miss, and will irretrievably lose him his cause. His judgment, his prudence, his self-control are assailed and pressed by such an overwhelming stress and energy of passion, that they are all but forced to give way : so mighty is the impulse of revenge within him, that even his iron strength of will can hardly withstand it : and, to brace his judgment against his passion, he has to summon up a counterpoising passion in aid of his judgment. Even his inexpressible hatred of the King is itself called in, to help him through the potent temptation, and to keep him from striking the King. This, I take it, is the meaning of the dreadful reasons and motives which he raves out for sparing Claudius. He will take him while in the act of committing such sins as will make sure the perdition of his soul. In all this, it seems to me, the providence of the drama is using one of Hamlet's maddest fits, to foreshadow the far deeper, fouler, more damning sins amidst which this execrable wretch ultimately falls.

Hamlet with his Mother.

Now that Hamlet is, beyond all peradventure, certified of the King's guilt, the next thing for him to do is, to come to

a full and perfect understanding with his mother. He must
see her by herself. He must search her breast to the bottom, he must "turn her eyes into her very soul," with his
burning eloquence of indignation, of shame, of reproof, of
remonstrance, of expostulation : he must arouse the better
feelings of the woman and the mother in her heart, and
through these, if possible, must redeem her from the blasting
curse of her present position : above all, he must know from
her directly, either through her words or her manner, whether
she was any way conspirant in the murder of his father,
and must also let her know, with an emphasis not to be re-
sisted, both his opinion of Claudius and how matters are
standing between Claudius and himself. While he is on the
point of doing this ; while, with his soul agitated to its inner-
most depths, he is talking with her ; while he is standing in
the room and beside the bed in which himself was born, and
which she has so shockingly dishonoured ; Polonius, on a
sudden, raises an outcry behind the hangings : Hamlet, supposing the voice to be the King's, is surprised, snatched,
swept quite away from himself with a whirlwind gust of passion : instantly, with the speed of lightning, out leaps his
sword from the scabbard, as of its own accord, and kills the
old intriguer.

How the Revenge is brought about.

By this instant lapse of self-control, Hamlet has lost his
lead in the game, and given Claudius a great advantage over
him ; which advantage, however, Claudius will so use as to
open a clear way for the final triumph of Hamlet's cause,
though at a fearful cost of life, his own among the rest.
Claudius is now to assume the offensive, and is so to carry
it as to achieve his own ruin. For, indeed, his guilt is of

such a kind, and is so placed, that it can have its proper retribution only through a process of further development. A
dreadful safety indeed! But he will prove far unequal to
the sharp exigency in which he will involve himself. Too
bad to repent, and too secure in his badness to be reached
by human avengement, there is, nevertheless, a Hand which
he cannot elude. That Hand is to work his punishment
through the springs of his own moral constitution. Hamlet's
piercing, unsleeping eye, now sharpened to its keenest edge,
is to be upon him, to penetrate his secretest designs, to trace
him through his darkest windings, as his evil genius. His
guilt is to entangle him, by an inward law, in a series of dia-
bolical machinations; remorse is to disconcert his judgment,
and put him to desperate shifts. Thus his first, most secret,
unprovable crime is to goad him on, from within, to perpe-
trating other crimes, — crimes so open and manifest as to
stand in no need of proof; and he is to go out of the world
in such a transport of wickedness, lying, poisoning, murdering, that "his heels shall kick at Heaven," sure enough.

Such is the stern, awful, inexorable moral logic of this
mighty drama. And its great wisdom lies in nothing more
than in the fact, the order, and the method of the hero's being
made to serve as the unconscious organ or instrument of the
providential retribution. He himself, indeed, is consciously
doing the best that can be done in his situation. Meanwhile the Nemesis of the play is working out the result
through him, without his knowing it, without his suspecting
it. Not till the hand of death is already upon him, does it
become possible for him to strike. Now, at length, the
seals are opened; now, for the first time, his hands are
untied, his passion, his avenging impulse, his will are set
free. All this he sees instantly just as it is: instantly, con-

sciously, he deals the stroke for which his Divine Helper has secretly prepared the way. He himself falls indeed, but falls as a pure and spotless victim, to feed the sacrificial fire of immortal hopes and aspirations in the human breast; so falls as to leave upon us the hallowed sense, that "flights of Angels sing him to his rest."

Hamlet's Self-Disparagement.

I must not dismiss the hero without adverting briefly to one or two other points. — Many people, I suspect, shape their opinions and feelings about Hamlet quite too much from what Hamlet, in some of his soliloquies, says against himself. In this, they seem to me to take him at his word just there where his word is least to be taken. For, surely, thus to turn his solitary self-communings, his thinkings-aloud, against him, is not fair. Instead of so taking him at his word, we ought to see him better than he then sees himself, and rather, with our calmer and juster vision, to step between him and his morbid self-accusings; to judge him and to maintain his cause upon reasons which he is himself too un-selfish, too right-hearted, too noble in mind, to accord their due weight in his thinkings. This holds especially in regard to his soliloquy beginning, "O, what a rogue and peasant slave am I!" where he surges through a long course of railing and storming at himself, bitterly charging himself with faults and vices which his whole conduct most certainly and most clearly acquits him of. This tempestuous strain of self-abuse springs in part from his madness, his disease, which vents itself in that way, and puts him thus to quarrelling with himself, because, in the extreme, unrelenting hardness of his case, he nevertheless will not, dare not go to accusing or arguing against his fate, or fall to quarrelling with what he regards as the inevitable orderings of Providence.

The truth is, Hamlet is suffering dreadfully : shame, indignation, grief, sympathy with his father's purgatorial pains, detestation, horror, at the triumphant murderer, a consuming, holy thirst of vengeance, impossible, as things stand, to be attained, — all these are crowding and pressing his soul together ; and his intolerable anguish, instead of easing itself by blaming, by resenting, by deploring his miserable lot, seeks such relief as it can by arraigning himself before himself, as deserving a lot far worse. He thus revenges upon himself, as it were, the inexorable cruelty of his position.

All this is what some of the Poet's critics cannot or will not see ; and Hamlet appears to them cold, hard-hearted, indifferent, because they are themselves either so hard or so locked up in their self-applauding critical perspicacity as to have no ear, no sense for his mute agony. And so they take him at his word ! not perceiving that what he says to himself against himself are just the things he would be sure *not* to say, if they were really true ; while the things which he does *not* say are so true, and so unutterably crushing in their truth, that he *must* be saying something else. Because he " has that within which passeth show," therefore what he *does* show is taken as a just index and exponent of what he has within.

Pathos of Hamlet's Situation.

This brings me to one of the most peculiar and most interesting features in the delineation of Hamlet. — In his intellectual powers, attainments, resources, Hamlet is highly self-conscious, though not at all touched with conceit. In his moral instincts, sentiments, principles, in his beautiful train of manly virtues, his courage, his honour, his reverence, his tenderness, his sense of truth and right, his human-heartedness, his generosity, his self-restraint, his self-sacrifice, —

in these he is nobly unconscious; and rather shows his full, deep possession of them by a modest sense, or fear, of his being deficient in them: for these things are apt to be most on the tongue where they are least in the heart. Hence, in part, the singular vein of pathos that permeates the delinea-tion. That pathos is altogether undemonstrative, silent; a deep undercurrent, hardly ever rising to the surface, so as to be directly visible, but kept down by its own weight. Hamlet, as I said before, suffers, suffers dreadfully; but he makes no sign, at least none when his suffering is greatest; or, if any at all, so very slight, as to be scarce heard amidst the louder noises of the play; as in what he says to Horatio, near the close: "Thou wouldst not think how ill all's here about my heart; but it is no matter: it is but foolery; but it is such a kind of gain-giving as would perhaps trouble a woman." Thus his suffering is not made audible to the sense: it is speechless, indeed unspeakable, and left for the inner eye, the intelligent heart, the sympathizing magnet within, to *infer*.

Such is the unspoken pathos of Hamlet's situation, — a pathos so deep, so pure, so refined, so soul-moving, if we have but the eye to see it, that I know not where else we shall find its like. Let us see, for a moment, to recur to a topic already discussed, — let us see how it is with him. If he could but forget the real nature of his task; if he could give free course to his mighty impulse of justice; then he might indeed have at least a respite to the torture that is wringing him. But, because his reason is so strong as to stay his hand, therefore he has to suffer such pain, — the pain of a most powerful will engaged in a mortal struggle against the insurgent forces of passion goading him onward. To quote again from Professor Werder: "To smite down the King, to sacrifice his own life by the blow, in order to be quit of his task at once, that were the easiest, the happiest thing for him ; but he *wills* to fulfill it, to *fulfill* it faithfully. What he rails at as 'pigeon-livered,' when the mortal nature, impatient of pain, weary of suffering, cries out in him, — all this is enduring courage, the courage of reason, springing from reverence for a holy duty, and from devotion thereto."

But, harsh and bitter as is his lot, Hamlet never complains of it, hardly breathes an audible sigh over it : nay, he will not, if he can help it, let either himself or others see it : heroically he bears it, heroically he hides it. Of self-pity, of self-compassion, he discovers not the slightest symptom ; and, so far from saying or doing any thing to stir pity or compassion in others, he is ever trying, though trying spontaneously and unconsciously, to disguise his inward state both from others and from himself ; — from himself in high strains of self-accusation ; from his true friends in smiles of benevolence, or in fine play of intellect ; from his foes and his false friends in caustic, frolicsome banter, and in pointed, stinging remonstrance or reproof. Even when his anguish is shrieking within him, he knits his lips down tight over it, and strangles the utterance. For, indeed, to his mind, it is not of the slightest consequence how much he suffers in this world, so he does his duty, his whole duty, and nothing but that ; and he is so all-intent upon that as to have no time, no heart, for self-commiseration. Now this utter oblivion of self in his vast, incommunicable sorrow is to me just the most pathetic thing in Shakespeare ; though, to be sure, the pathos is much less pronounced than in other cases : but I deem it all the better for that.

It is partly to relieve or divert off his sense of woe that his mind is so continually " voyaging through strange seas of

thought "; sometimes in outpourings of statesman-like wisdom, such as would add to the fame of a Burke or a Webster; sometimes in profound moralizings on life and death,
on duty and immortality, such as would give a richer bloom
to the laurels of a Cicero, a Marcus Aurelius, a Jeremy Taylor, or a Sir Thomas Browne; sometimes in well-seasoned
discourse on the player's art and on the right virtues of liter-
ary style, such as "shames the schools"; now in flashes of
wit more than Attic; now in jets of humour the freshest, the
raciest, the mellowest, the most suggestive, ever delivered.

All this, to be sure, Hamlet does not himself say; no!
nor does the Poet say it for him in words; but the Poet says
it through the ineffable dramatic logic of the play, — says it
by a speaking silence. a mute eloquence, far more powerful
and penetrating than words. It is the "austere and solid
sweetness" of a great, strong, delicate soul perfectly self-
contained.

General Remarks on Hamlet.

Intellectually, and morally too, Hamlet is represented as,
in the language of our time, much in advance of his age;
his mind casting far onwards to an era of purer, richer,
brighter civilization. He conceives a mould of statesman-
ship, a style of public order, and a tone of social converse,
such as the time affords him no examples of. The coarse
and brutal manners of his nation, infecting even the Court,
he both scorns and deplores, and this on grounds of taste,
of policy, of honour, and of right. And the effects which
such things have on national character and well-being are
discoursed by him with rare discernment and reach of
thought. His mind is indeed penetrated with the best efficacies of Christian morality and refinement.

In Shakespeare's time the Drama was an intense national passion, all grades of the English people, from the throne downwards, taking a lively interest in it, and some of the finest gentlemen and choicest spirits of the age lending it their hearty support, apparently regarding it as a powerful engine of public enlightenment and progress : all which was in fact one cause why the Drama came to such a glorious efflorescence in that age. It was therefore in strict keeping with the best thoughts of the time that the Poet made his favorite intellectual hero, prince though he be, deeply versed in the theory of the dramatic art, and much concerned to have the representatives of it well used ; as when he tells Polonius, " After your death you were better have a bad epitaph, than their ill report while you live." Hamlet's idea seems to be, " Let me have the making of a nation's plays, and I care little who makes its laws." His mind was indeed meant to be large enough, and his taste catholic enough, to include all generous disciplines and liberal preparations in its scope ; and Shakespeare evidently thought no scorn to endow such a man with his own exquisite science in the walk which his " sweet and cunning hand " was to render so illustrious.

Laertes.

Laertes makes a very peculiar and most emphatic contrast to Hamlet. We cannot exactly call Laertes a noble character, yet he has noble streaks in him. The respect in which he holds his father, and the entire and unreserved affection he bears his sister, set him well in our esteem as a son and a brother : beyond these he can hardly be said to show any sentiments or principles worthy of regard. He takes as ardently to the gayeties of the French capital as Hamlet does to the studious walks and shades of Wittenberg

Though incapable of any thing so serious as friendship, he is nevertheless a highly companionable fellow, at least among those of like resort. He is never pestered at all with moral scruples : life has no dark and difficult problems to him : he has no philosophy at all, does not even know what the word means : truth, as such, is neither beautiful nor venerable in his sight : in his heat and stress of destructive impulse, he does not see far enough to apprehend any causes for deliberation or delay. In regard to the death of his father, he snatches eagerly at the conclusion shaped for him by the King, without pausing to consider the grounds of it, or to weigh the merits of the case, because it offers a speedy chance of discharging his revenge ; and he is reckless alike of means and of consequences, in fact cares nothing for others or even for himself, here or hereafter, so he may quickly ease his breast of the mad rapture with which it is panting. He has a burning resentment of personal wrongs, real or supposed, but no proper sense of justice ; indeed, he can nowise enter into any question of so grave a nature as that : hence in the exigency that overtakes him, " wild sword-law " becomes at once his religion.

The blame of the treacherous plot for assassinating Hamlet, on the express ground of his " being remiss, most generous, and free from all contriving," properly belongs to the King : but the further infamy of anointing his sword in order to clinch the nail of his purpose would go hard with Laertes, but that his trance of passion at Ophelia's madness and death in a great measure, if not entirely, takes away his responsibility. In his transport of grief and rage he is as much beside himself as Hamlet is in his wildest paroxysms of disorder ; and the most suggestive point of contrast between them is in reference to the opposite manner in which the moral character of each transpires under the eclipse of reason. Observe, also, how the two men differ in their ends: Laertes dies repenting of the base and hateful wrong he has done to Hamlet, and begging his forgiveness; Hamlet dies pitying Laertes, and — forgiving him !

The King.

Enough, perhaps, has already been said of Claudius; but there is one further point in his character, so suggestive of wholesome thought, that it ought to receive some passing notice. — The words " all may be well," with which he pro · logues his act of devotion, are very significant, as showing that his prayer is an attempt to make religion a substitute for duty. As often happens in real life, he betakes himself to a sentimental repentance as absolving him from " doing works meet for repentance." For who has not seen men resorting to very emphatic exercises of religion, as virtually dispensing with the law of good and pious works? It is observable that the King's fit of devotion operates to ease him through his course of crime, instead of deterring him from it. Such are the subtle tricks men practise on themselves, to soothe the pangs of guilt without amendment of life. The King goes from his closet to plot further crimes ! Thus his prayer is " like a spendthrift sigh that hurts by easing"; that is to say, he endeavours to satisfy or appease his conscience with a falsetto cry of penitence. Strange it should be so, but so it is !

The Ghost.

The Ghost is a powerful element in this great drama, shedding into it a peculiar and preternatural grandeur; but that power acts through the finest organs of the soul, working so deeply on the moral and imaginative forces, that the coarse arts of criticism can do but little with it. What an air of dread expectancy waits upon the coming and the motions of that awful shade! How grave and earnest, yet how calm and composed its speech! as if it came indeed from the other world, and brought the lessons of that world in its mouth. The stately walk, the solemn, slowly-measured words, the unearthly cast and temper of the discourse, are all ghost-like. The popular currency of many of the Ghost's sayings shows how profoundly they sink into our souls, and what a weight of ethical meaning attaches to them. Observe, too, how choicely Horatio hits the key-note of the part, and attempers us to its influences: —

> What art thou, that usurp'st this time of night,
> Together with that fair and warlike form
> In which the majesty of buried Denmark
> Did sometime march?

But indeed the whole matter preparatory to the Ghost's interview with Hamlet, its first appearance on the scene, its sad and silent steps, its fading at the crowing of the cock, and the subdued reflections that follow, ending with the speech,

> But look, the Morn, in russet mantle clad,
> Walks o'er the dew of yond high eastern hill;

all this is managed with consummate skill.

Horatio.

Horatio is one of the very noblest and most beautiful of Shakespeare's male characters: there is not a single loose stitch in his make-up: he is at all times superbly self-contained: he feels deeply, but never gushes nor runs over: as true as a diamond, as modest as a virgin, and utterly unselfish ; a most manly soul, full alike of strength, tenderness, and solidity. But he moves so quietly in the drama, that his rare traits of character have received scant justice. Much of the best spirit and efficacy of the scenes is owing to his presence. He is the medium whereby some of the hero's finest and noblest qualities are conveyed to us ; yet himself so clear and transparent, that he scarcely catches the attention. The great charm of his unselfishness is, that he seems not to be himself in the least aware of it ; " as one, in suffering all, that suffers nothing." His mild scepticism " touching the dreaded sight twice seen of us," is exceedingly graceful and scholarly. And, indeed, all that comes from him marks the presence of a calm, clear head keeping touch and time perfectly with a good heart.

Polonius.

Polonius is Shakespeare's version, sharply individualized, of a politician somewhat past his faculties ; shrewd, careful, conceited, meddlesome, and pedantic. Hamlet does him some injustice ; partly as thinking that the old man has wantonly robbed him of his heart's best object, and not making due allowance, as indeed lovers seldom do in such cases, for the honest though perhaps erring solicitude of a father's love. Therewithal he looks upon him as a supple time-server and ducking observant, which indeed he is, of whoever chances to be in power, ever ready to " crook the pregnant hinges of the knee where thrift may follow fawning." As such he of course has the utmost contempt for him ; which contempt his disease lets loose from the bands of respect, while his intellect engineers it with the greatest fluency and point.

Polonius has his mind richly stored with prudential and

politic wisdom ; which however shows somewhat absurdly in him, because, to use a figure of Coleridge's, it is like a light in the stern of a ship, that illumines only that part of the course already left behind. For, as Dr. Johnson aptly remarks, he is " knowing in retrospect, and ignorant in foresight." A man of one method, political engineering ; with his fingers ever itching to work the machine of policy ; and with little perception of times and occasions ; he is called to act where such arts and methods are peculiarly unfitting, and therefore he overreaches himself.

To such a mind the hero's character can hardly be other than an inscrutable enigma. It takes a whole man to understand Hamlet, and Polonius is but the attic storey of a man ! Assuming Hamlet to be thus and so, Polonius reasons and acts just right in regard to him ; but the fact is, he cannot *see* him ; and so, his premises being all wrong, the very justness of his reasoning only carries the further astray. But, in the directions he gives his man Reynaldo for angling out the truth about his absent son, the old politician is perfectly at home ; and his mind seems to revel in the mysteries of wire-pulling and trap-setting. He understands, no man better, " how your bait of falsehood takes the carp of truth." But to such modes of dealing Hamlet is quite impracticable. And he takes a mad pleasure in fooling and plaguing the old fox !

A chronic fanaticism of intrigue having blunted in Polonius the powers of special insight and discernment in what is before him, he therefore perceives not the unfitness of his old methods to the new exigency ; while his long experience of success in " hunting the trail of policy " makes him feel quite sure of succeeding now. To quote Dr. Johnson again, " such a man is positive and confident, because he knows that his mind was once strong, but knows not that it has become weak." Antiquated managers, indeed, like Polonius, seldom have much strength but as they fall back upon the resources of memory : out of these, the ashes, so to speak, of extinct faculties, they may appear wise long after the springs of real wisdom are dried up within them ; as a man who *has lost his sight* may seem to distinguish colours, provided he does not speak of the particular colours before him.

Polonius has great knowledge of the world ; though even here his mind has come to rest mainly in generalities. Accordingly the pithy maxims he gives Laertes, to " character in his memory," are capital in their way ; nothing could be better : yet they are but the well-seasoned fruits of general experience and reflection ; and there is no apparent reason why he should speak them at that time, except that they were strong in his mind. One would suppose that in such an act of paternal blessing he would try to breathe some fire of noble sentiment into his son ; whereas he thinks of nothing higher than cold precepts of worldly prudence ; which seem indeed to be the essence of religion with him. And he imagines that such thoughts will be a sufficient breakwater against the passions of youth !

Note, also, what a precious, characteristic specimen of unconscious grannyism he blunders out when he undertakes to explain "the very cause of Hamlet's lunacy." Here, with his hands brimfull of the most serious business, he is pleased, notwithstanding, to spend the time in dallying with artful quirks of thought and speech, — a piece of pedantry and impertinence which has often reminded me of the man who " could speak no sense in several languages." In this instance, again, he shows a good memory of what he had learned at the university; but he manifestly has no live organs to perceive the rights of the occasion. Such is the natural effect of " dotage encroaching upon wisdom."

Ophelia.

The pathetic sweetness of Ophelia " divided from herself and her fair judgment" touches the soul with surpassing delicacy. But the touch is full of power withal. Her madness is totally different from Hamlet's; but the delineation of it, so science assures us, is no less true to nature, and evinces an insight no less profound of pathological laws. The violence her feelings suffered in the constrained repulse of her lover after she had " suck'd the honey of his music vows"; her tender grief at his subsequent condition, which is all the greater that she thinks herself the cause of it; the shock of her father's sudden and violent death, — the father whom she loves with such religious entireness, — and this by the hand of that same lover, and in consequence of the madness into which, as she believes, her own action has cast him; — all these causes join in producing her lapse of reason, and all reappear more or less in what comes from her afterwards. Her insanity is complete, unconscious, and such as, it is said, never ends but with the sufferer's death. There is no method in it: she is like one walking and talking in her sleep; her mind still busy, but its sources of activity all within; literally " incapable of her own distress." The verses she sings are fragments of old ballads which she had heard in her childhood, when she understood not the meaning of them, and which had faded from her memory, but are now revived just enough for her inward eye to catch the words. The immodesty of some of them is surpassingly touching, because it tells us, as nothing else could, that she is utterly unconscious of what she is saying. The fine threads of association by which they are now brought to her mind may be felt, but cannot be described. And the sweet, guileless, gentle spirit of the dear girl casts a tender sanctity over the whole expression.

This delineation shows the Poet under an aspect very peculiar and well worth the noting. His genius here appears literally angelic in its steps and tones of purity and reverence and human-heartedness. He gives just enough to start our tenderest sympathies, but nothing to entertain a prurient curiosity; barely hinting the nature of the disease, and then drawing the veil of silence over it, like some protecting spirit of humanity, sent to guard its sacredest possessions from unholy eyes and irreverent hands. In all this we have what may be fitly termed the Shakespeare of Shakespeare; — I mean his ineffable delicacy and cleanness of moral perception, and his angelic awe of moral beauty.

The central idea or formal cause of Ophelia's character stands in perfect simplicity, — the pure whiteness of perfect truth. This is her wisdom, — the wisdom, not of reflection, but of instinctive reason, — a spontaneous beating of her heart in unison with the soul of Nature, and all the better for being so. And her free docility to paternal counsel and full submission to paternal command are in no sort the result of weakness; filial duty and filial affection being the native element of her young life; so that she instinctively shrinks from forsaking that element, and indeed never thinks of doing so, any more than she does of disowning the laws of gravity and respiration.

Ophelia's situation much resembles Imogen's; their characters are in marked contrast. Both appear amidst the corruptions of a wicked court, and both pass through them unhurt; the one because she knows not of them, the other because she both knows and hates them. And the reason why Ophelia knows not of them is because her simplicity of character makes her susceptive only of that which is simple.

The space Ophelia fills in the reader's thoughts is strangely disproportionate to that which she fills in the play. Her very silence utters her; unseen, she is missed, and so thought of the more; in her absence she is virtually present in what others bring from her. Whatever grace comes from Polonius and the Queen is of her inspiring: Laertes is scarce regarded but as he loves his sister: of Hamlet's soul, too, she is the sunrise and the morning hymn. The soul of innocence and gentleness, virtue radiates from her insensibly, as fragrance is exhaled from flowers. It is in such forms that Heaven most frequently visits us.

Ophelia's insanity is one of those mysterious visitings over which we can only brood in dumb compassion; which Heaven alone has a heart adequately to pity, and a hand effectually to heal. Its pathos were too much to be borne, but for the incense that rises from her crushed spirit as she turns "thought and affliction, passion, Hell itself to favour and to prettiness."—Of her death what shall be said? The "snatches of old tunes" with which she chaunts, as it were, her own burial service, are like smiles gushing from the heart of woe. I must leave her with the words of Hazlitt: "O rose of May! O flower too soon faded! Her love, her madness, her death, are described with the truest touches of tenderness and pathos. It is a character which nobody but Shakespeare could have drawn, and to the conception of which there is not the smallest approach, except in some of the old romantic ballads."

The Queen.

The Queen's affection for this lovely being is one of those unexpected strokes of art, so frequent in Shakespeare, which surprise us into reflection by their naturalness. That Ophelia should disclose a vein of goodness in the Queen, was necessary, perhaps, to keep us both from misprising the influence of the one and from exaggerating the wickedness of the other. The love she thus inspires tells us that her helplessness springs from innocence, not from weakness, and so prevents the pity which her condition moves from lessening the respect due to her character.

Almost any other author would have depicted Gertrude without a single alleviating trait. Beaumont and Fletcher would probably have made her simply frightful or loathsome, and capable only of exciting abhorrence or disgust; if, indeed, in her monstrous depravity she had not rather failed to excite any feeling. Shakespeare, with far more effect as well as far more truth, exhibits her with such a mixture of good and bad as neither disarms censure nor precludes pity. Herself dragged along in the terrible train of consequences which her own guilt had a hand in starting, she is hurried away into the same dreadful abyss along with those whom she loves, and against whom she has sinned. In her tenderness towards Hamlet and Ophelia we recognize the virtues of the mother without in the least palliating the guilt of the wife ; while the crimes in which she is a partner almost disappear in those of which she is the victim.

Conclusion.

This play has many and varied scenic excellences, of which only a few of the less obvious need be specified. — In

the platform scenes the chills of a northern winter midnight
seem creeping over us as the heartsick sentinels pass in view,
and, steeped in moonlight and drowsiness, exchange their
meeting and parting salutations. The thoughts and images
that rise up in their minds are just such as the anticipation of
preternatural visions would be likely to inspire. And the
sensations one has in reading these scenes are not unlike
those of a child passing a graveyard by moonlight. Out of
the dim and drowsy moonbeams apprehension creates its own
objects ; the fancies embody themselves in surrounding facts ;
fears giving shape to outward things, while those things give
outwardness to the fears.—The heterogeneous, oddly-assorted
elements that are brought together in the grave-digging scene ;
the strange mixture of songs and witticisms and dead-men's
bones, and the still stranger transitions of the sprightly, the
meditative, the solemn, the playful, the grotesque, make up
such a combination as Shakespeare only could conceive.
Here we have the hero's profound discourse of thought, his
earnest moral reflectiveness, and his most idiomatic humour, all working out together. As illustrating his whole
character, in all its depth and complexity, the scene is one
of the richest and wisest in the play.

HAMLET, PRINCE OF DENMARK.

PERSONS REPRESENTED.

CLAUDIUS, King of Denmark.
HAMLET, his Nephew, Son of the former King.
POLONIUS, Lord Chamberlain.
HORATIO, Friend to Hamlet.
LAERTES, Son of Polonius.
VOLTIMAND,
CORNELIUS,
ROSENCRANTZ,
GUILDENSTERN,   } Courtiers.
OSRIC, a Courtier.
Another Courtier.
A Priest.

MARCELLUS,
BERNARDO,   } Officers.
FRANCISCO, a Soldier.
REYNALDO, Servant to Polonius.
A Captain. Ambassadors.
The Ghost of Hamlet's Father.
FORTINBRAS, Prince of Norway.
Two Grave-diggers.

GERTRUDE, Mother of Hamlet, and Queen.
OPHELIA, Daughter of Polonius.

Lords, Ladies, Officers, Soldiers, Players, Sailors, Messengers, and Attendants. SCENE, Elsinore.

ACT I.

SCENE I. — *Elsinore. A Platform before the Castle.*

FRANCISCO *at his Post. Enter to him* BERNARDO.

Bern. WHO's there?
Fran. Nay, answer me :[1] stand, and unfold yourself.
Bern. Long live the King!
Fran. Bernardo?

[1] Answer *me*, as I have the right to challenge *you*. Bernardo then gives in answer the watchword, "Long live the King!"

Bern. He.

Fran. You come most carefully upon your hour.

Bern. 'Tis now struck twelve ; get thee to bed, Francisco

Fran. For this relief much thanks : 'tis bitter cold,
And I am sick at heart.

Bern. Have you had quiet guard?

Fran.   Not a mouse stirring.   10

Bern. Well, good night.
If you do meet Horatio and Marcellus,
The rivals[2] of my watch, bid them make haste.

Fran. I think I hear them. — Stand, ho !   Who is there?

Enter HORATIO *and* MARCELLUS.

Hora. Friends to this ground.

Marc.   And liegemen to the Dane.

Fran. Give you good night.[3]

Marc.   O, farewell, honest soldier :
Who hath relieved you?

Fran.   Bernardo has my place.
Give you good night.   [*Exit.*

Marc.   Holla ! Bernardo !

Bern.   Say, —
What, is Horatio there?

Hora.   A piece of him.   20

Bern. Welcome, Horatio ; welcome, good Marcellus.

---

[2] *Rivals* are associates or partners.   A brook, rivulet, or river, *rivus*,
being a natural boundary between different proprietors, was owned by them
in common ; that is, they were *partners* in the right and use of it.   From the
strifes thus engendered, the *partners* came to be *contenders :* hence the ordinary sense of *rival*.

[3] This salutation is an abbreviated form of, " May God give you a good
night " ; which has been still further abbreviated in the phrase, " Good
night."

~~Hora~~. *Marc.* What, has this thing[4] appear'd again to-night?

Bern. I have seen nothing.

Marc. Horatio says 'tis but our fantasy,
And will not let belief take hold of him
Touching this dreaded sight, twice seen of us:
Therefore I have intreated him along
With us to watch the minutes of this night,
That, if again this apparition come,
He may approve our eyes,[5] and speak to it.

Hora. Tush, tush, 'twill not appear.

Bern.   Sit down awhile; 30
And let us once again assail your ears,
That are so fortified against our story,
What[6] we two nights have seen.

Hora.   Well, sit we down,
And let us hear Bernardo speak of this.

Bern. Last night of all,
When yond same star that's westward from the pole[7]
Had made his[8] course t' illume that part of heaven

---

[4] There is a temperate scepticism, well befitting a scholar, in Horatio's "has this *thing* appeared again to-night." *Thing* is the most general and indefinite substantive in the language. Observe the gradual approach to what is more and more definite. "Dreaded sight" cuts off a large part of the indefiniteness, and "this apparition" is a further advance to the particular. The matter is aptly ordered for what Coleridge calls "*credibilizing* effect."

[5] That is, *make good* our vision, or *prove* our eyes to be *true*. *Approve* was often thus used in the sense of *confirm*.

[6] "*With an account of* what," is the meaning; the language being elliptical.

[7] Of course the *polar star*, or north star, is meant, which appears to stand still, while the other stars in its neighbourhood seem to revolve around it.

[8] *His* was continually used for *its* in Shakespeare's time, the latter not being then an accepted word, though it was just creeping into use. The English Bible abounds in instances of *his* so used; as, "the fruit-tree yielding fruit after *his* kind"; and, "giveth to every seed *his* own body."

Where now it burns, Marcellus and myself,
The bell then beating one,—

Enter the GHOST.

Marc. Peace, break thee off; look, where it comes again !

Bern. In the same figure, like the King that's dead.

Marc. Thou art a scholar; speak to it, Horatio.[9]

Bern. Looks it not like the King? mark it, Horatio.

Hora. Most like: it harrows me[10] with fear and wonder.

Bern. It would[11] be spoke to.

Marc.　　　　　　　　　　Question it, Horatio.

Hora. What art thou that usurp'st this time of night,
Together with that fair and warlike form
In which the Majesty of buried Denmark
Did sometimes[12] march? by Heaven I charge thee, speak !

Marc. It is offended.

Bern.　　　　　　　　See, it stalks away !

Hora. Stay ! speak, speak ! I charge thee, speak !

　　　　　　　　　　　　　　　　[*Exit* GHOST.

Marc. 'Tis gone, and will not answer.

Bern. How now, Horatio ! you tremble and look pale :
Is not this something more than fantasy?
What think you on't?

[9] It was believed that a supernatural being could only be spoken to with effect by persons of learning; exorcisms being usually practiced by the clergy in Latin. So in *The Night Walker* of Beaumont and Fletcher : " Let's call the butler up, for he speaks Latin, and that will daunt the Devil."

[10] To *harrow* is to *distress*, to *vex*, to *disturb*. To *harry* and to *harass* have the same origin. Milton has the word in *Comus* : " Amazed I stood *harrow'd* with grief and fear."

[11] *Would* and *should* were often used indiscriminately. I am not clear, however, whether the meaning here is, " It *wants* to be spoke to," or " It *ought* to be spoke to." Perhaps both.

[12] *Sometimes* and *sometime* were used indiscriminately, and often, as here in the sense of *formerly*.

Hora. Before my God, I might not this believe
Without the sensible and true avouch
Of mine own eyes.

    Marc.   Is it not like the King?

    Hora. As thou art to thyself:
Such was the very armour he had on
When he th' ambitious Norway combated;
So frown'd he once, when, in an angry parle,
He smote the sledded Polacks[13] on the ice.
'Tis strange.

    Marc. Thus twice before, and jump[14] at this dead hour,
With martial stalk hath he gone by our watch.

    Hora. In what particular thought to work I know not;
But, in the gross and scope of my opinion,
This bodes some strange eruption to our State.[15]

    Marc. Good now,[16] sit down, and tell me, he that knows,
Why this same strict and most observant watch
So nightly toils the subject[17] of the land,
And why such daily cast of brazen cannon,
And foreign mart for implements of war;

[13] *Polacks* was used for *Polanders* in Shakespeare's time. *Sledded* is *sledged;* on a *sled* or *sleigh.* — *Parle,* in the preceding line, is the same as *parley.*

[14] *Jump* and *just* were synonymous in the time of Shakespeare. So in Chapman's *May Day,* 1611: "Your appointment was *jumpe* at three with me."

[15] Horatio means that, in a general interpretation of the matter, this foreshadows some great evil or disaster to the State; though he cannot conceive in what particular shape the evil is to come.

[16] " *Good* now " was often used precisely as the phrase " *well* now." Also, *good* for *well.* So in *The Tempest,* i. 1: " *Good,* speak to the mariners." And again: " *Good,* yet remember whom thou hast aboard."

[17] The Poet sometimes uses an adjective with the sense of the plural substantive; as here *subject* for *subjects.* — *Toils* is here a transitive verb. — *Mart,* in the next line but one, is *trade.*

Why such impress[18] of shipwrights, whose sore task
Does not divide the Sunday from the week :
What might be toward,[19] that this sweaty haste
Doth make the night joint-labourer with the day?
Who is't that can inform me?

 Hora.   That can I ;
At least, the whisper goes so.[20] Our last King,   8D
Whose image even but now appear'd to us,
Was, as you know, by Fortinbras of Norway,
Thereto prick'd on[21] by a most emulate pride,
Dared to the combat ; in which our valiant Hamlet —
For so this side of our known world esteem'd him —
Did slay this Fortinbras ; who, by a seal'd compáct,
Well ratified by law and heraldry,[22]
Did forfeit, with his life, all those his lands
Which he stood seized of,[23] to the conqueror :
Against the which a moiety competent[24]   9 0

[18] *Impress* here means pressing or forcing of men into the service. — *Divide*, next line, is *distinguish*. Of course, *week* is put for *week-days.*

[19] *Toward*, here, is *at hand*, or *forthcoming.* Often so used.

[20] That is, " so as I am going to tell you."

[21] *Prick'd on* refers to Fortinbras ; the sense being, "by Fortinbras, *who was* prick'd on thereto."

[22] " Law *and* heraldry " is the same as " *the* law *of* heraldry " ; what is sometimes called " the code of honour." Private duels were conducted according to an established code, and heralds had full authority in the matter. The Poet has many like expressions. So in *The Merchant*, v. 1 : " I was beset with shame *and* courtesy " ; which means " with *the* shame of *discourtesy.*" Also in *King Lear*, i. 2 : " This policy *and reverence of* age makes the world bitter," &c. ; meaning " This policy, or *practice, of reverencing* age," &c.

[23] This is the old legal phrase, still in use, for *held possession of,* or *was the rightful owner of.*

[24] *Moiety competent* is *equivalent portion.* The proper meaning of *moiety* is *half ;* so that the sense here is, half of the entire value put in pledge on both sides. — *Gaged* is *pledged.*

Was gagèd by our King ; which had return'd
To the inheritance of Fortinbras,
Had he been vanquisher ; as, by the same co-mart [25]
And carriage of the article design'd, [26]
His fell to Hamlet.   Now, sir, young Fortinbras,
Of unimprovèd mettle [27] hot and full,
Hath in the skirts of Norway here and there
Shark'd up [28] a list of lawless resolutes,
For food and diet, to some enterprise
That hath a stomach in't ; [29] which is no other —
As it doth well appear unto our State —
But to recover of us, by strong hand
And terms compulsative, those foresaid lands
So by his father lost : and this, I take it,
Is the main motive of our preparations,
The source of this our watch, and the chief head
Of this post-haste and romage [30] in the land.

[25] *Co-mart* is *joint-bargain* or *mutual agreement;* the same as *compact* a little before. So, in the preceding speech, *mart* for *trade, purchase,* or *bargain.*

[26] *Design'd* in the sense of the Latin *designatus ; marked out* or *drawn up. Carriage* is *purport* or *drift.*

[27] *Mettle,* in Shakespeare, is *spirit, temper, disposition.—Unimproved* is commonly explained *unimpeached, unquestioned;* and so, it appears, the word was sometimes used. But it may here mean *rude, wild, uncultured;* since Fortinbras, as "like will to like," may well be supposed of a somewhat *lawless* spirit.

[28] *Shark'd up* is *snapped up,* or *raked together;* the idea being, that Fortinbras has gathered eagerly, wherever he could, a band of desperadoes, hard cases, or roughs, who were up to any thing bold and adventurous, and required no pay but their keep.

[29] *Stomach* was often used in the sense of *courage,* or appetite for danger or for fighting. So in *Julius Cæsar,* v. 1 ; "If you dare fight to-day, come to the field ; if not, when you have *stomachs.*"

[30] *Romage,* now spelt *rummage,* is used for ransacking, or making a thorough search.

Bern. I think it be no other but e'en so.

Well may it sort[31] that this portentous figure

Comes armèd through our watch, so like the King   *110*

That was and is the question of these wars.

Hora. A mote it is to trouble the mind's eye.

In the most high and palmy[32] state of Rome,

A little ere the mightiest Julius fell,

The graves stood tenantless, and the sheeted dead

Did squeak and gibber in the Roman streets :

So,[33] stars with trains of fire ; and dews of blood ;

Disasters in the Sun ; and the moist star,[34]

Upon whose influence Neptune's empire stands,

Was sick almost to doomsday[35] with eclipse :   *120*

And even the like precurse of fierce[36] events,

As harbingers preceding still the fates

And prologue to the omen[37] coming on,

Have Heaven and Earth together demonstrated

Unto our climature[38] and countrymen. —

---

[31] *Sort*, probably, for *happen*, or *fall out*. Often so. The word was sometimes used for *suit*, *fit*, or *agree;* which *may be* the sense here.

[32] *Palmy* is *victorious;* the *palm* being the old badge of victory.

[33] *So* is here equivalent, apparently, to *in like sort*, or *like manner*, and naturally draws in the sense of *there were;* unless we choose to regard these words as understood. See Critical Notes.

[34] "The moist star" is the Moon; so called, no doubt, either from the dews that attend her shining, or from her connection with the tides. — "Disasters in the Sun" is astrological, referring to the calamities supposed to be portended by certain aspects or conditions of that luminary.

[35] *Doomsday* is the old word for *judgment-day*. The meaning is that the Moon was sick almost unto death.

[36] The Poet repeatedly uses *fierce* in the general sense of *violent*, *swift*, *excessive*, *vehement*. So he has "*fierce* vanities," "*fierce* abridgment," and "*fierce* wretchedness." — *Precurse* for *precursor*, *forerunner*.

[37] *Omen* is here a *portentous* or *ominous event*.

[38] *Climature* for *clime* or *climate;* used in a local sense.

But soft, behold ! lo, where it comes again !

Re-enter the GHOST.

I'll cross it, though it blast me.[39] — Stay, illusion !
If thou hast any sound, or use of voice,
Speak to me :
If there be any good thing to be done,
That may to thee do ease and grace to me,
Speak to me :
If thou art privy to thy country's fate,
Which happily foreknowing[40] may avoid,
O, speak !
Or if thou hast uphoarded in thy life
Extorted treasure in the womb of Earth,
For which, they say, you spirits oft walk in death,
Speak of it :   [*Cock crows.*
         stay, and speak ! — Stop it, Marcellus.
  Marc. Shall I strike at it with my partisan ?[41]
  Hora. Do, if it will not stand.
  Bern.   'Tis here !
  Hora.   'Tis here !
  Marc. 'Tis gone !   [*Exit* GHOST.
We do it wrong, being so majestical,

---

[39] It was believed that a person crossing the path of a spectre became
subject to its malignant influence. Lodge's *Illustrations of English History*,
speaking of Ferdinand, Earl of Derby, who died by witchcraft, as was supposed, in 1594, has the following : " On Friday there appeared a tall man,
who twice crossed him swiftly ; and when the earl came to the place where
he saw this man, he fell sick."

[40] Which *happy* or *fortunate foreknowledge* may avoid : a participle and
adverb used with the sense of a substantive and adjective. — It was an old
superstition that, if a man had " devoured widows' houses " or the portion
of orphans, he could not lie quiet in his grave.

[41] *Partisan* was a *halbert* or *pike ;* a weapon used by watchmen

To offer it the show of violence ;
For it is, as the air, invulnerable,
And our vain blows malicious mockery.

    Bern. It was about to speak, when the cock crew.

    Hora. And then it started like a guilty thing
Upon a fearful summons. I have heard,
The cock, that is the trumpet to the morn,   *150*
Doth with his lofty and shrill-sounding throat
Awake the god of day ; and at his warning,
Whether in sea or fire, in earth or air,
Th' extravagant and erring [42] spirit hies
To his confine : [43] and of the truth herein
This present object made probation.[44]

    Marc. It faded on the crowing of the cock.
Some say that ever, 'gainst that season comes
Wherein our Saviour's birth is celebrated,
The bird of dawning singeth all night long :   *160*
And then, they say, no spirit dare stir abroad ;
The nights are wholesome ; then no planets strike,

---

    [42] *Extravagant* is *extra-vagans*, wandering about, going beyond bounds.
Erring is *erraticus*, straying or roving up and down.

    [43] *Confine* for *place of confinement.* — This is a very ancient belief. Pru-
dentius, born in 348, has a hymn, *Ad Gallicinium*, which aptly illustrates
the text : —

        Ferunt, vagantes Dæmonas,   Hoc esse signum præscii
        Lætos tenebris Noctium,   Norunt repromissæ Spei,
        Gallo canente exterritos   Qua nos soporis liberi
        Sparsim timere, et cedere.   Speramus adventum Dei.

Still more apposite is the following from the old Sarum service : —

        Preco diei jam sonat,   Hoc excitatus Lucifer
        Noctis profundæ pervigil,   Solvit polum caligine ;
        Nocturna lux viantibus,   Hoc omnis errorum chorus
        A nocte noctem segregans.   Viam nocendi deserit.
                                 Gallo canente, spes redit, &c.

    [44] *Probation* for *proof.* Repeatedly so.

No fairy takes,[45] nor witch hath power to charm,
So hallow'd and so gracious is the time.

Hora. So have I heard and do in part believe it.
But, look, the morn, in russet mantle clad,
Walks o'er the dew of yond high eastern hill : [46]
Break we our watch up ; [47] and, by my advice,
Let us impart what we have seen to-night
Unto young Hamlet ; for, upon my life,
This spirit, dumb to us, will speak to him.
Do you consent we shall acquaint him with it,
As needful in our loves, fitting our duty?

Marc. Let's do't, I pray ; and I this morning know
Where we shall find him most conveniently.   [*Exeunt.*

SCENE II. — *A Room of State in the Castle.*

Enter the KING, *the* QUEEN, HAMLET, POLONIUS, LAERTES,
VOLTIMAND, CORNELIUS, Lords, *and* Attendants.

King. Though yet of Hamlet our dear brother's death
The memory be green, and that[1] it us befitted

---

[45] *Take* was used for *blast, infect,* or *smite with disease.* So in *King Lear,* ii. 4: "Strike her young bones, you *taking* airs, with lameness." — *Gracious,* in Shakespeare, sometimes means *full of grace* or of the *Divine favour.*

[46] These last three speeches are admirably conceived. The speakers are in a highly kindled state: when the Ghost vanishes, their terror presently subsides into an inspiration of the finest quality, and their intense excitement, as it passes off, blazes up in a subdued and pious rapture of poetry.

[47] This, let the grammarians say what they will, is a clear instance of the first person plural, in the imperative mood. The same has occurred once before : " Well, *sit we down,* and *let us hear* Bernardo speak of this."

[1] Instead of *that,* present usage would repeat *though.* But in such cases the old language in full was *though that, if that, since that, when that,* &c.; and Shakespeare, in a second clause, very often uses the latter word instead of repeating the first. The same thing often occurs in Burke, who died in 1797.

To bear our hearts in grief, and our whole kingdom
To be contracted in one brow of woe,
Yet so far hath discretion fought with nature
That we with wiser sorrow think on him,
Together with remembrance of ourselves.
Therefore our sometime [2] sister, now our Queen,
Th' imperial jointress [3] of this warlike State,
Have we, as 'twere with a defeated joy, —
With one auspicious and one dropping eye ; [4]
With mirth in funeral and with dirge in marriage,
In equal scale weighing delight and dole ; —
Taken to wife : nor have we herein barr'd
Your better wisdoms, which have freely gone
With this affair along : [5] For all, our thanks.

　　Now follows that you know : [6] Young Fortinbras,
Holding a weak supposal of our worth,
Or thinking by our late dear brother's death
Our State to be disjoint [7] and out of frame,

---

[2] *Sometime*, in the sense of *former*, or *formerly*. See page 48, note 12.

[3] *Jointress* is the same as *heiress*. The Poet herein follows the history, which represents the former King to have come to the throne by marriage; so that whatever of hereditary claim Hamlet has to the crown is in right of his mother. See the Introduction, page 7.

[4] The same thought occurs in *The Winter's Tale*, v. 2: "She had *one eye declined* for the loss of her husband, *another elevated* that the oracle was fulfill'd." There is an old proverbial phrase, "To laugh with one eye, and cry with the other."

[5] Note the strained, elaborate, and antithetic style of the King's speech thus far. As he is there shamming and playing the hypocrite, he naturally tries how finely he can word it. In what follows, he speaks like a man, his mind moving with simplicity and directness as soon as he comes to plain matters of business.

[6] "Now follows that *which* you know *already*." *That* was continually used where we should use *what*.

[7] *Disjoint* for *disjointed*. The Poet has many preterites so formed.

Colleaguèd[8] with the dream of his advantage,
He hath not fail'd to pester us with message,
Importing the surrender of those lands
Lost by his father, with all bands[9] of law,
To our most valiant brother.   So much for him.   25
Now for ourself, and for this time of meeting:
Thus much the business is: We have here writ
To Norway, uncle of young Fortinbras, —
Who, impotent and bed-rid, scarcely hears
Of this his nephew's purpose, — to suppress   30
His further gait herein; in that[10] the levies,
The lists, and full proportions, are all made
Out of his subject: — And we here dispatch
You, good Cornelius, and you, Voltimand,
For bearers of this greeting to old Norway;   35
Giving to you no further personal power
To[11] business with the King more than the scope
Of these dilated articles allow.[12]
Farewell, and let your haste commend your duty.

Corn. }
Volt. }   In that and all things will we show our duty.   40

8 *Colleaguèd* does not refer to, or, as we should say, agree with *Fortin-bras*, but with *supposal*, or rather with the whole sense of the three preceding lines. So that the meaning is, "his supposal of our weakness, or of our unsettled condition, *united* with his expectation of advantage."

9 *Band* and *bond* were the same, and both used for *obligation*.

10 *Gait* is *course, progress;* which is much the same as *walk.—In that* has the sense of *because* or *inasmuch as*. Often so.

11 *To* was often thus used where we should use *for*. So a little before, in "taken *to* wife," and a little after in "bow them *to* your gracious leave."

12 The scope of these articles when dilated or explained in full. Such elliptical expressions are common with the Poet. The rules of modern grammar would require *allows* instead of *allow;* but in old writers, when the noun and the verb have a genitive intervening, it is very common for the verb to take the number of the genitive.

King. We doubt it nothing ; heartily farewell. —

[*Exeunt* VOLTIMAND *and* CORNELIUS.

And now, Laertes, what's the news with you?
You told us of some suit : what is't, Laertes?
You cannot speak of reason [13] to the Dane,
And lose your voice : what wouldst thou beg, Laertes,
That shall not be my offer, not thy asking?
The head is not more native to the heart,
The hand more instrumental to the mouth,
Than is the throne of Denmark to thy father. [14]
What wouldst thou have, Laertes?

Laer.   Dread my lord, [15]
Your leave and favour to return to France ;
From whence though willingly I came to Denmark,
To show my duty in your coronation,
Yet now, I must confess, that duty done,
My thoughts and wishes bend again toward France,
And bow them to your gracious leave and pardon.

King. Have you your father's leave? — What says Polonius?

Polo. He hath, my lord, wrung from me my slow leave
By laboursome petition ; and at last
Upon his will I seal'd my hard [16] consent :
I do beseech you, give him leave to go.

King. Take thy fair hour, Laertes ; time be thine,

---

[13] That is, cannot speak *what is reasonable.*

[14] The various parts of the body enumerated are not more *allied, more
necessary* to each other, than the King of Denmark is bound to your father
to do him service.

[15] We should say "my dread lord." Shakespeare abounds in such inver-
sions. So "good my lord," "dear my brother," "sweet my sister," &c.

[16] *Hard* for *reluctant, difficult ;* like *slow* just before.

And thy best graces spend it at thy will ![17] —
But now, my cousin Hamlet, and my son, —

    Ham. [*Aside.*] A little more than kin, and less than kind.[18]

    King. — How is it that the clouds still hang on you?

    Ham. Not so, my lord ; I am too much i' the sun.[19]

    Queen. Good Hamlet, cast thy nighted colour off,
And let thine eye look like a friend on Denmark.
Do not for ever with thy vailèd lids[20]
Seek for thy noble father in the dust.
Thou know'st 'tis common ; all that live must die,
Passing through nature to eternity.

    Ham. Ay, madam, it is common.

    Queen.   If it be,
Why seems it so particular with thee?

    Ham. Seems, madam ! nay, it is ; I know not *seems*.
'Tis not alone my inky cloak, good mother,

[17] "Take an auspicious hour, Laertes ; be your time your own, and thy best virtues guide thee in spending of it at thy will."

[18] The King is "a little more than kin" to Hamlet, because, in being at once his uncle and his father, he is *twice* kin. And he is "less than kind," because his incestuous marriage, as Hamlet views it, is *unnatural* or *out of nature.* The Poet repeatedly uses *kind* in its primitive sense of *nature.* So, "your cuckoo sings by *kind*," and, "fitted by *kind* for rape and villainy." — *Cousin* was used in the general sense of *kinsman*, especially for *nephew* and *niece*, as well as in its modern sense.

[19] Hamlet seems to have a twofold, perhaps a threefold meaning here. First, he intends a sort of antithesis to the King's, "How is it that the clouds still hang on you?" Second, he probably alludes to the old proverbial phrase of being *in the sun*, or *in the warm sun*, which used to signify the state of being without the charities of home and kindred, — exposed to the social inclemencies of the world. Hamlet regards himself as exiled from these charities, as having lost both father and mother. Perhaps he also intends a sarcastic quibble between *sun* and *son*.

[20] With *downcast eyes.* To *vail* is to *lower*, to *let fall.*

Nor customary suits of solemn black,
Nor windy suspiration of forced breath,
No, nor the fruitful river in the eye,
Nor the dejected haviour of the visage,
Together with all forms, modes, shows of grief,
That can denote me truly : these, indeed, seem,
For they are actions that a man might play :
But I have that within which passeth show ;
These but the trappings and the suits of woe.

  King. 'Tis sweet and cómmendable in your nature, Ham-
   let,
To give these mourning duties to your father :
But, you must know, your father lost a father ;
That father lost, lost his ; and the survivor bound
In filial obligation for some term
To do obsequious [21] sorrow : but to persevere
In obstinate condolement is a course
Of impious stubbornness ; 'tis unmanly grief :
It shows a will most incorrect [22] to Heaven,
A heart unfortified, a mind impatient,
An understanding simple and unschool'd :
For what we know must be, and is as common
As any the most vulgar thing to sense,
Why should we in our peevish opposition
Take it to heart ? Fie ! 'tis a fault to Heaven,
A fault against the dead, a fault to Nature,
To reason most absurd ; whose common theme
Is death of fathers, and who still hath cried,
From the first corse till he that died to-day,
This must be so. We pray you, throw to earth

---

[21] The Poet uses *obsequious* as having the sense of *obsequies.*
[22] *Incorrect* is here used in the sense of *incorrigible.*

This unprevailing[23] woe, and think of us
As of a father ; for let the world take note,
You are the most immediate to our throne ;
And with no less nobility of love
Than that which dearest father bears his son
Do I impart toward you.[24]   For your intent
In going back to school in Wittenberg,[25]
It is most retrograde to our desire ;
And we beseech you, bend you to remain
Here, in the cheer and comfort of our eye,
Our chiefest courtier, cousin, and our son.

   Queen. Let not thy mother lose her prayers, Hamlet :
I pray thee, stay with us ; go not to Wittenberg.

   Ham. I shall in all my best obey you, madam.

   King. Why, 'tis a loving and a fair reply :
Be as ourself in Denmark. — Madam, come ;
This gentle and unforced accord of Hamlet
Sits smiling to my heart : in grace whereof,
No jocund health that Denmark drinks to-day,
But the great cannon to the clouds shall tell ;
And the King's rouse[26] the heavens shall bruit again,

23 *Unprevailing* was used in the sense of *unavailing*.

24 "Impart towards you," seems rather odd language, especially as *impart* has no object. The meaning probably is, "I take you into a partnership," or, "I invest you with a participation of the royal dignity, as heir-presumptive." — "Nobility of love" is merely a generous or heightened phrase for *love.* See Critical Notes.

25 *School* was applied to places not only of academical, but also of professional study ; and in the olden time men were wont to spend their whole lives in such cloistered retirements of learning. So that we need not suppose Hamlet was "going back to school" as an undergraduate.

26 A *rouse* was a deep draught to one's health, wherein it was the custom to empty the cup or goblet. Its meaning, and probably its origin, was the same as *carouse.* To *bruit* is to *noise ;* used with *again,* the same as *echo* or *reverberate.*

Respeaking earthly thunder.   Come away.

                     [Exeunt all but HAMLET.

   Ham. O, that this too-too solid flesh would melt,
Thaw, and resolve [27] itself into a dew !
Or that the Everlasting had not fix'd
His canon 'gainst self-slaughter !   O God ! O God !
How weary, stale, flat, and unprofitable
Seem to me all the uses of this world !
Fie on't ! O fie ! 'tis an unweeded garden,
That grows to seed ; things rank and gross in nature
Possess it merely. [28]   That it should come to this !
But two months dead ! — nay, not so much, not two :
So excellent a king ; that was, to this,
Hyperion to a satyr ; [29] so loving to my mother,
That he might not beteem [30] the winds of heaven
Visit her face too roughly.   Heaven and Earth !
Must I remember ? why, she would hang on him,
As if increase of appetite had grown
By what it fed on : and yet, within a month, —
Let me not think on't, — Frailty, thy name is woman ! —
A little month, or e'er [31] those shoes were old
With which she follow'd my poor father's body,

---

   [27] *Resolve* in its old sense of *dissolve*. The three words *melt, thaw,* and
resolve, all signifying the same thing, are used merely for emphasis, — *melt,
melt, melt.*

   [28] *Merely* in one of the Latin senses of *mere; wholly, entirely.*

   [29] *Hyperion*, which literally means *sublimity*, was one of the names of
Apollo, the most beautiful of all the gods, and much celebrated in classic
poetry for his golden locks. Here, as often, *to* has the force of *compared to,*
or *in comparison with.*

   [30] *Beteem* is an old word for *permit* or *suffer.*

   [31] *Or ever* was in common use for *before, sooner than.* So in Daniel, vi.
24 : " And the lions brake all their bones in pieces *or ever* they came to the
bottom of the den."

Like Niobe, all tears ; [32] — why, she, even she —
O God ! a beast, that wants discourse of reason, [33]
Would have mourn'd longer — married with my uncle,
My father's brother ; but no more like my father
Than I to Hercules : within a month ;
Ere yet the salt of most unrighteous tears
Had left the flushing [34] in her gallèd eyes,
She married.   O, most wicked speed, to post
With such dexterity to incestuous sheets !
It is not, nor it cannot come to, good :
But break, my heart, for I must hold my tongue.

    Enter HORATIO, MARCELLUS, *and* BERNARDO.

  Hora. Hail to your lordship !
  Ham.   I'm glad to see you well :
Horatio,— or I do forget myself.
  Hora. The same, my lord, and your poor servant ever.
  Ham. Sir, my good friend ; I'll change that name with
      you : [35]
And what make you [36] from Wittenberg, Horatio ?—
Marcellus ?

---

[32] Niobe was the wife of Amphion, King of Thebes. As she had twelve
children, she went to crowing one day over Latona, who had only two,
Apollo and Diana. In return for this, all her twelve were slain by Latona's
two ; and Jupiter, in pity of her sorrow, transformed her into a rock, from
which her tears issued in a perennial stream.

[33] *Discourse of reason*, in old philosophical language, is *rational* discourse,
or *discursive* reason ; the faculty of pursuing a train of thought, or of passing from thought to thought in the way of inference or conclusion.

[34] Shakespeare has *leave* repeatedly in the sense of *leave off*, or *cease*.
Flushing is the redness of the eyes caused by what the Poet elsewhere calls
" eye-offending brine."

[35] As if he had said, " No, not my poor servant : we are *friends ;* that is
the style I will exchange with you."

[36] " What *make* you ? " is old language for " What *do* you ? "

Marc. My good lord,—

Ham. I'm very glad to see you.—[*To* BERNARDO.]
        Good even, sir.[37]—
But what, in faith, make you from Wittenberg?

Hora. A truant disposition, good my lord.

Ham. I would not hear your enemy say so;
Nor shall you do mine ear that violence,
To make it truster of your own report
Against yourself: I know you are no truant.
But what is your affair in Elsinore?
We'll teach you to drink deep ere you depart.

Hora. My lord, I came to see your father's funeral.

Ham. I pray thee, do not mock me, fellow-student;
I think it was to see my mother's wedding.

Hora. Indeed, my lord, it follow'd hard upon.

Ham. Thrift, thrift, Horatio! the funeral baked meats [38]
Did coldly furnish forth the marriage tables.
Would I had met my dearest [39] foe in Heaven
Or ever I had seen that day, Horatio!
My father!—methinks I see my father.

Hora. O, where, my lord?

Ham.   In my mind's eye, Horatio.

[37] The words, *Good even, sir*, are evidently addressed to Bernardo, whom
Hamlet has not before known; but as he now meets him in company with
old acquaintants, like a true gentleman, as he is, he gives him a salutation
of kindness. — Marcellus has said before of Hamlet, "I this *morning* know
where we shall find him." But *good even* was the common salutation after
noon.

[38] Scott, in *The Bride of Lammermoor*, has made the readers of romance
familiar with the old custom of "funeral baked meats," which was kept up
in Scotland till a recent period. — *Thrift* means *economy:* all was done
merely to save cost.

[39] In Shakespeare's time *dearest* was applied to any person or thing that
excites the liveliest interest, whether of love or hate.

Hora. I saw him once; he was a goodly king.

Ham. He was a man, take him for all in all,
I shall not look upon his like again.

Hora. My lord, I think I saw him yesternight.

Ham. Saw who?

Hora. My lord, the King your father.

Ham. The King my father!

Hora. Season your admiration [40] for a while
With an attentive ear, till I deliver,
Upon the witness of these gentlemen,
This marvel to you.

Ham.   For God's love, let me hear.

Hora. Two nights together had these gentlemen,
Marcellus and Bernardo, on their watch,
In the dead vast [41] and middle of the night,
Been thus encounter'd: A figure like your father,
Arm'd at all points, exactly, cap-a-pie,
Appears before them, and with solemn march
Goes slow and stately by them: thrice he walk'd
By their oppress'd and fear-surprisèd eyes,
Within his truncheon's length; whilst they, distill'd
Almost to jelly with the act of fear, [42]
Stand dumb, and speak not to him. This to me
In dreadful secrecy impart they did;
And I with them the third night kept the watch:
Where, as they had deliver'd, both in time,

[40] *Admiration* in the Latin sense of *wonder* or *astonishment.* — *Season* is *qualify* or *temper.*

[41] *Vast* is *void* or *vacancy.* So in *The Tempest,* i. 2: "Urchins shall, for that *vast* of night that they may work," &c.

[42] To *distill* is to fall in drops, to melt; so that *distill'd* is a very natural and fit expression for the cold sweat caused by intense fear. "The *act of fear*" is the *action* or the *effect* of fear.

Form of the thing, each word made true and good,
The apparition comes.　I knew your father;
These hands are not more like.

  Ham.   But where was this?
  Marc. My lord, upon the platform where we watch'd.
  Ham. Did you not speak to it?
  Hora.   My lord, I did;
But answer made it none: yet once methought
It lifted up its head and did address
Itself to motion, like as it would speak;
But even then the morning cock crew loud,
And at the sound it shrunk in haste away,
And vanish'd from our sight.

  Ham.   'Tis very strange.
  Hora. As I do live, my honour'd lord, 'tis true;
And we did think it writ down in our duty
To let you know of it.

  Ham. Indeed, indeed, sirs, but this troubles me.
Hold you the watch to-night?

  Marc. }
  Bern. }   We do, my lord.

  Ham. Arm'd, say you?
  Marc. }
  Bern. } Arm'd, my lord.

  Ham. From top to toe?
  Marc. }
  Bern. }   My lord, from head to foot.

  Ham. Then saw you not his face?
  Hora. O, yes, my lord; he wore his beaver up.[43]
  Ham. What, look'd he frowningly?

---

[43] The beaver was a movable part of the helmet, which could be drawn
down over the face or pushed up over the forehead.

Hora. A countenance more in sorrow than in anger.

Ham. Pale, or red?

Hora. Nay, very pale.

Ham.   And fix'd his eyes upon you?

Hora. Most constantly.

Ham.   I would I had been there.

Hora. It would have much amazed you.

Ham. Very like, very like.   Stay'd it long?

Hora. While one with moderate haste might tell[44] a hundred.

Marc.
Bern. } Longer, longer.

Hora. Not when I saw't.

Ham.   His beard was grizzled? — no?

Hora. It was, as I have seen it in his life,
A sable silver'd.

Ham.   I'll watch to-night ;
Perchance 'twill walk again.

Hora.   I warrant it will.

Ham. If it assume my noble father's person,
I'll speak to it, though Hell itself should gape,
And bid me hold my peace.   I pray you all,
If you have hitherto conceal'd this sight,
Let it be tenable[45] in your silence still ;
And whatsoever else shall hap to-night,
Give it an understanding, but no tongue :
I will requite your loves.   So, fare you well :
Upon the platform, 'twixt eleven and twelve,
I'll visit you.

All.   Our duty to your Honour.

---

[44] To *tell* was continually used for to *count*.

[45] *Tenable* for *retained*.   The Poet has many like instances of confusion

Ham. Your loves, as mine to you ; farewell. —

       [*Exeunt all but* HAMLET.

My father's spirit in arms ! all is not well ;

I doubt[46] some foul play : would the night were come !

Till then sit still, my soul.   Foul deeds will rise,

Though all the Earth o'erwhelm them, to men's eyes. [*Exit.*

   SCENE III. — *A Room in Polonius's House.*

    Enter LAERTES *and* OPHELIA.[1]

Laer. My necessaries are embark'd ; farewell :

And, sister, as the winds give benefit

And convoy is assistant,[2] do not sleep,

But let me hear from you.[3]

 Ophe.   Do you doubt that ?

 Laer. For Hamlet and the trifling of his favour,

Hold it a fashion and a toy in blood,

A violet in the youth of primy nature,

Forward, not permanent, sweet, not lasting,

The pérfume and supplyance of a minute ;[4]

No more.

---

of forms; as *admired* for *admirable,* that is, *wonderful,* in *Macbeth,* iii. 4 : " Broke the good meeting with most *admired* disorder.

[46] *Doubt* in the sense of *fear* or *suspect.* Repeatedly so.

[1] This scene must be regarded as one of Shakespeare's lyric movements in the play, and the skill with which it is interwoven with the dramatic parts is peculiarly an excellence with our Poet. *You experience the sensation of a pause, without the sense of a stop.* — COLERIDGE.

[2] *Convoy* is used for *conveyance.* Communication with France being by sea, of course there needed both a ship to carry letters, and a wind to drive the ship.

[3] That is, "*without letting* me hear from you." The Poet repeatedly uses *but* in this way; the exceptive *but,* from *be out.* The usage is very common in Scotch : Burns has it frequently

[4] A mere pastime, to *supply* or *fill up* the passing hour ; a sweet play, to

Ophe. No more but so?

Laer.   Think it no more:[5]

For nature, crescent, does not grow alone
In thews[6] and bulk, but, as this temple waxes,
The inward service of the mind and soul
Grows wide withal.[7]   Perhaps he loves you now;
And now no soil nor cautel[8] doth besmirch
The virtue of his will: but you must fear;
His greatness weigh'd, his will is not his own;
For he himself is subject to his birth:[9]
He may not, as unvalued persons do,
Carve for himself; for on his choice depends
The safety and the health of the whole State;
And therefore must his choice be circumscribed
Unto the voice and yielding of that body
Whereof he is the head.[10]   Then, if he says he loves you,
It fits your wisdom so far to believe it
As he in his particular act and place
May give his saying deed;[11] which is no further
Than the main voice of Denmark goes withal.
Then weigh what loss your honour may sustain,

beguile the present idle time.   Instead of *supplyance*, the Poet elsewhere has *supplyment* in much the same sense.

[5] "Take for granted that such is the case, till you have clear proof to the contrary." — *Crescent* is *growing, increasing*.

[6] *Thews* is an old word for *sinews* or *muscles*.

[7] The idea is, that Hamlet's love is but a youthful fancy which, as his mind comes to maturity, he will outgrow.   The passage would seem to infer that the Prince is not so old as he is elsewhere represented to be.

[8] *Cautel* is a debauched relation of *caution*, and means *fraud* or *deceit*.

[9] Subject to the *conditions* which his birth entails upon him.

[10] His choice of a wife must be limited by the approval or consent of the nation.

[11] So far only as he, in his public and official character, shall make his promise good.

If with **too credent** ear you list his songs,[12]
Or lose your heart, or your chaste treasure open
To his unmaster'd importunity.
Fear it, Ophelia, fear it, my dear sister;
And keep you in the rear of your affection,
Out of the shot and danger of desire.
Th' unchariest maid is prodigal enough,
If she unmask her beauty to the Moon:
Virtue itself scapes not calumnious strokes:
The canker galls the infants of the Spring,
Too oft before their buttons be disclosed;[13]
And in the morn and liquid dew of youth
Contagious blastments are most imminent.
Be wary, then; best safety lies in fear:
Youth to itself rebels, though none else near.

    Ophe. I shall th' effect of this good lesson keep,
As watchman to my heart. But, good my brother,
Do not, as some ungracious pastors[14] do,
Show me the steep and thorny way to Heaven,
Whiles, like a puff'd and reckless libertine,
Himself the primrose path of dalliance treads,
And recks not his own read.[15]

    Laer.   O, fear me not.
I stay too long: but here my father comes. —

Enter POLONIUS.

---

[12] "If with too *credulous* ear you *listen to* his songs."

[13] In Shakespeare's time, *canker* was often used of the worm that kills the early buds before they open out into flowers. Perhaps it here means a disease that sometimes infests plants, and *eats* out their life. — *Buttons* is *buds*, and *disclose* is used in the sense of *open* or *unfold*.

[14] Pastors that *have not the grace* to practice what they preach.

[15] *Regards* not his own *lesson*.

A double blessing is a double grace ;
Occasion smiles upon a second leave.

    Polo. Yet here, Laertes? aboard, aboard, for shame !
The wind sits in the shoulder of your sail,
And you are stay'd for.   There ; my blessing with thee !
And these few precepts in thy memory
See thou chárácter.[16]   Give thy thoughts no tongue,
Nor any unproportion'd thought his act.[17]
Be thou familiar, but by no means vulgar.[18]
The friends thou hast, and their adoption tried,
Grapple them to thy soul with hoops of steel ;
But do not dull thy palm with entertainment
Of each new-hatch'd, unfledged comráde.[19]   Beware
Of entrance to a quarrel ; but, being in,
Bear't that th' opposèd may beware of thee.
Give every man thine ear, but few thy voice :
Take each man's censure,[20] but reserve thy judgment.
Costly thy habit as thy purse can buy,
But not express'd in fancy ; rich, not gaudy :
For the apparel oft proclaims the man ;
And they in France of the best rank and station
Are most select and generous, chief in that.[21]
Neither a borrower nor a lender be :
For loan oft loses both itself and friend ;

   [16] To *character* is to *engrave* or *imprint.*

   [17] *Unproportion'd* for *unhandsome* or *unfitting.   His,* again, for *its.*   See page 47, note 8.

   [18] *Vulgar* is here used in its old sense of *common.*

   [19] " Do not *blunt* thy feeling by taking every new acquaintance by the hand, or by admitting him to the intimacy of a friend."

   [20] *Censure* was continually used for *opinion,* or *judgment.*

   [21] That is, most select and generous, but chiefly or especially so in the matter of dress.

And borrowing dulls the edge of husbandry.
This above all : To thine own self be true ;
And it must follow, as the night the day,
Thou canst not then be false to any man.[22]
Farewell ; my blessing season [23] this in thee !
   Laer. Most humbly do I take my leave, my lord.
   Polo. The time invites you ; go, your servants tend.
   Laer. Farewell, Ophelia ; and remember well
What I have said to you.
   Ophe.   'Tis in my memory lock'd,
And you yourself shall keep the key of it.
   Laer. Farewell.   *[Exit.*
   Polo. What is't, Ophelia, he hath said to you?
   Ophe. So please you, something touching the Lord Ham·
     let.
   Polo. Marry,[24] well bethought :
'Tis told me, he hath very oft of late
Given private time to you ; and you yourself
Have of your audience been most free and bounteous.
If it be so, — as so 'tis put on me,

[22] This is regarded by many as a very high strain of morality. I cannot
see it so; though, to be sure, it is as high as Polonius can go: it is the
height of worldly wisdom, — a rule of being wisely selfish. In the same
sense, "honesty is the best policy"; but no truly honest man ever acts on
that principle; and a man who fixes upon no higher rule than that of being true to himself will never be really true to himself. This is one of the
cases wherein a man must aim at the greater, else he will not attain the less.
In other words, a man will never be really true to himself, unless it be a
matter of conscience with him to be true to something higher than himself.
A *passion* for rectitude is the only thing that will serve. See iii. 4, note 16.

   [23] *Season* is here used, apparently, in the sense of *ingrain ;* the idea being that of so *steeping* the counsel into his mind that it will not fade out.

   [24] *Marry* was continually used as a general intensive, like *heracle* and
edepol in Latin. The usage sprang from the custom of swearing by St
Mary the Virgin Mother.

And that in way of caution, — I must tell you,
You do not understand yourself so clearly
As it behoves my daughter and your honour.
What is between you? give me up the truth.

Ophe. He hath, my lord, of late made many tenders
Of his affection to me.

Polo. Affection ! pooh ! you speak like a green girl,
Unsifted[25] in such perilous circumstance.
Do you believe his — *tenders*, as you call them?

Ophe. I do not know, my lord, what I should think.

Polo. Marry, I'll teach you : think yourself a baby ;
That you have ta'en these tenders for true pay,
Which are not sterling.[26]   Tender yourself more dearly ;[27]
Or — not to crack the wind of the poor phrase,
Running it thus[28] — you'll tender me a fool.

Ophe. My lord, he hath impórtuned me with love
In honourable fashion ; —

Polo. Ay, fashion you may call it ; go to, go to.[29]

Ophe. — And hath given countenance to his speech, my
    lord,
With almost all the holy vows of Heaven.

Polo. Ay, springes to catch woodcocks.[30]   I do know

---

[25] *Unsifted* is *untried, inexperienced.* We still speak of *sifting* a matter in the same sense.

[26] Polonius is using *tender* in different senses ; here in a business or financial sense, as in the phrase "legal tender." So our "greenbacks," though legal tender, have not been *sterling ;* that is, have been *below par.*

[27] "Take better care of yourself." To *tender* a thing is, in one sense, to be tender or careful of it. Shakespeare has the word repeatedly so.

[28] Polonius is likening the phrase to a poor nag, which, if run too hard, will be *wind-broken.*

[29] *Go to* is an old phrase of varying import ; sometimes meaning *hush up,* sometimes *come on,* sometimes *go ahead.*

[30] This was a proverbial phrase. There is a collection of epigrams under

When the blood burns, how prodigal the soul
Lends the tongue vows: these blazes, daughter,
Giving more light than heat, extinct in both,
Even in their promise, as it is a-making,
You must not take for fire.[31]   From this time
Be somewhat scanter of your maiden presence;
Set your entreatments at a higher rate
Than a command to parley.[32]   For Lord Hamlet,
Believe so much in him, that he is young;
And with a larger tether[33] may he walk
Than may be given you.   In few,[34] Ophelia,
Do not believe his vows; for they are brokers,[35] —
Not of that dye which their investments show,
But mere implorators of unholy suits,
Breathing like sanctified and pious bawds,[36]
The better to beguile.   This is for all, —
I would not, in plain terms, from this time forth,
Have you so slander[37] any moment's leisure,

that title: the woodcock being accounted a witless bird, from a vulgar notion
that it had no brains. "Springes to catch woodcocks" means arts to entrap
simplicity. *Springe* is, properly, *snare* or *trap*. — *Blood*, in the next line, is
put for *passion*. Often so.

31 Here, as often, *fire* is two syllables: the verse requires it so.

32 Be more difficult of access, and let the *suits to you* for that purpose be
of higher respect than a command to parley.

33 That is, with a *longer line;* a horse, fastened by a string to a stake, is
tethered.

34 In few *words;* in *short.*

35 *Brokers*, as the word is here used, are *go-betweens*, or *panders;* the
same as *bawds*, a little after.

36 So in *As You Like It*, ii. 3: "Your virtues are *sanctified and holy trai-
tors* to you." This joining of words that are really contradictory, or qualify-
ing of a noun with adjectives that literally quench it, sometimes gives great
strength of expression. Even so grave a writer as Hooker speaks of *stealing*
certain benefits upon men "through a kind of *heavenly fraud.*"

37 That is, so disgrace, or misuse, as to *cause* slander.

As to give words or talk with the Lord Hamlet.
Look to't, I charge you : come your ways.

   Ophe. I shall obey, my lord.   [*Exeunt.*

Scene IV. — *The Platform.*

Enter Hamlet, Horatio, *and* Marcellus.

   Ham. The air bites shrewdly ; it is very cold.

   Hora. It is a nipping and an eager[1] air.

   Ham. What hour now?

   Hora.   I think it lacks of twelve.

   Ham. No, it is struck.

   Hora. Indeed? I heard it not : it then draws near the
      season
Wherein the spirit held his wont to walk.

   [*A flourish of trumpets, and ordnance shot off within.*
What does this mean, my lord?

   Ham. The King doth wake to-night, and takes his rouse,[2]
Keeps wassail, and the swaggering up-spring reels ; [3]
And, as he drains his draughts of Rhenish down,
The kettle-drum and trumpet thus bray out
The triumph of his pledge.

   Hora.   Is it a custom?

   Ham. Ay, marry is't ;
But to my mind, though I am native here

---

  [1] *Eager* was used in the sense of the French *aigre*, sharp, biting.

  [2] To *wake* is to *hold a late revel* or *debauch*. A *rouse* is what we now call
a *bumper.* — *Wassail* originally meant a drinking to one's health ; from *wæs
hæl*, health be to you : hence it came to be used for any festivity of the
bottle and the bowl.

  [3] Reels *through* the swaggering *up-spring*, which was the name of a rude,
boisterous German dance, as appears from a passage in Chapman's *Alphon-
sus :* "We Germans have no changes in our dances ; an almain and an *up-
spring*, that is all."

And to the manner born, it is a custom
More honour'd in the breach than the observance.
This heavy-headed revel east and west [4]
Makes us traduced and tax'd of other nations :
They clepe us drunkards, and with swinish phrase
Soil our addition ; [5] and indeed it takes
From our achievements, though perform'd at height,
The pith and marrow of our attribute. [6]
So, oft it chances in particular men, [7]
That for some vicious mole of nature in them,
As in their birth, — wherein they are not guilty,
Since nature cannot choose his origin ; —

[4] The sense of *east and west* goes with what follows, not what precedes :
"brings reproach upon us in all directions." To *tax* was often used for to
charge, to *accuse*.

[5] *Clepe* is an old Saxon word for *call.* — The Poet often uses *addition* for
title ; so that the meaning is, they sully our title by likening us to swine.
The character here ascribed to the Danes appears to have had a basis of fact.
Heywood, in his *Drunkard Opened,* 1635, speaking of "the vinosity of nations," says the Danes have made profession thereof from antiquity, and are
the first upon record "that have brought their wassel bowls and elbowdeep
healths into this land."

[6] That is, of our *reputation*, or of what *is attributed* to us.

[7] Hamlet is now wrought up to the highest pitch of expectancy; his
mind is sitting on thorns; and he seeks relief from the pain of that over-
intense feeling by launching off into a strain of general and abstract reflection. His state of mind, distracted between his eager anticipation and his
train of thought, aptly registers itself in the irregular and broken structure
of his language. Coleridge remarks upon the passage as follows : "The
unimportant conversation with which this scene opens is a proof of Shakespeare's minute knowledge of human nature. It is a well-established fact,
that, on the brink of any serious enterprise, or event of moment, men almost
invariably endeavour to elude the pressure of their own thoughts by turning
aside to trivial objects and familiar circumstances : thus this dialogue on
the platform begins with remarks on the coldness of the air, and inquiries,
obliquely connected indeed with the expected hour of the visitation, but
thrown out in a seeming vacuity of topics, as, to the striking of the clock,
and so forth."

By the o'ergrowth of some complexion,
Oft breaking down the pales and forts of reason ;[8]
Or by some habit that too much o'er-leavens
The form of plausive[9] manners ; — that these men, —   20
Carrying, I say, the stamp of one defect,
Being nature's livery, or fortune's star,[10] —
Their virtues else — be they as pure as grace,
As infinite as man may undergo —
Shall in the general censure take corruption
From that particular fault ; the dram of leav'n
Doth all the noble substance of 'em sour,
To his own scandal ;[11] —

[8] The idea is, of some native aptitude indulged and fostered too much, so that it breaks down the proper guards and strongholds of reason. Here, as in some other cases, *pales* is *palings*. And *complexion* was often used, as here, to signify any constitutional *texture, aptitude,* or *predisposition.*

[9] *Plausive* for *approvable,* or that which is to be applauded; the active form with the passive sense. This indiscriminate use of active and passive forms, both in adjectives and participles, was very common. So Milton has *unexpressive* for *inexpressible,* and Shakespeare has *deceivable* for *deceptive.*

[10] Alluding to the old astrological notion, of a man's character or fortune being determined by the star that was in the ascendant on the day of his birth. — *Livery* is properly a *badge-dress;* of course, here put for a man's *distinctive idiom.* — Note the change of the subject from *these men* to *their virtues.*

[11] *His,* again, for *its,* referring to *substance,* or, possibly, to *leav'n.* Of course *'em* refers to *virtues.* So that the meaning is, that the dram of leaven sours all the noble substance of their virtues, insomuch as to bring reproach and scandal on that substance itself. The Poet seems to have had in mind Saint Paul's proverbial saying, 1 *Corinthians,* v. 6: "A little leaven leaveneth the whole lump." And so in Bacon's *Henry the Seventh :* "And, as a little *leaven* of new distaste doth commonly *soure* the whole lumpe of former *merites,* the King's wit began now to suggest unto his passion," &c. This is said in reference to Sir William Stanley, whose prompt and timely action gained the victory of Bosworth Field. Some years after, he became a suitor for the earldom of Chester; whereupon, as Bacon says, "his suit did end not only in a denial, but in a *distaste*" on the part of the King. See Critical Notes.

Hora.   Look, my lord, it comes !

Enter the GHOST.

Ham. Angels and ministers of grace defend us !—
Be thou a spirit of health or goblin damn'd ;
Bring with thee airs from Heaven or blasts from Hell ;
Be thy intents wicked or charitable ;
Thou comest in such a questionable [12] shape,
That I will speak to thee : I'll call thee Hamlet,
King, father : royal Dane, O, answer me !
Let me not burst in ignorance ; but tell
Why thy canónized bones, hearsèd in death,
Have burst their cerements ; [13] why the sepulchre,
Wherein we saw thee quietly in-urn'd,
Hath oped his ponderous and marble jaws,
To cast thee up again.   What may this mean,
That thou, dead corse, again in cómplete steel
Revisit'st thus the glimpses of the Moon,
Making night hideous ; and we fools of Nature
So horridly to shake our disposition
With thoughts beyond the reaches of our souls ? [14]
Say, why is this ? wherefore ? what should we do ?

                         [GHOST *beckons* HAMLET.

[12] "A *questionable* shape" is a shape that may be *questioned*, or *con-versed with*.   In like manner the Poet often uses *question* for *conversation*.

[13] *Canonized* means made sacred by the *canonical* rites of sepulture.— *Cerements* is a dissyllable.   It is from a Latin word meaning *wax*, and was so applied from the use of wax or pitch in sealing up coffins or caskets so as to make them waterproof.

[14] "We fools of Nature," in the sense here implied, is, we who cannot by nature know the mysteries of the supernatural world.   Strict grammar would require *us* instead of *we*. — The general idea of the passage seems to be, that man's intellectual eye is not strong enough to bear the unmuffled light of eternity.

Hora. It beckons you to go away with it,
As if it some impartment did desire
To you alone.

    Marc. Look, with what courteous action
It waves you to a more removèd[15] ground :
But do not go with it.

    Hora.   No, by no means.

    Ham. It will not speak ; then I will follow it.

    Hora. Do not, my lord.

    Ham.   Why, what should be the fear ?
I do not set my life at a pin's fee ;
And for my soul, what can it do to that,
Being a thing immortal as itself?
It waves me forth again : I'll follow it.

    Hora. What if it tempt you toward the flood, my lord,
Or to the dreadful summit of the cliff
That beetles o'er his base[16] into the sea,
And there assume some other horrible form,
Which might deprive your sovereignty of reason,[17]
And draw you into madness?[18] think of it :
The very place puts toys[19] of desperation,
Without more motive, into every brain
That looks so many fathoms to the sea,
And hears it roar beneath.

---

[15] *Removèd* for *remote, secluded, retired.*

[16] *Overhangs its* base.   So in Sidney's *Arcadia:* "Hills lift up their *beetle* brows, as if they would overlooke the pleasantnesse of their under prospect."

[17] To " deprive your sovereignty of reason " is to *depose* your *government* of reason, or take it away.   The word was often used thus.

[18] It was anciently believed that evil spirits sometimes assumed the guise of deceased persons, to draw men into madness and suicide, as is here apprehended of the Ghost.

[19] *Toys* is *freaks, whims,* or *fancies ;* here meaning any sudden mad impulse to suicide.

Ham.   It waves me still. —
Go on ; I'll follow thee.
   Marc. You shall not go, my lord.
   Ham.   Hold off your hands !
   Hora. Be ruled ; you shall not go.
   Ham.   My fate cries out,
And makes each petty artery [20] in this body
As hardy as the Némean lion's nerve.
Still am I call'd. — Unhand me, gentlemen ; —
                 [*Breaking away from them.*
By Heaven, I'll make a ghost of him that lets [21] me !
I say, away ! — Go on ; I'll follow thee.
              [*Exeunt* GHOST *and* HAMLET.
   Hora. He waxes desperate with imagination.
   Marc. Let's follow ; 'tis not fit thus to obey him.
   Hora. Have after. — To what issue will this come ?
   Marc. Something is rotten in the State of Denmark.
   Hora. Heaven will direct it.
   Marc.   Nay,[22] let's follow him.   [*Exeunt.*

SCENE V. — *Another Part of the Platform.*

Enter the GHOST *and* HAMLET.

Ham. Where wilt thou lead me ? speak ; I'll go no fur
   ther.
   Ghost. Mark me.
   Ham.   I will.
   Ghost.   My hour is almost come,

---

[20] *Artery, nerve,* and *sinew* were used interchangeably in the Poet's time.
[21] The old *let,* now obsolete, meaning to *hinder.*
[22] *Nay* refers to Horatio's " Heaven will direct it," and means, " let us not
leave it to Heaven, but look after it ourselves."

When I to sulphurous and tormenting flames
Must render up myself.

   Ham.   Alas, poor Ghost !

   Ghost. Pity me not, but lend thy serious hearing
To what I shall unfold.

   Ham.   Speak ; I am bound to hear.

   Ghost. So art thou to revenge, when thou shalt hear.

   Ham. What ?

   Ghost. I am thy father's spirit,
Doom'd for a certain term to walk the night,
And for the day confined to fast in fires,[1]
Till the foul crimes done in my days of nature
Are ourirnt and purged away.   But that I am forbid
To tell the secrets of my prison-house,
I could a tale unfold whose lightest word
Would harrow up thy soul ; freeze thy young blood ;
Make thy two eyes, like stars, start from their spheres ;
Thy knotted and combinèd locks to part,
And each particular hair to stand on end,
Like quills upon the fretful porpentine :[2]
But this eternal[3] blazon must not be
To ears of flesh and blood.   List, list, O, list !
If thou didst ever thy dear father love, —

   Ham. O God !

   Ghost. — Revenge his foul and most unnatural murder.

   Ham. Murder !

---

[1] Chaucer in the *Persones Tale* says, " The misese of hell shall be *in defaute of mete and drinke.*" So, too, in *The Wyll of the Devyll:* " Thou shalt lye in frost and fire, with sicknes and *hunger.*"

[2] Such is the old form of the word, and so Shakespeare always has it.

[3] The Poet repeatedly has *eternal* in the sense of *infernal,* like our Yankee *'tarnal ;* and such is probably the meaning here ; though some think it means " the mysteries of eternity."

Ghost. Murder most foul, as in the best it is ;
But this most foul, strange, and unnatural.

Ham. Haste me to know't, that I, with wings as swift
As meditation or the thoughts of love,
May sweep to my revenge.

Ghost.   I find thee apt ;
And duller shouldst thou be than the fat weed
That roots itself in ease on Lethe wharf,[4]
Wouldst thou not stir in this.   Now, Hamlet, hear :
'Tis given out that, sleeping in my orchard,[5]
A serpent stung me ; so the whole ear of Denmark
Is by a forgèd process of my death
Rankly abused ; but know, thou noble youth,
The serpent that did sting thy father's life
Now wears his crown.

Ham.   O my prophetic soul ![6]
My uncle !

Ghost. Ay, that incestuous, that adulterate beast,
With witchcraft of his wit, with traitorous gifts, —
O wicked wit and gifts, that have the power
So to seduce ! — won to his shameful lust
The will of my most seeming-virtuous Queen :
O Hamlet, what a falling-off was there !
From me, whose love was of that dignity,
That it went hand in hand even with the vow
I made to her in marriage ; and to decline
Upon a wretch whose natural gifts were poor

---

[4] Of course "Lethe wharf" is the place on the banks of the river Lethe
where the old boatman, Charon, had his moorings. — In the preceding line,
shouldst for *wouldst.*   See page 48, note 11.

[5] *Orchard* and *garden* were synonymous.

[6] Hamlet has suspected "some foul play," and now his suspicion seems
prophetic, or as if inspired.

To[7] those of mine!

But virtue, as it never will be moved,

Though lewdness court it in a shape of Heaven,

So lust, though to a radiant angel link'd,

Will sate itself in a celestial bed,

And prey on garbage.

But, soft! methinks I scent the morning air;

Brief let me be.   Sleeping within my orchard,

My custom always in the afternoon,

Upon my sécure[8] hour thy uncle stole,

With juice of cursèd hebenon[9] in a vial,

And in the porches of my ears did pour

The leperous distilment; whose effect[10]

Holds such an enmity with blood of man,

That swift as quicksilver it courses through

The natural gates and alleys of the body;[11]

And with a sudden vigour it doth posset

And curd, like eager[12] droppings into milk,

[7] *To*, again, for *compared to*. See page 62, note 29.

[8] *Secure* has the sense of the Latin *securus; unguarded, unsuspecting.*

[9] *Hebenon* is probably derived from *henbane*, the oil of which, according to Pliny, dropped into the ears, disturbs the brain; and there is sufficient evidence that it was held poisonous. So in Anton's *Satires*, 1606: "The *poison'd henbane*, whose cold juice doth kill."

[10] *Effect* for *efficacy*, or *effectiveness;* the effect put for the cause.

[11] The Poet here implies as much as was then known touching the circulation of the blood. So in *Julius Cæsar*, ii. 1: "As dear to me as are the ruddy drops that visit my sad heart." Harvey's great discovery was not published till 1628, twelve years after the Poet's death. The lawyers claim Shakespeare as of their house: I suspect the physicians have an equal right to him.

[12] *Eager* has occurred before in the sense of *sharp, biting*. "Eager droppings" are drops of *acid.* — A *posset* is described by Randle Holme as follows: "Hot milk poured on ale or sack, having sugar, grated bisket, and eggs, with other ingredients boiled in it, which goes to a curd." So that to *posset* is to *coagulate* or *curdle.*

The thin and wholesome blood: so did it mine ;
And a most instant tetter bark'd [13] about,
Most lazar-like, with vile and loathsome crust,
All my smooth body.
Thus was I, sleeping, by a brother's hand
Of life, of crown, of Queen, at once dispatch'd :
Cut off even in the blossom of my sins,
Unhousell'd, disappointed, unanel'd ; [14]
No reckoning made, but sent to my account
With all my imperfections on my head.

   Ham. O, horrible ! O, horrible ! most horrible !

   Ghost. If thou hast nature [15] in thee, bear it not ;
Let not the royal bed of Denmark be
A couch for luxury and damnèd incest.
But, howsoever thou pursuest this act,
Taint not thy mind, [16] nor let thy soul contrive
Against thy mother aught : leave her to Heaven,
And to those thorns that in her bosom lodge
To prick and sting her. Fare thee well at once !
The glow-worm shows the matin to be near,

---

  [13] *Bark'd* means *formed a bark* or *scab.* — *Instant* in the sense of the Latin *instans ;* urgent, importunate, *itching.* — The meaning of *lazar-like* is well illustrated in *Paradise Lost,* xi. 477–488.

  [14] *Unhousell'd* is without having received the sacrament. *Disappointed* is *unappointed, unprepared.* A man well furnished for an enterprise is said to be well-*appointed. Unanel'd* is without extreme unction. So in Cavendish's *Life of Wolsey :* "Then we began to put him in mind of Christ's passion ; and sent for the abbot of the place to *anneal* him." These "last offices" were thought to have much effect in mitigating the pains of Purgatory.

  [15] *Nature* for *natural affection.* A very frequent usage.

  [16] This part of the injunction is well worth noting : time and manner are left to Hamlet ; only he is to keep himself clean from crime and from dishonour : his revenge must be righteous, and according to the demands of justice, not merely personal.

And 'gins to pale his uneffectual fire : [17]

Adieu, adieu, adieu ! remember me.   [*Exit.*

   Ham. O all you host of Heaven !   O Earth ! what else ?

And shall I couple Hell ?   O, fie ! [18]   Hold, hold, my heart ;

And you, my sinews, grow not instant old,

But bear me stiffly up. — Remember thee !

Ay, thou poor Ghost, while memory holds a seat

In this distracted globe. [19]   Remember thee !

Yea, from the table [20] of my memory

I'll wipe away all trivial fond recórds,

All saws of books, all forms, all pressures past,

That youth and observation copied there ;

And thy commandment all alone shall live

Within the book and volume of my brain,

Unmix'd with baser matter : yes, by Heaven ! —

O most pernicious woman ! —

O villain, villain, smiling, damnèd villain !

My tables, [21] — meet it is I set it down,

That one may smile, and smile, and be a villain ;

At least I'm sure it may be so in Denmark. —

So, uncle, there you are. [22] — Now to my word ;

---

   [17] *Uneffectual* because it gives light without heat, does not *burn.* — *Matin,* properly morning-prayer, is here put for *morning.*

   [18] Hamlet invokes Heaven and Earth, and then asks whether he shall invoke Hell also. "O, fie!" refers to the latter, and implies a strong negative.

   [19] By *this globe* Hamlet means his *head.*

   [20] *Table* for what we call *tablet.* — *Saws* is *sayings ; pressures, impressions.*

   [21] " *Tables,* or books, or registers for memory of things " were used in Shakespeare's time by all ranks of persons, and carried in the pocket; what we call *memorandum-books.*

   [22] This, I think, has commonly been taken in too literal and formal a way, as if Hamlet were carefully writing down the axiomatic saying he has just uttered. I prefer Professor Werder's view of the matter : " Hamlet

It is *Adieu, adieu! remember me:*
I have sworn't.

    Hora. [*Within.*] My lord, my lord,—

    Marc. [*Within.*] Lord Hamlet,—

    Hora. [*Within.*] Heaven secure him!

    Marc. [*Within.*] So be it!

    Hora. [*Within.*] Illo, ho, ho, my lord!

    Ham. Hillo, ho, ho, boy! come, bird, come.[23]

Enter HORATIO *and* MARCELLUS.

    Marc. How is't, my noble lord?

    Hora.   What news, my lord?

    Ham. O, wonderful!

    Hora. Good my lord, tell it.

    Ham. No; you'll reveal it.

    Hora. Not I, my lord, by Heaven.

    Marc. Nor I, my lord.

    Ham. How say you, then? would heart of man once
      think it?—

But you'll be secret?

    Hora. }
    Marc. }   Ay, by Heaven, my lord.

    Ham. There's ne'er a villain dwelling in all Denmark
But he's an arrant knave.[24]

pulls out his tablets, and jabs the point of his pencil once or twice into the leaf, because he cannot do the same to the King with his sword, as he would like to do,—nothing further; only such marks, such a sign, does he make. That stands for 'So, uncle, there you are!' And although he says he must write it down for himself, he does not literally write; that does not accord with his mood and situation."

23 This is the call which falconers use to their hawk in the air when they would have him come down to them.

24 Dr. Isaac Ray, a man of large science and ripe experience in the treatment of insanity, says of Hamlet's behaviour in this scene, that "it betrays

Hora. There needs no ghost, my lord, come from the
    grave
To tell us this.

Ham.   Why, right ; you are i' the right ;
And so, without more circumstance [25] at all,
I hold it fit that we shake hands and part :
You, as your business and desire shall point you, —
For every man hath business and desire,
Such as it is ; — and, for mine own poor part,
Look you, I'll go pray.

Hora. These are but wild and whirling words, my lord

Ham. I'm sorry they offend you, heartily ;
Yes, faith, heartily.

Hora.   There's no offence, my lord.

Ham. Yes, by Saint Patrick,[26] but there is, Horatio,
And much offence too. Touching this vision here,
It is an honest ghost,[27] that let me tell you ;
For your desire to know what is between us,
O'ermaster't as you may.[28] And now, good friends,
As you are friends, scholars, and soldiers,
Give me one poor request.

---

the excitement of delirium, — the wandering of a mind reeling under the
first stroke of disease."

25 *Circumstance* is sometimes used for *circumlocution.* So in *Othello,* i.
1 : " A bombast *circumstance* horribly stuff'd with epithets of war." But it
was also used for *circumstantial detail;* and such is probably the meaning
here.

26 Warburton has ingeniously defended Shakespeare for making the
Danish Prince swear by *St. Patrick,* by observing that the whole northern
world had their learning from Ireland.

27 Hamlet means that the Ghost is a real ghost, just what it appears to
be, and not " the Devil " in " a pleasing shape," as Horatio had apprehended
it to be. See page 79, note 18.

28 That is, o'ermaster your *desire :* " subdue it as you best can."

Hora. What is't, my lord? we will.

Ham. Never make known what you have seen to-night.

Hora. }
Marc. } My lord, we will not.

Ham. Nay, but swear't.

Hora. In faith, my lord, not I.

Marc. Nor I, my lord, in faith.

Ham.   Upon my sword.

Marc. We've sworn, my lord, already.[29]

Ham. Indeed, upon my sword, indeed.

Ghost. [*Beneath.*] Swear.

Ham. Ha, ha, boy! say'st thou so? art thou there, true
    penny?[30] —

Come on, — you hear this fellow in the cellarage, —
Consent to swear.

Hora.   Propose the oath, my lord.

Ham. Never to speak of this that you have seen:
Swear by my sword.

Ghost. [*Beneath.*] Swear.

Ham. *Hic et ubique!* then we'll shift our ground. —
Come hither, gentlemen,
And lay your hands again upon my sword,
Never to speak of this that you have heard:
Swear by my sword.

Ghost. [*Beneath.*] Swear.

Ham. Well said, old mole! canst work i' the ground so
    fast?

---

[29] The oath they have already sworn is *in faith*. But this has not enough
of ritual solemnity in it, to satisfy Hamlet. The custom of swearing by the
sword, or rather by the cross at the hilt of it, is very ancient. The Saviour's
name was sometimes inscribed on the handle. So that swearing by one's
sword was the most solemn oath a Christian soldier could take.

[30] *True-penny* is an old familiar term for a right honest fellow.

A worthy pioneer !31 — Once more remove, good friends.

   Hora. O day and night ! but this is wondrous strange.

   Ham. And therefore as a stranger give it welcome.

There are more things in Heaven and Earth, Horatio,

Than are dreamt of in your philosophy.32

But come :

Here, as before, never, so help you Mercy,

How strange or odd soe'er I bear myself, —

As I perchance hereafter shall think meet

To put an antic disposition on,33 —

That you, at such times seeing me, never shall,

With arms encumber'd thus, or this head-shake,

Or by pronouncing of some doubtful phrase,

as, *Well, well, we know ;* or, *We could, an if* 34 *we would ;*

or, *If we list to speak ;* or, *There be, an if they might ;*

Or such ambiguous giving-out, to note

That you know aught of me : — this not to do,

So Grace and Mercy at your most need help you,

Swear.

---

31 Alluding to one of the offices of military engineers, which is to *pioneer*
an army ; that is, to go before and clear the road.

32 Strictly speaking, *your* is redundant here. Hamlet means *any* philosophy. The Poet often uses the pronouns in that way. So in v. 1, of this
play : " And *your* water is a sore decayer of *your* whoreson dead body."   In
the text, however, I suspect that *your* is meant to convey a mild sneer at
philosophy, which has sometimes been as arrogant as science is in some of
her modern representatives.

33 This has been taken as proving that Hamlet's " antic disposition " is
merely assumed for a special purpose. But our ripest experts in the matter
are far from regarding it so. They tell us that veritable madmen are sometimes inscrutably cunning in arts for disguising their state ; saying, in effect,
" To be sure, you may find me acting rather strangely at times, but you
must not think me crazy ; I know what I am about, and have a purpose in it."

34 *An if* is merely an old reduplication, and is equivalent simply to *if*
So the Poet uses *if*, or *an*, or *an if*, indifferently.

Ghost. [*Beneath.*] Swear.

[*They kiss the hilt of* HAMLET'S *sword.*

Ham. Rest, rest, perturbèd spirit ! — So, gentlemen,
With all my love I do commend me to you ;
And what so poor a man as Hamlet is
May do t' express his love and friending to you,
God willing, shall not lack.   Let us go in together ;
And still your fingers on your lips, I pray.
The time is out of joint : — O cursèd spite,
That ever I was born to set it right ! —
Nay, come ; let's go together.   [*Exeunt.*

ACT II.

SCENE I. — *A Room in Polonius's House.*

Enter POLONIUS *and* REYNALDO.

Polo. Give him this money and these notes, Reynaldo.
Reyn. I will, my lord.
Polo. You shall do marvellous wisely, good Reynaldo,
Before you visit him, to make inquiry
Of his behaviour.
Reyn.   My lord, I did intend it.
Polo. Marry, well said, very well said.   Look you, sir,
Inquire me first what Danskers [1] are in Paris,
And how, and who ; what means, and where they keep ; [2]
What company, at what expense ; and finding,
By this encompassment and drift of question,

---

[1] *Dansker* is *Dane ; Dansk* being the ancient name of Denmark. — Here
me is used very much as *your* in the preceding scene.   See page 89, note 3.
[2] The Poet repeatedly uses *keep* in the sense of *lodge* or *dwell.*

That they do know my son, come you more nearer
Than your particular demands will touch it : [3]
Take you, as 'twere, some distant knowledge of him ;
As thus, *I know his father and his friends,*
And in part him ; — do you mark this, Reynaldo?

Reyn. Ay, very well, my lord.

Polo. *And in part him ; but,* you may say, *not well :*
But, if 't be he I mean, he's very wild ;
Addicted so and so.   And there put on him
What forgeries you please ; marry, none so rank
As may dishonour him ; take heed of that ;
But, sir, such wanton, wild, and usual slips
As are companions noted and most known
To youth and liberty.

Reyn.   As gaming, my lord?

Polo. Ay, or drinking, fencing, swearing,
Quarrelling, drabbing ; you may go so far.

Reyn. My lord, that would dishonour him.

Polo. Faith, no ; as you may season it in the charge.
You must not put another[4] scandal on him
Than he is open to incontinency ;
That's not my meaning : but breathe his faults so quaintly,[5]
That they may seem the taints of liberty ;
The flash and outbreak of a fiery mind ;

---

[3] This seems illogical, and would be so in any mouth but a politician's, as implying that general inquiries would come to the point faster than particular ones. But here, again, *your* is used as explained in note 32, page 89. The scheme here laid down is, to *steal* upon the truth by roundabout statements and questions ; or, as it is afterwards said, " By indirections find directions out."

[4] *Another* must here be taken as equivalent to *a further.*

[5] *Quaintly,* from the Latin *comptus,* properly means *elegantly,* but is here used in the sense of *adroitly* or *ingeniously.*

A savageness in unreclaimèd blood,
Of general assault.[6]

    Reyn.   But, my good lord, —

    Polo. Wherefore should you do this?

    Reyn.   Ay, my lord,
I would know that.

    Polo.   Marry, sir, here's my drift;
And, I believe, it is a fetch of warrant :[7]
You laying these slight sullies on my son,
As 'twere a thing a little soil'd i' the working,
Mark you,
Your party in convérse, him you would sound,
Having ever seen in the prenominate crimes
The youth you breathe of guilty,[8] be assured
He closes with you in this consequence :
Good sir, or so ; or *friend*, or *gentleman*, —
According to the phrase or the addition
Of man and country ; —

    Reyn.   Very good, my lord.

    Polo. And then, sir, does he this, — he does — what was
I about to say? — By the Mass,[9] I was about to say something : — where did I leave?

    Reyn. At *closes in the consequence;* at *friend or so*, and
gentleman.

    Polo. At *closes in the consequence*, — ay, marry ;
He closes with you thus : *I know the gentleman;*

---

    [6] A wildness of untamed blood, such as youth is generally assailed by.

    [7] "A fetch of warrant" is an allowable stratagem or artifice.

    [8] Having *at any time* seen the youth you *speak* of guilty in the *forenamed vices.* — "Closes with you in this consequence" means, apparently, *agrees* with you in this *conclusion.* — *Addition* again for *title.*

    [9] *Mass* is the old name of the Lord's Supper, and is still used by the Roman Catholics. It was often sworn by, as in this instance.

I saw him yesterday, or 'tother day,
Or then, or then ; with such or such ; and, as you say,
There was he gaming, there o'ertook in's rouse,
There falling out at tennis : or, perchance,
I saw him enter such a house of sale..

See you now,
Your bait of falsehood takes this carp of truth ; [10]
And thus do we of wisdom and of reach,
With windlaces and with assays of bias,[11]
By indirections find directions out :
So, by my former lecture and advice,
Shall you my son. You have me, have you not ? [12]

   Reyn. My lord, I have.
   Polo.   God b' wi' you ! [13] fare you well.
   Reyn. Good my lord !
   Polo. Observe his inclination in yourself.[14]

[10] The shrewd old wire-puller is fond of angling arts. The *carp* is a species of fish.

[11] "Of wisdom and of reach " is here equivalent to *by cunning and over-reaching.* — *Windlaces* is here used in the sense of taking a winding, circuit-ous, or roundabout course to a thing, instead of going *directly* to it ; or, as we sometimes say, " beating about the bush," instead of coming straight to the point. This is shown by a late writer in the *Edinburgh Review,* who quotes two passages in illustration of it from Golding's translation of Ovid, which is known to have been one of the Poet's books. Here is one of the quotations : —

      The winged god, beholding them returning in a troupe,
      Continu'd not directly forth, but gan me down to stoupe,
      And fetch'd a *windlass* round about.

"Assays of bias " are *trials* of *inclination.* A bias is a weight in one side of a bowl, which keeps it from rolling straight to the mark, as in ninepins.

[12] " You *understand* me, do you not ? "

[13] The old phrase, " God be with you," is here in the process of abbrevi-ation to what we now use, — " Good by."

[14] " Use your own eyes upon him, as well as learn from others." Or the meaning may be, " comply with his inclinations in order to draw him out." *Observe* sometimes has this sense of *yielding to,* and so *flattering.*

Reyn. I shall, my lord.

Polo. And let him ply his music.[15]

Reyn. Well, my lord.

Polo. Farewell! — [*Exit* REYNALDO.

Enter OPHELIA.

How now, Ophelia! what's the matter?

Ophe. O, my lord, my lord, I have been so affrighted!

Polo. With what, i' the name of God?

Ophe. My lord, as I was sewing in my closet,
Lord Hamlet, with his doublet all unbraced;[16]
No hat upon his head; his stockings foul'd,
Ungarter'd, and down-gyvèd to his ankle;[17]
Pale as his shirt; his knees knocking each other;
And with a look so piteous in purpórt
As if he had been loosèd out of Hell
To speak of horrors, — he comes before me.

Polo. Mad for thy love?

Ophe. My lord, I do not know;
But, truly, I do fear it.

Polo. What said he?

Ophe. He took me by the wrist and held me hard;
Then goes he to the length of all his arm,
And, with his other hand thus o'er his brow,
He falls to such perusal of my face
As he would draw it.[18] Long time stay'd he so;
At last, — a little shaking of mine arm,
And thrice his head thus waving up and down, —

[15] " Eye him sharply, but *slyly*, and let him fiddle his secrets all out."

[16] *Unbraced* is the same as our *unbuttoned*.

[17] Hanging down like the loose cincture that confines the fetters or gyves round the ankles.

[18] " To such a *study* of my face as *if* he would *make a picture* of it."

He raised a sigh so piteous and profound,
That it did seem to shatter all his bulk,[19]
And end his being : that done, he lets me go ,
And, with his head over his shoulder turn'd,
He seem'd to find his way without his eyes ;
For out o' doors he went without their help,
And, to the last, bended their light on me.

Polo. Come, go with me : I will go seek the King.
This is the very ecstasy[20] of love,
Whose violent property fordoes[21] itself,
And leads the will to desperate undertakings,
As oft as any passion under heaven
That does afflict our natures.   I am sorry, —
What, have you given him any hard words of late ?

Ophe. No, my good lord ; but, as you did command,
I did repel his letters, and denied
His access to me.

Polo.   That hath made him mad.
I'm sorry that with better heed and judgment
I had not quoted him.[22]   I fear'd he did but trifle,
And meant to wreck thee ; but beshrew[23] my jealousy !
By Heaven, it is as proper to our age
To cast beyond ourselves in our opinions,[24]
As it is common for the younger sort

[19] Here *bulk* is put for *breast*. The usage was common.

[20] All through this play, *ecstasy* is *madness*. It was used for any violent perturbation of mind.

[21] *Fordo* was the same as *undo* or *destroy*.

[22] To *quote* is to *note*, to *mark*, or *observe*.

[23] *Beshrew* was much used as a mild form of imprecation ; about the same as *confound it!* or, *a plague upon it!*

[24] In this admirable scene, Polonius, who is throughout the skeleton of his former skill in state-craft, hunts the trail of policy at a dead scent, supplied by the weak fever-smell in his own nostrils. — COLERIDGE.

To lack discretion.[25]   Come, go we to the King:
This must be known ; which, being kept close, might move
More grief to hide than hate to utter love.[26]   [*Exeunt.*

SCENE II. — *A Room in the Castle.*

Enter the KING, *the* QUEEN, ROSENCRANTZ, GUILDENSTERN,
and Attendants.

King. Welcome, dear Rosencrantz and Guildenstern !
Moreover that [1] we much did long to see you,
The need we have to use you did provoke
Our hasty sending.   Something have you heard
Of Hamlet's transformation ; so I call it,
Since nor th' exterior nor the inward man
Resembles that it was.   What it should be,
More than his father's death, that thus hath put him
So much from th' understanding of himself,
I cannot dream of.   I entreat you both,
That, being of so young days brought up with him,
And since so neighbour'd to his youth and humour,[2]
That you vouchsafe your rest here in our Court
Some little time ; so by your companies
To draw him on to pleasures, and to gather,
So much as from occasion you may glean,

[25] We old men are as apt to overreach ourselves with our own policy, as
the young are to miscarry through inconsideration.

[26] The sense is rather obscure, but appears to be, " By keeping Hamlet's
love secret, we may cause more of grief to others, than of hatred on his part
by disclosing it."   The Poet sometimes strains language pretty hard in order to close a scene with a rhyme.

[1] *Moreover that* for *besides that.*   Not so elsewhere, I think.

[2] And having since had so near an opportunity of studying his inclination and character during his youth.

Whether aught to us unknown afflicts him thus,
That, open'd, lies within our remedy.

Queen. Good gentlemen, he hath much talk'd of you ;
And sure I am two men there are not living
To whom he more adheres.   If it will please you
To show us so much gentry[3] and good will
As to expend your time with us awhile,
For the supply and profit of our hope,[4]
Your visitation shall receive such thanks
As fits a king's remembrance.

Rosen.   Both your Majesties
Might, by the sovereign power you have of us,
Put your dread pleasures more into command
Than to entreaty.

Guild.   But we both obey ;
And here give up ourselves, in the full bent,
To lay our service freely at your feet,
To be commanded.

King. Thanks, Rosencrantz and gentle Guildenstern.

Queen. Thanks, Guildenstern and gentle Rosencrantz :
And I beseech you instantly to visit
My too-much-changèd son. — Go, some of you,
And bring these gentlemen where Hamlet is.

Guild. Heavens make our presence and our practices
Pleasant and helpful to him !

Queen.   Ay, amen !

[*Exeunt* ROSEN., GUILDEN., *and some* Attendants

Enter POLONIUS.

Polo. Th' ambassadors from Norway, my good lord,
Are joyfully return'd.

---

[3] *Gentry* for *courtesy, gentleness,* or *good-breeding.*
[4] " The supply and profit" is the *feeding* and *realizing.*

King. Thou still hast been the father of good news.

Polo. Have I, my lord? Assure you, my good liege,

I hold my duty, as I hold my soul,

Both to my God and to my gracious King : [5]

And I do think — or else this brain of mine

Hunts not the trail of policy so sure

As it hath used to do — that I have found

The very cause of Hamlet's lunacy.

King. O, speak of that ; that do I long to hear.

Polo. Give, first, admittance to th' ambassadors ;

My news shall be the fruit to that great feast.

King. Thyself do grace to them, and bring them in.—

[*Exit* POLONIUS

He tells me, my dear Gertrude, he hath found

The head and source of all your son's distemper.

Queen. I doubt [6] it is no other but the main, —

His father's death, and our o'erhasty marriage.

King. Well, we shall sift him. —

Re-enter POLONIUS, *with* VOLTIMAND *and* CORNELIUS.

Welcome, my good friends !

Say, Voltimand, what from our brother Norway?

Volt. Most fair return of greetings and desires.

Upon our first, he sent out to suppress

His nephew's levies ; which to him appear'd

To be a preparation 'gainst the Polack ;

But, better look'd into, he truly found

It was against your Highness : whereat grieved, —

That so his sickness, age, and impotence

Was falsely borne in hand,[7] — sends out arrests

---

[5] I hold my duty both to my God and to my King, as I do my soul.

[6] *Doubt,* again, for *suspect* or *fear.* See page 68, note 46.

[7] To *bear in hand* is to delude by false assurances or expectations.

On Fortinbras ; which he, in brief, obeys ;
Receives rebuke from Norway ; and, in fine,
Makes vow before his uncle never more   70
To give th' assay of arms against your Majesty.
Whereon old Norway, overcome with joy,
Gives him three thousand crowns in annual fee ; [8]
And his commission to employ those soldiers,
So levied as before, against the Polack :
With an entreaty, herein further shown,   [*Giving a paper.*
That it might please you to give quiet pass
Through your dominions for this enterprise,
On such regards of safety and allowance [9]
As therein are set down.

    King.   It likes us [10] well ;   80
And at our more consider'd time [11] we'll read,
Answer, and think upon this business :
Meantime we thank you for your well-took labour.
Go to your rest ; at night we'll feast together :
Most welcome home ! [*Exeunt* VOLTIMAND *and* CORNELIUS.

    Polo.   This business is well ended. —
My liege, and madam, to expostulate [12]
What majesty should be, what duty is,
Why day is day, night night, and time is time,
Were nothing but to waste night, day, and time.
Therefore, since brevity is the soul of wit,   90

[8] *Fee* was often used for *fee-simple*, which is the strongest tenure in English law, and means an estate held in absolute right.

[9] That is, on such *pledges* of safety to the country, and on such *terms* of permission. The passage of an army through a country is apt to cause great trouble and damage to the people.

[10] " It likes us " for " it pleases us," or " we like it."   Often so.

[11] That is, " when we have had time for *further consideration.*"   The Poet has several like expressions in this play.

[12] *Expostulate* in the Latin sense of *argue* or *discuss.*

And tediousness the limbs and outward flourishes,
I will be brief :   Your noble son is mad :
Mad call I it ; for, to define true madness,
What is't but to be nothing else but mad?
But let that go.

    Queen.   More matter, with less art.

    Polo. Madam, I swear I use no art at all.
That he is mad, 'tis true : 'tis true 'tis pity ;
And pity 'tis 'tis true : a foolish figure ;
But farewell it, for I will use no art.
Mad let us grant him, then : and now remains
That we find out the cause of this effect, —
Or rather say, the cause of this defect,
For this effect defective comes by cause :
Thus it remains, and the remainder thus.
Perpend : [13]
I have a daughter, — have while she is mine, —
Who, in her duty and obedience, mark,
Hath given me this : now gather, and surmise.

    [Reads.] *To the celestial and my soul's idol, the most beauti-*
            fied Ophelia : —

That's an ill phrase, a vile phrase ; *beautified* is a vile phrase :
but you shall hear.   Thus :

    [Reads.] *In her excellent white bosom, these,*[14] *&c.*

    Queen. Came this from Hamlet to her?

    Polo. Good madam, stay awhile ; I will be faithful.

    [Reads.]   *Doubt thou the stars are fire ;*
                Doubt that the Sun doth move ;

---

[13] *Perpend* is *weigh* or *consider.*

[14] The word *these* was usually added at the end of the superscription of
letters.   Hamlet's letter is somewhat in the euphuistic style which was fash-
ionable in the Poet's time.

> *Doubt* [15] *truth to be a liar;*
> *But never doubt I love.*

*O dear Ophelia, I am ill at these numbers. I have not
art to reckon* [16] *my groans; but that I love thee best, O most
best, believe it. Adieu.*

> *Thine evermore, most dear lady, whilst this*
> > *machine is to him,*[17] HAMLET.

This in obedience hath my daughter shown me;
And, more above, hath his solicitings,
As they fell out by time, by means, and place,
All given to mine ear.

 King.   But how hath she
Received his love?

 Polo.   What do you think of me?

 King. As of a man faithful and honourable.

 Polo. I would fain prove so. But what might you think, —
When I had seen this hot love on the wing,
(As I perceived it, I must tell you that,
Before my daughter told me,) — what might you,
Or my dear Majesty your Queen here, think,
If I had play'd the desk or table-book; [18]
Or given my heart a winking, mute and dumb; [19]
Or look'd upon this love with idle sight; —

---

[15] *Doubt*, again, as note 6. In the two preceding lines the word has its ordinary sense.

[16] Hamlet is *tacitly* quibbling: he first uses *numbers* in the sense of *verses*, and here *implies* the other sense.

[17] That is, "while he is living." *Machine* for *body*.

[18] By keeping dark about the matter. A desk or table-book does not prate of what it contains. A table-book is a case or set of tablets, to carry in the pocket, and write memoranda upon. See page 85, note 21.

[19] "If I had given my heart a *hint* to be mute about their passion."
"*Conniventia, a winking at; a sufferance; a feigning not to see or know.*"

What might you think? No, I went round[20] to work;
And my young mistress thus I did bespeak:
Lord Hamlet is a prince, out of thy star;[21]
This must not be: and then I precepts gave her,
That she should lock herself from his resort,
Admit no messengers, receive no tokens.
Which done, she took the fruits of my advice;
And he, repulsèd, — a short tale to make, —
Fell into a sadness; then into a fast;
Thence to a watch; thence into a weakness;
Thence to a lightness; and, by this declension,
Into the madness wherein now he raves,
And all we mourn for.

  King.   Do you think 'tis this?

  Queen. It may be, very likely.

  Polo. Hath there been such a time — I'd fain know that —
That I have positively said *'Tis so,*
When it proved otherwise?

  King.   Not that I know.

  Polo. [*Pointing to his head and shoulder.*] Take this
    from this, if this be otherwise.
If circumstances lead me, I will find
Where truth is hid, though it were hid indeed
Within the centre.[22]

  King.   How may we try it further?

  Polo. You know, sometimes he walks for hours together
Here in the lobby.

[20] To be *round* is to be *plain, downright, outspoken.*

[21] Not within thy *destiny;* alluding to the supposed influence of the stars on the fortune of life.

[22] *Centre* here means, no doubt, the Earth, which, in the old astronomy, was held to be literally the centre of the solar system. The Poet has the word repeatedly in that sense.

Queen.   So he does indeed.

Polo. At such a time I'll loose my daughter to him :
Be you and I behind an arras[23] then ;
Mark the encounter : if he love her not,
And be not from his reason fall'n thereon,
Let me be no assistant for a State,
But keep a farm and carters.

King.   We will try it.

Queen. But look where sadly the poor wretch[24] comes
    reading.

Polo. Away, I do beseech you, both away :
I'll board[25] him presently. —

          [*Exeunt* KING, QUEEN, *and* Attendants.

Enter HAMLET, *reading.*

          O, give me leave :

How does my good Lord Hamlet ?

Ham. Well, God-'a-mercy.

Polo. Do you know me, my lord ?

Ham. Excellent well ; you're a fishmonger.[26]

Polo. Not I, my lord.

Ham. Then I would you were so honest a man.

Polo. Honest, my lord !

[23] In Shakespeare's time the chief rooms of houses were lined with tapestry hangings, which were suspended on frames, some distance from the walls, to keep them from being rotted by the damp. These tapestries were called *arras* from the town *Arras*, in France, where they were made.

[24] *Wretch* was the strongest term of endearment in the language ; generally implying, however, a dash of pity. So in *Othello*, iii. 3, the hero, speaking of Desdemona, exclaims in a rapture of tenderness, " Excellent *wretch*, perdition catch my soul, but I do love thee ! "

[25] To *board* him is to *accost* or *address* him.

[26] *Fishmonger* meant an angler as well as a dealer in fish. Hamlet probably means that Polonius has come to *fish out* his secret.

Ham. Ay, sir; to be honest, as this world goes, is to be one man pick'd out of ten thousand.

Polo. That's very true, my lord.

Ham. For if the Sun breed maggots in a dead dog, being a good kissing carrion,[27] — Have you a daughter?

Polo. I have, my lord.

Ham. Let her not walk i' the sun : conception is a blessing ; but not as your daughter may conceive. Friend, look to 't.

Polo. How say you by that?[28] — [*Aside.*] Still harping on my daughter : yet he knew me not at first ; he said I was a fishmonger : he is far gone, far gone : and truly in my youth I suffered much extremity for love ; very near this. I'll speak to him again. — What do you read, my lord?

Ham. Words, words, words.

Polo. What is the matter, my lord?

Ham. Between who?

Polo. I mean, the matter that you read, my lord.

Ham. Slanders, sir : for the satirical rogue says here that old men have gray beards ; that their faces are wrinkled ; their eyes purging thick amber and plum-tree gum ; and that they have a plentiful lack of wit, together with most weak hams : all which, sir, though I most powerfully and

27 " A good *kissing* carrion " is, no doubt, a carrion good *for kissing*, or good *to kiss*. So in *The Merry Wives*, v. 5, we have the compound " *kissing*-comfits," which were candies flavoured so as to perfume the breath, and thus render the lips sweet for kissing, or to kiss. And so we often say " good hay-making weather," meaning, of course, weather good for hay-making, or good to make hay. In my first edition of Shakespeare, 1856, I so explained the passage ; but afterwards, in my School edition of *Hamlet*, 1870, I receded from that explanation, out of deference to the judgment of others. I am now obliged to Professor Hiram Corson for recalling me to it.

28 " *How say* you by that ? " is " *What mean* you by that ? "

potently believe, yet I hold it not honesty[29] to have it thus
set down ; for you yourself, sir, should be old as I am, if
like a crab you could go backward.[30]

Polo. [*Aside.*] Though this be madness, yet there is
method in't. — Will you walk out of the air, my lord?

Ham. Into my grave?

Polo. Indeed, that is out o' the air. — [*Aside.*] How
pregnant[31] sometimes his replies are ! a happiness that often
madness hits on, which reason and sanity could not so pros-
perously be deliver'd of. I will leave him, and suddenly
contrive the means of meeting between him and my daughter. — My honourable lord, I will most humbly take my
leave of you.

Ham. You cannot, sir, take from me any thing that I will
more willingly part withal ; — [*Aside.*] except my life, except
my life, except my life.

Polo. Fare you well, my lord.

Ham. These tedious old fools !

Enter Rosencrantz *and* Guildenstern.

Polo. You go to seek the Lord Hamlet ; there he is.

Rosen. [*To* Polo.] God save you, sir ! [*Exit* Polonius

Guild. My honour'd lord !

Rosen. My most dear lord !

Ham. My excellent-good friends ! How dost thou,
Guildenstern? — Ah, Rosencrantz ! — Good lads, how do ye
both?

Rosen. As the indifferent[32] children of the Earth.

---

[29] Shakespeare sometimes uses *honesty* with the sense of the adjective
right, or *honourable*.

[30] That is, "if you could *turn your life* backward, and grow young."

[31] *Pregnant*, here, is pithy, *full of meaning*, or of *pertinency*.

[32] *Indifferent*, here, has the sense of *middling*, — *tolerably well off*

Guild. Happy, in that we are not over-happy ;
On Fortune's cap we're not the very button.

Ham. Nor the soles of her shoe?

Rosen. Neither, my lord.

Ham. Then you live about her waist, or in the middle of
her favours?   What's the news?

Rosen. None, my lord, but that the world's grown honest.

Ham. Then is doomsday near : but your news is not true.
Let me question more in particular : What have you, my
good friends, deserved at the hands of Fortune, that she
sends you to prison hither?

Guild. Prison, my lord !

Ham. Denmark's a prison.

Rosen. Then is the world one.

Ham. A goodly one ; in which there are many confines,
wards, and dungeons, Denmark being one o' the worst.

Rosen. We think not so, my lord.

Ham. Why, then 'tis none to you ; for there is nothing
either good or bad, but thinking makes it so : to me it is a
prison.

Rosen. Why, then your ambition makes it one ; 'tis too
narrow for your mind.

Ham. O God, I could be bounded in a nut-shell, and
count myself a king of infinite space, were it not that I have
bad dreams.

Guild. Which dreams indeed are ambition ; for the very
substance of the ambitious [33] is merely the shadow of a
dream.

---

[33] This is obscure : but "the very substance of the ambitious" probably
means the substance of *that which* the ambitious *pursue*, not that of which
they *are made*.   The obscurity grows from an uncommon use of the objective genitive.

Ham. A dream itself is but a shadow.

Rosen. Truly, and I hold ambition of so airy and light a quality, that it is but a shadow's shadow.

Ham. Then are our beggars bodies, and our monarchs and outstretched heroes the beggars' shadows. Shall we to the Court? for, by my fay, I cannot reason.[34]

Rosen. ⎫
Guild. ⎬ We'll wait upon you.

Ham. No such matter: I will not sort you with the rest of my servants; for, to speak to you like an honest man, I am most dreadfully attended.[35] But, in the beaten way of friendship, what make you at Elsinore?[36]

Rosen. To visit you, my lord; no other occasion.

Ham. Beggar that I am, I am even poor in thanks; but I thank you: and sure, dear friends, my thanks are too dear at a halfpenny. Were you not sent for? Is it your own inclining? Is it a free visitation? Come, deal justly with me: come, come; nay, speak.

Guild. What should we say, my lord?

Ham. Why, any thing, — but to the purpose. You were sent for; and there is a kind of confession in your looks which your modesties have not craft enough to colour.[37] I know the good King and Queen have sent for you.

---

[34] Hamlet is here playing or fencing with words, and seems to lose himself in the riddles he is making. The meaning is any thing but clear; perhaps was not meant to be understood. But *bodies* is no doubt put for *substance* or *substances*. And perhaps the sense will come thus: *Substance* and *shadow* are antithetic and correlative terms, and Hamlet assumes *beggar* and *king* to be so too. As a shadow must be cast by some substance; so our beggars are the substances antithetic and correlative to the shadows cast by them. All which infers that our kings and heroes are but the shadows of our beggars. — *Fay* is merely a diminutive of *faith.*

[35] Referring, perhaps, to the "bad dreams" spoken of a little before.

[36] "What *is your business at* Elsinore?" See page 63. note 36.

[37] To *colour* is to *disguise* to *conceal.*

Rosen. To what end, my lord?

Ham. That you must teach me. But let me conjure you, by the rights of our fellowship, by the consonancy of our youth, by the obligation of our ever-preserved love, and by what more dear a better proposer could charge you withal, be even and direct with me, whether you were sent for, or no.

Rosen. [*Aside to* GUILDEN.] What say you?

Ham. [*Aside.*] Nay, then I have an eye of you.[38] — If you love me, hold not off.

Guild. My lord, we were sent for.

Ham. I will tell you why; so shall my anticipation prevent your discovery, and your secrecy to the King and Queen moult no feather.[39] I have of late — but wherefore I know not — lost all my mirth, forgone all custom of exercises; and indeed it goes so heavily with my disposition, that this goodly frame, the Earth, seems to me a sterile promontory; this most excellent canopy, the air, look you, this brave[40] o'erhanging firmament, this majestical roof fretted with golden fire, — why, it appears no other thing to me than a foul and pestilent congregation of vapours. What a piece of work is man! how noble in reason! how infinite in faculties! in form and moving how express and admirable! in action how like an angel! in apprehension how like a god! the

---

[38] "I will watch you sharply." *Of* for *on;* a common usage.

[39] Hamlet's fine sense of honour is well shown in this. He will not tempt them to any breach of confidence; and he means that, by telling them the reason, he will forestall and prevent their disclosure of it. — *Moult* is an old word for *change;* used especially of birds when casting their feathers. So in Bacon's *Natural History:* "Some birds there be, that upon their *moulting* do turn colour; as robin-redbreasts, after their moulting, grow red again by degrees."

[40] Here, as often, *brave* is *grand, splendid.*

beauty of the world ! the paragon of animals ! And yet, to me, what is this quintessence of dust ? man delights not me ; no, nor woman neither, though by your smiling you seem to say so.

Rosen. My lord, there was no such stuff in my thoughts.

Ham. Why did you laugh then, when I said *man delights not me ?*

Rosen. To think, my lord, if you delight not in man, what lenten entertainment [41] the players shall receive from you : we coted [42] them on the way, and hither are they coming to offer you service.

Ham. He that plays the king shall be welcome, — his Majesty shall have tribute of me ; the adventurous knight shall use his foil and target ; the lover shall not sigh gratis ; the humorous man [43] shall end his part in peace ; the Clown shall make those laugh whose lungs are tickle o' the sear ; [44]

---

[41] " *Lenten* entertainment " is entertainment for the season of *Lent*, when players were not allowed to perform in public, in London.

[42] To *cote* is, properly, to *overpass*, to *outstrip*. So Scott, in *Old Mortality*, note J.: " This horse was so fleet, and its rider so expert, that they are said to have outstripped and *coted*, or turned, a hare upon the Bran-Law."

[43] *Humorous man* here means a man made unhappy by his own crotchets. *Humour* was used for any wayward, eccentric impulse causing a man to be full of ups and downs, or of flats and sharps. Such characters were favourites on the stage. The melancholy Jaques in *As You Like It* is an instance.

[44] *Tickle* is *delicate, sensitive, easily moved*. *Sear*, also spelt *sere* and *serre*, is the catch of a gun-lock, that holds the hammer cocked or half-cocked. Here, as often, *o'*, that is, *of*, is equivalent to *in respect of*. The image is of a gunlock with the hammer held so lightly by the catch as to go off at the slightest pressure on the trigger ; and the general idea is of persons so prone to laughter, that the least touch or gleam of wit is enough to make them explode. The same thought occurs in *The Tempest*, ii. 1 : " I did it to minister occasion to these gentlemen, who are of such *sensible* and nimble lungs, that they always use to laugh at nothing." Here, as in many other places, *sensible* is *sensitive*. In the text, Hamlet is slurring the extem-

and the lady shall say her mind freely, or the blank-verse
shall halt for't.[45]   What players are they?

Rosen. Even those you were wont to take delight in, the
tragedians of the city.

Ham. How chances it they travel? their residence, both
in reputation and profit, was better both ways.[46]

Rosen. I think their innovation comes by the means of
the late inhibition.[47]

Ham. Do they hold the same estimation they did when
I was in the city? are they so follow'd?

Rosen. No, indeed, they are not.

Ham. How comes it? do they grow rusty?

Rosen. Nay, their endeavour keeps in the wonted pace;
but there is, sir, an eyrie of children, little eyases,[48] that cry
out on the top of question,[49] and are most tyrannically

porized witticisms of the Clowns, by a sort of ironical praise. For this
explanation I am indebted to the "Clarendon Press Series," which quotes
from Howard's *Defensative against the Poyson of supposed Prophecies,* 1620:
" Discovering the moods and humors of the vulgar sort to be so loose and
tickle of the seare."

[45] That is, the poet's feet shall go lame from her overworking them.

[46] The London theatrical companies, when not allowed to play in the
city, were wont to travel about the country, and exercise their craft in the
towns. This was less reputable, and at the same time brought less pay, than
residing in the city.

[47] Referring, no doubt, to an order of the Privy Council, issued in June,
1600.   By this order the players were *inhibited* from acting in or near the
city during the season of Lent, besides being very much restricted at all
other seasons, and hence " chances it they travel," or *stroll* into the country.

[48] *Eyrie,* from *eyren,* eggs, properly means a *brood,* but sometimes a *nest.*
Eyases are unfledged hawks.

[49] " Cry out on the top of question " means, I have no doubt, *exclaim
against those who are at the top of their profession,* who stand highest in the
public esteem, who are most talked or conversed about as having surpassed
all others. Shakespeare uses *cry out on,* or *cry on,* nearly if not quite always
in the sense of *exclaim against,* or *cry down.* So in the last scene of this

clapped for't : these are now the fashion ; and so berattle [50] the common stages, — so they call them, — that many wearing rapiers are afraid of goose-quills, and dare scarce come thither. [51]

Ham. What, are they children? who maintains 'em? how are they escoted? [52] Will they pursue the quality no longer 340 than they can sing? will they not say afterwards, if they should grow themselves to common players, — as it is most like, if their means are no better, — their writers do them wrong, to make them exclaim against their own succession? [53]

play : " This quarry *cries on* havoc." He also very often uses *top*, both noun and verb, in the sense of to *excel* or *surpass*. He also has *question* repeatedly in the sense of *talk* or *conversation.* — For this explanation I am mainly indebted to Mr. Joseph Crosby, of Zanesville, O., who remarks to me upon the whole sentence as follows : " A brood of young hawks, unfledged nestlings, that exclaim against, or lampoon, the best productions of the dramatic pen ; little chits, that declaim squibs, and turn to ridicule their seniors and betters, both actors and authors, and are vociferously applauded for it."

[50] To *berattle* is to *berate*, to *squib.* Here, again, I quote from Mr. Crosby : " It is no wonder the regular profession suffer, when children thus ' carry it away,' and are all ' the fashion ' ; berating the adult performers, and getting ' most tyrannically clapp'd for it ' ; so much so, that the well-deserving writers for the ' common stages,' grown-up men ' wearing rapiers, are afraid of goose-quills,' (applied to the penny-a-liners for the boys,) and dare scarce come to the play-house any more."

[51] The allusion is to the children of St. Paul's and of the Revels, whose performing of plays was much in fashion at the time this play was written. From an early date, the choir-boys of St. Paul's, Westminster, Windsor, and the Chapel Royal, were engaged in such performances, and sometimes played at Court. The complaint here is, that these juveniles abuse " the common stages," that is, the public theatres.

[52] *Escoted* is *paid ;* from the French *escot,* a *shot* or *reckoning.* — *Quality* is *profession* or *calling ;* often so used. — " No longer than they can sing " means no longer than they keep the voices of boys.

[53] *Run down* the profession to which they are themselves to *succeed.* This fully accords with, and approves, the explanation given in note 49. As Mr. Crosby observes, " it appears that a contest was waging between the

Rosen. Faith, there has been much to-do on both sides ;
and the nation holds it no sin to tarre [54] them to controversy :
there was for a while no money bid for argument, unless the
poet and the player went to cuffs in the question.[55]

Ham. Is't possible?

Guild. O, there has been much throwing about of brains.[56]

Ham. Do the boys carry it away?[57]

Rosen. Ay, that they do, my lord ; Hercules and his load
too.

Ham. It is not very strange ; for mine uncle is King of
Denmark, and those that would make mows at him while my
father lived give twenty, forty, fifty, an hundred ducats a-piece
for his picture in little. 'Sblood,[58] there is something in this
more than natural, if philosophy could find it out.

                              [*Flourish of trumpets within.*

Guild. There are the players.

patrons of these boy-players, who wrote their parts for them, and the writers
for 'the common stages,' whom the children so berated and disparaged."

[54] The Poet has *to-do* repeatedly in the exact sense of *ado*. — To *tarre* is
to *set on*, to incite ; a word borrowed from the setting-on of dogs.

[55] The meaning is not "unless the poet and the player" went to fighting
each other, but unless *both* the *writers* and the *actors* joined together in
pelting and running down the full-grown regular performers. Here, as
often, *argument* is the subject-matter or plot of a play, and so is put for the
play itself. *Question*, again, often means *conversation*, and is here put, apparently, for the *dialogue*. So that the meaning of the whole seems to be,
"The public would not patronize these juvenile performances, unless both
the 'eyases' and the 'goosequills,' (that is, the boy-actors and their writers,)
in their dialogue, went to abusing or berating the authors and actors of the
'common stages.'"—CROSBY.

[56] Bandying of wit, or pelting each other with words.

[57] That is, carry all the world before them : there is, perhaps, an allusion
to the *Globe* theatre, the sign of which is said to have been Hercules carrying the globe.

[58] '*Sblood* is an old diluted and disguised oath, originally *God's blood*.
So, also, are '*swounds* or '*zounds*, '*sfoot*, '*slight*.

Ham. Gentlemen, you are welcome to Elsinore. Your hands, come : the appurtenance of welcome is fashion and ceremony : let me comply with you in this garb ; lest my extent to the players,[59] which, I tell you, must show fairly outward, should more appear like entertainment than yours. You are welcome ; but my uncle-father and aunt-mother are deceived.

Guild. In what, my dear lord ?

Ham. I am but mad north-north-west ; when the wind is southerly I know a hawk from a handsaw.[60]

Enter POLONIUS,

Polo. Well be with you, gentlemen !

Ham. Hark you, Guildenstern ; — and you too ; — at each ear a hearer : that great baby you see there is not yet out of his swaddling-clouts.

Rosen. Happily he's the second time come to them ; for they say an old man is twice a child.

Ham. I will prophesy he comes to tell me of the players ; mark it. — You say right, sir : o' Monday morning ; 'twas so indeed.[61]

Polo. My lord, I have news to tell you.

Ham. My lord, I have news to tell you. When Roscius was an actor in Rome, —

[59] To *comply with*, as here used, evidently means to be *formally civil* or *polite to*, or to *compliment*. We have it again in the same sense, in **v. 2,** where Hamlet says of Osric, " He did *comply with* his dug before he suck'd it." — *Appurtenance* is *appertainings*, or *proper appendages*. — *Garb* is *style* or *manner*. Repeatedly so. — " My *extent* to the players " means *extension* of courtesy and civility to them.

[60] " To know a hawk from a handsaw " was a proverb in Shakespeare's time. *Handsaw* is merely a corruption of *hernshaw*, which means a *heron*.

[61] This is spoken in order to blind Polonius as to what they have been talking about.

Polo. The actors are come hither, my lord.

Ham. Buz, buz![62]

Polo. Upon mine honour, —

Ham. Then came each actor on his ass, —

Polo. — the best actors in the world, either for tragedy, comedy, history, pastoral, pastoral-comical, historical-pastoral, tragical-historical, tragical-comical-historical-pastoral, scene individable, or poem unlimited;[63] Seneca cannot be too heavy, nor Plautus too light. For the law of writ and the liberty,[64] these are the only men.

Ham. O Jephthah, judge of Israel, what a treasure hadst thou!

Polo. What treasure had he, my lord?

Ham. Why,

> *One fair daughter, and no more,*
> *The which he lov'd passing well.*

Polo. [*Aside.*] Still on my daughter.

Ham. Am I not i' the right, old Jephthah?

[62] Hamlet affects to discredit the news: all a mere *buzzing* or *rumour*. Polonius then assures him, "On my honour"; which starts the poor joke, "If they are come on your honour,' then came each actor on his ass'"; these latter words being probably a quotation from some ballad.

[63] *Individable* for *undivided;* just as we have *tenable* for *retained*, i. 2: "Let it be *tenable* in your silence still." The Poet has many like instances of the endings *-able* or *-ible* and *-ed* used indiscriminately. In the text, *scene* and *poem* are evidently used as equivalent terms. In the Greek Tragedy there was no division into scenes; the scene continued the same, or *undivided*, all through the piece. But in the Gothic Drama, as Shakespeare found and fixed it, the changes of scene are without definite limitations. This seems to be the difference meant. Seneca was considered the best of the Roman tragic writers, and Plautus of the comic.

[64] "The meaning," says Collier, "probably is, that the players were good, whether at written productions or at extemporal plays, where liberty was allowed to the performers to invent the dialogue, in imitation of the Italian *commedie al improviso.*"

Polo. If you call me Jephthah, my lord, I have a daughter that I love passing well.

Ham. Nay, that follows not.

Polo. What follows, then, my lord?

Ham. Why, *As by lot, God wot;* and then, you know, *It came to pass, as most like it was,*[65] — the first row of the pious chanson[66] will show you more; for look, where my abridgments come.[67] —

Enter four or five Players.

You are welcome, masters; welcome, all. I am glad to see ye well. Welcome, good friends. — O, my old friend! thy face is valanced since I saw thee last:[68] comest thou to beard me in Denmark? — What, my young lady and mis-

---

[65] Hamlet is teasing the old fox, and quibbling between a logical and a literal sequence. The lines he quotes are from an old ballad, entitled *Jephtha, Judge of Israel.* A copy of the ballad, as Shakespeare knew it, was reprinted in Evan's *Old Ballads,* in 1810; the first stanza being as follows: —

> I have read that many years agoe,
>   When Jephtha, judge of Israel,
> Had one fair daughter and no moe,
>   Whom he loved passing well;
>   As by lot, God wot,
>   It came to passe, most like it was,
>   Great warrs there should be,
> And who should be the chiefe but he, but he.

[66] *Chanson* is something to be *sung* or *chanted;* and "the first *row*" probably means the first *column,* or, perhaps, *stanza.*

[67] Perhaps Hamlet calls the players "my *abridgments*" in the same sense and for the same reason as he afterwards calls them "the abstracts and brief chroniclers of the time." He may have the further meaning of *abridging* or *cutting short* his talk with Polonius. Or, again, he may mean that their office is to *abridge the time,* or make it seem short; to minister *pastimes.*

[68] *Valanced* is *fringed,* and here means that the player has lately grown a beard.

tress ! By'r Lady, [69] your ladyship is nearer to heaven than
when I saw you last, by the altitude of a chopine.[70] Pray
God, your voice, like a piece of uncurrent gold, be not
crack'd within the ring.[71] — Masters, you are all welcome.
We'll e'en to't like French falconers, fly at any thing we
see : [72] we'll have a speech straight. , Come, give us a taste
of your quality ; come, a passionate speech.

1 Play. What speech, my lord?

Ham. I heard thee speak me a speech once, — but it
was never acted ; or, if it was, not above once, for the play,
I remember, pleased not the million ; 'twas caviar to the
general ; [73] but it was — as I received it, and others, whose
judgments in such matters cried in the top of mine [74] — an
excellent play, well digested in the scenes, set down with as

[69] *By'r Lady* is a contraction of *by our I ady*, referring to the Virgin Mary.
In the Poet's time, female parts were acted by boys; and Hamlet is ad-
dressing one whom as a boy he had seen playing some heroine.

[70] *Chopine* was the name of an enormously thick-soled shoe which Spanish and Italian ladies were in the habit of wearing, in order, as would seem,
to make themselves as tall as the men, perhaps taller; or it may have been,
to keep their long skirts from mopping the sidewalks too much. The fashion is said to have been used at one time by the English.

[71] The old gold coin was thin and liable to crack. There was a *ring* or
circle on it, within which the sovereign's head was stamped; if the crack
extended beyond this ring, it was rendered uncurrent: it was therefore a
simile applied to any other injured object. There is some humour in ap-
plying it to *a cracked voice*.

[72] From this it would seem that the English custom in falconry was, first
to let off some bird into the air, and then to fly the hawk after it; the
French, to fly the hawk at any bird that might happen to be on the wing
within ken.

[73] *Caviar* was the pickled roes of certain fish of the sturgeon kind, called
in Italy *caviale*, and much used there and in other countries. Great quan-
tities were prepared on the river Volga formerly. As a dish of high season-
ing and peculiar flavour, it was not relished by the *many;* that is, the *gen
tral.*

[74] Meaning, probably, were *better than mine.* See page 110, note 49.

much modesty as cunning. I remember, one said there
were no sallets in the lines to make the matter savoury,[75] nor
no matter in the phrase that might indict the author of affectation; but call'd it an honest method, as wholesome as
sweet, and by very much more handsome than fine. One
speech in it I chiefly loved : 'twas Æneas' tale to Dido ; and
thereabout of it especially where he speaks of Priam's slaughter. If it live in your memory, begin at this line : let me
see, let me see,—

  The rugged Pyrrhus, like th' Hyrcanian beast,—

'tis not so ; — it begins with *Pyrrhus :*

  The rugged Pyrrhus,—*he whose sable arms,*
  Black as his purpose, did the night resemble
  When he lay couchèd in the ominous horse,—
  Hath now this dread and black complexion smear'd
  With heraldry more dismal : head to foot
  Now is he total gules ; [76] *horridly trick'd*
  With blood of fathers, mothers, daughters, sons,
  Baked and impasted with the parching streets,
  That lend a tyrannous and damnèd light
  To their lord's murder. Roasted in wrath and fire,
  And thus o'er-sizèd with coagulate gore,
  With eyes like carbuncles, the hellish Pyrrhus
  Old grandsire Priam seeks.

So, proceed you.

 Polo. Fore God, my lord, well spoken, with good accent
and good discretion.

---

[75] No impertinent high-seasoning or false brilliancy, to give it an unnatural relish. *Sallet* is explained " a pleasant and merry word that maketh folk
to laugh."—This passage shows that the Poet understood the essential
poverty of " fine writing."

[76] *Gules* is *red*, in the language of heraldry : to *trick* is to colour.

1 Play.   *Anon he finds him*
Striking too short at Greeks ; his antique sword,
Rebellious to his arm, lies where it falls,
Repugnant to command : unequal match'd,
Pyrrhus at Priam drives ; in rage strikes wide ;
But with the whiff and wind of his fell sword
Th' unnervèd father falls.   Then senseless Ilium,
Seeming to feel this blow, with flaming top
Stoops to his base ; and with a hideous crash
Takes prisoner Pyrrhus' ear : for, lo ! his sword,
Which was declining on the milky head
Of reverend Priam, seem'd i' the air to stick :
So, as a painted tyrant, Pyrrhus stood,
And like a neutral to his will and matter,
Did nothing.
But, as we often see, against some storm,
A silence in the heavens, the rack[77] *stand still,*
The bold winds speechless, and the orb below
As hush as death, anon the dreadful thunder
Doth rend the region ; [78] *so, after Pyrrhus' pause,*
Arousèd vengeance sets him new a-work ;
And never did the Cyclops' hammers fall
On Mars's armour, forged for proof eterne,[79]
With less remorse than Pyrrhus' bleeding sword
Now falls on Priam.
Out, out, thou harlot, Fortune !   All you gods,

---

[77] *Rack*, from *reek*, is used by old writers to signify the highest and therefore lightest clouds. So in Fletcher's *Women Pleased*, iv. 2 : "Far swifter than the sailing *rack* that gallops upon the wings of angry winds." So that the heavens must be silent indeed, when "the rack stands still."

[78] *Region*, here, is *sky*, or the *air*. So in the last speech of this scene : " I should have fatted all the *region* kites," &c.

[79] For *eternal resistance* to assault. As we say *shot-proof, water-proof.*

In general synod, take away her power;
Break all the spokes and fellies from her wheel,
And bowl the round nave down the hill of heaven
As low as to the fiends! [80]

Polo. This is too long.

Ham. It shall to the barber's, with your beard. — Pr'ythee
say on: he's for a jig [81] or a tale of bawdry, or he sleeps
Say on; come to Hecuba.

1 Play. *But who, O, who had seen the mobled Queen —*

Ham. *The mobled Queen?*

Polo. That's good; *mobled Queen* [82] is good.

1 Play. *— Run barefoot up and down, threatening the flames*
With bisson rheum; [83] *a clout about that head*
Where late the diadem stood; and for a robe,
About her lank and all o'er-teemèd loins,
A blanket in th' alarm of fear caught up; —
Who this had seen, with tongue in venom steep'd
'Gainst Fortune's state would treason have pronounced:

[80] This admirable substitution of the epic for the dramatic, giving such
reality to the dramatic diction of Shakespeare's own dialogue, and author-
ized, too, by the actual style of the tragedies before his time, is well worthy
of notice. The fancy that a burlesque was intended sinks below criticism:
the lines, as epic narrative, are superb. — In the thoughts, and even in the
separate parts of the diction, this description is highly poetical: in truth,
taken by itself, that is its fault, that it is too poetical! — the language of lyric
vehemence and epic pomp, and not of the drama. But if Shakespeare had
made the diction truly dramatic, where would have been the contrast between *Hamlet* and the play in *Hamlet?* — COLERIDGE.

[81] *Giga*, in Italian, was a fiddle or crowd; *gigaro*, a fiddler, or minstrel.
Hence a *jig* was a ballad, or ditty, sung to the fiddle.

[82] *Mobled* is *hastily* or *carelessly dressed*. To *mob* or *mab* is still used in
the north of England for to dress in a slatternly manner; and Coleridge
says "*mob*-cap is still a word in common use for a morning cap."

[83] *Bisson* is *blind*. *Bisson rheum* is therefore *blinding tears*.

But if the gods themselves did see her then,
When she saw Pyrrhus make malicious sport
In mincing with his sword her husband's limbs,
The instant burst of clamour that she made —
Unless things mortal move them not at all —
Would have made milch the burning eyes of heaven,
And passion in the gods.[84]

Polo. Look, whether he has not turn'd his colour, and has tears in's eyes. — Pray you, no more.

Ham. 'Tis well; I'll have thee speak out the rest soon. — Good my lord, will you see the players well bestowed? Do you hear? let them be well used, for they are the abstracts and brief chronicles of the time:[85] after your death you were better have a bad epitaph than their ill report while you live.

Polo. My lord, I will use them according to their desert.

Ham. God's bodykins,[86] man, much better! Use every man after his desert, and who should 'scape whipping? Use them after your own honour and dignity: the less they deserve, the more merit is in your bounty. Take them in.

Polo. Come, sirs.

Ham. Follow him, friends; we'll hear a play to-morrow. [*Exit* POLONIUS *with all the* Players *but the First.*] — Dost thou hear me, old friend? can you play *The Murder of Gonzago*?

[84] By a hardy poetical license this expression means, "Would have *filled with tears* the burning eyes of heaven." — *Passion*, here, is *compassion*, or sympathetic sorrow.

[85] The condensed efficacies and representatives of the age. In Shakespeare's time, the Drama, including both authors and actors, was a sort of Fourth Estate in the realm; perhaps as much so as the Newspaper Press is now.

[86] *Bodykins* is merely a diminutive of *body*.

1 Play. Ay, my lord.

Ham. We'll ha't to-morrow night. You could, for a need, study a speech of some dozen or sixteen lines, which I would set down and insert in't, could you not?

1 Play. Ay, my lord.

Ham. Very well. Follow that lord; and look you mock him not. [*Exit* Player.] — My good friends, I'll leave you till night : you are welcome to Elsinore.

Rosen. Good my lord !

Ham. Ay, so, God b' wi' ye ! —

[*Exeunt* ROSENCRANTZ *and* GUILDENSTERN.

Now I am alone.

O, what a rogue and peasant slave am I !
Is it not monstrous, that this player here,
But in a fiction, in a dream of passion,
Could force his soul so to his own conceit,[87]
That from her working all his visage wann'd ;
Tears in his eyes, distraction in's aspéct,
A broken voice, and his whole function suiting
With forms to his conceit? and all for nothing !
For Hecuba !
What's Hecuba to him, or he to Hecuba,
That he should weep for her? What would he do,
Had he the motive and the cue [88] for passion
That I have? He would drown the stage with tears,
And cleave the general ear with horrid speech ;
Make mad the guilty, and appal the free,
Confound the ignorant, and amaze indeed

---

[87] *Conceit* is used repeatedly by the Poet for *conception* or *imagination.*

[88] The *hint* or *prompt-word*, a technical phrase among players. "A prompter," says Florio, " one who keepes the booke for the plaiers, and teacheth them or schollers their *kue.*"

The very faculties of eyes and ears. Yet I,
A dull and muddy-mettled rascal, peak,
Like John-a-dreams, unpregnant of my cause,
And can say nothing;[89] no, not for a king
Upon whose property and most dear life
A damn'd defeat was made.[90] Am I a coward?
Who calls me villain? breaks my pate across?
Plucks off my beard, and blows it in my face?
Tweaks me by th' nose? gives me the lie i' the throat,
As deep as to the lungs?[91] who does me this?
Ha!
'Swounds, I should take it; for it cannot be
But I am pigeon-liver'd, and lack gall
To make oppression bitter;[92] or, ere this,
I should have fatted all the region kites[93]
With this slave's offal.[94] Bloody, bawdy villain!

[89] This John was probably distinguished as a sleepy, apathetic fellow, a sort of dreaming or droning simpleton or flunky. The only other mention of him that has reached us is in Armin's *Nest of Ninnies*, 1608: "His name is John, indeed, says the cinnick, but neither John a-nods nor *John a-dreams*, yet either, as you take it."

[90] Thus Chapman, in his *Revenge for Honour:* "That he might in the meantime make a sure *defeat* on our good aged father's life."

[91] This was giving one the lie with the most galling additions and terms of insult, or belabouring him with extreme provocation, and then rubbing it in; so that the not resenting it would stamp him as the most hopeless of cowards. So in *King Richard II.*, when Norfolk would drive home his charge upon Bolingbroke with the utmost force, he exclaims, "As low as to thy heart, through the false passage of thy throat, thou liest."

[92] "Lack gall to make me feel the bitterness of oppression"; or, perhaps, to make oppression bitter to the oppressor. — The gentleness of doves and pigeons was supposed to proceed from their having no gall in them.

[93] All the kites of the *airy* region, the sky. See page 118, note 78.

[94] This soliloquy is said to mean, forsooth, that thus far Hamlet has mistaken and blundered about the whole thing. Pray, have people no ears for the agony of a human being, which is so intolerable, that it drives him to

Remorseless, treacherous, lecherous, kindless [95] villain !
O vengeance ! —
Why, what an ass am I !   This is most brave,
That I, the son of a dear father murder'd,
Prompted to my revenge by Heaven and Hell,[96]
Must, like a trull, unpack my heart with words,
And fall a-cursing, like a very drab,
A scullion !
Fie upon't ! foh !   About, my brain ! [97] — I've heard
That guilty creatures sitting at a play
Have by the very cunning of the scene
Been struck so to the soul, that presently
They have proclaim'd their malefactions ;
For murder, though it have no tongue, will speak

the extremity of falling out with himself? no appreciation of a situation in
which righteous indignation, because it cannot reach its object, turns against
itself, in order to give itself vent, and to cool the heated sense of the impossibility of acting, by self-reproach and all manner of self-depreciation ?   That
he can *say* nothing for a king upon whose property and most dear life a
damned defeat has been made, — that is the very horror of his position, —
to be forced to speak not a syllable directly to the point : if he had chosen
to do only that, most assuredly and instantly he would have lost the game.
The actor, *he* can talk of Priam's death and Hecuba's grief, — talk of them
so movingly !   Had he *his* (Hamlet's) motive, *his* cue for passion, he would
drown the stage with tears, make mad the guilty, &c., because he, in the
freedom of the actor, of the objective, can act !   But Hamlet cannot do that ;
he can act no play, but a real thing, directly, out of his own consciousness ;
and must suffer wreck, because he can adduce no proof of the reality.   He
must be silent ; he can operate only indirectly, by means of a reflected
image ; must let the play-actors speak and act for him ; and can himself
only *look on* and *observe*. — WERDER.

[95] *Kindless* is *unnatural*.   See page 59, note 18. — Observe how Hamlet
checks himself in this strain of objurgation, and then, in mere shame of what
he has just done, turns to ranting at himself for having ranted.

[96] By all the best and all the worst passions of his nature.

[97] "*About*, my brain." is nothing more than " *to work*, my brain."   The
phrase to go *about* a thing, is still common.

With most miraculous organ.   I'll have these players
Play something like the murder of my father
Before mine uncle : I'll observe his looks ;
I'll tent him to the quick : if he but blench,[98]
I know my course.   The spirit that I have seen
May be the Devil : and the Devil hath power
T' assume a pleasing shape ; yea, and perhaps,
Out of my weakness and my melancholy, —
As he is very potent with such spirits, —
Abuses me to damn me.[99]   I'll have grounds
More relative than this : [100] the play's the thing
Wherein I'll catch the conscience of the King.

                                        [*Exit.*

ACT III.

SCENE I. — *A Room in the Castle.*

Enter the KING, *the* QUEEN, POLONIUS, OPHELIA, ROSEN-
CRANTZ, *and* GUILDENSTERN.

King. And can you, by no drift of circumstance,[1]
Get from him why he puts on this confusion,

---

[98] To *tent* was to *probe* a wound.   To *blench* is to *shrink* or *start.*

[99] That Hamlet was not alone in the suspicion here started, appears from Sir Thomas Browne's *Religio Medici :* " I believe that those apparitions and ghosts of departed persons are not the wandering souls of men, but the unquiet walks of devils, prompting and suggesting us into mischief, blood, and villainy ; instilling and stealing into our hearts that the blessed spirits are not at rest in their graves, but wander, solicitous of the affairs of the world." — To *abuse*, in the Poet's language, is to *deceive*, or *practise upon* with illusions.

[100] Grounds standing in closer and clearer relation with the matter alleged by the Ghost.

[1] Course of indirect, roundabout inquiry.

Grating so harshly all his days of quiet
With turbulent and dangerous lunacy?

Rosen. He does confess he feels himself distracted;
But from what cause he will by no means speak.

Guild. Nor do we find him forward to be sounded;
But, with a crafty madness, keeps aloof,
When we would bring him on to some confession
Of his true state.

Queen.　　　　Did he receive you well?

Rosen. Most like a gentleman.

Guild. But with much forcing of his disposition.

Rosen. Most free of question,[2] but of our demands
Niggard in his reply.

Queen.　　　　Did you assay him
To any pastime?

Rosen. Madam, it so fell out that certain players
We o'er-raught [3] on the way : of these we told him;
And there did seem in him a kind of joy
To hear of it.   They are about the Court;
And, as I think, they have already order
This night to play before him.

Polo.　　　　　　'Tis most true :
And he beseech'd me to entreat your Majesties
To hear and see the matter.

King. With all my heart ; and it doth much content me
To hear him so inclined. —
Good gentlemen, give him a further edge,
And drive his purpose on to these delights.

[2] Here, as often, *of* is probably equivalent to *in respect of.* Also in " *of* our demands." *Question* may here mean *inquiry*, or *conversation;* and either of these senses accords well enough with the occasion referred to. See Critical Notes.

[3] *O'er-raught* is *overtook; raught* being an old form of *reached.*

Rosen. We shall, my lord.

         [*Exeunt* ROSENCRANTZ *and* GUILDENSTERN.

  King.   Sweet Gertrude, leave us too ;

For we have closely[4] sent for Hamlet hither,

That he, as 'twere by accident, may here

Affront[5] Ophelia.

Her father and myself, lawful espials,

Will so bestow ourselves that, seeing, unseen,

We may of their encounter frankly judge ;

And gather by him, as he is behaved,

If't be the affliction of his love or no

That thus he suffers for.

  Queen.   I shall obey you. —

And for your part, Ophelia, I do wish

That your good beauty be the happy cause

Of Hamlet's wildness ; so shall I hope your virtues

Will bring him to his wonted way again,

To both your honours.

  Ophe.   Madam, I wish it may. [*Exit* QUEEN.

  Polo. Ophelia, walk you here. — Gracious, so please you,

We will bestow ourselves. — [*To* OPHE.] Read on this book ;

That show of such an exercise may colour

Your loneliness. We're oft to blame in this, —

'Tis too much proved, — that with devotion's visage

And pious action we do sugar o'er

The Devil himself.

  King. [*Aside.*] O, 'tis too true !

How smart a lash that speech doth give my conscience !

---

  4 *Closely* is *secretly ;* sent in such a way as not to let Hamlet know from whom the message came : a *got-up* accident.

  5 *Affront* was sometimes used for *meet*, or, as it is explained a little after, *encounter.* So in *Cymbeline*, iv. 3 : "Your preparation can *affront* no less than what you hear of."

The harlot's cheek, beautied with plastering art,
Is not more ugly to the thing that helps it[6]
Than is my deed to my most painted word.
O heavy burden !

 Polo. I hear him coming : let's withdraw, my lord.
     [*Exeunt* KING *and* POLONIUS.

    Enter HAMLET.

 Ham. To be, or not to be, — that is the question :
Whether 'tis nobler in the mind to suffer
The slings and arrows of outrageous fortune,
Or to take arms against a sea of troubles,
And by opposing end them?   To die, — to sleep, —
No more ; and by a sleep to say we end
The heart-ache, and the thousand natural shocks
That flesh is heir to, — 'tis a consummation
Devoutly to be wish'd.   To die, — to sleep ; —
To sleep ! perchance to dream ! — ay, there's the rub ;[7]
For in that sleep of death what dreams may come
When we have shuffled off this mortal coil,[8]
Must give us pause : there's the respect
That makes calamity of so long life ; [9]
For who would bear the whips and scorns of time,
Th' oppressor's wrong, the proud man's contumely,
The pangs of disprized love, the law's delay,

 [6] Not more ugly *in comparison with* the thing that helps it.

 [7] *Rub* is *obstruction, hindrance.*   The word was borrowed from the bowl-ing-alley, where it was used of any thing that deflected the bowl from its aim.

 [8] "This mortal *coil*" is the tumult and bustle of this mortal life; or, as Wordsworth has it, "the fretful stir unprofitable, and the fever of the world." Perhaps *coil* here means, also, the body.

 [9] That is, the *consideration* that induces us to undergo the calamity of so long a life.   This use of *respect* is very frequent.

The insolence of office, and the spurns
That patient merit of th' unworthy takes,
When he himself might his quietus [10] make
With a bare bodkin? who'd these fardels [11] bear,
To grunt and sweat under a weary life,
But that the dread of something after death, —
The undiscover'd country from whose bourn
No traveller returns,[12] — puzzles the will,
And makes us rather bear those ills we have
Than fly to others that we know not of?
Thus conscience does make cowards of us all;
And thus the native hue of resolution
Is sicklied o'er with the pale cast of thought; [13]
And enterprises of great pith and moment
With this regard their currents turn awry,
And lose the name of action. — Soft you now!
The fair Ophelia! — Nymph, in thy orisons
Be all my sins remember'd.

> *Ophe.*   Good my lord,
> How does your Honour for this many a day?

---

[10] The allusion is to the term *quietus est*, used in settling accounts at exchequer audits. Thus in Sir Thomas Overbury's character of *a Franklin*. " Lastly, to *end* him, he cares not when his end comes; he needs not feare his audit, for his *quietus* is in heaven." — *Bodkin* was the ancient term for a small dagger.

[11] *Fardel* is an old word for *burden* or *bundle*.

[12] *Bourn* is *boundary*. So in *Troilus and Cressida*, ii. 3: "I will not praise thy wisdom, which, like a *bourn*, a pale, a shore, confines thy spacious and dilated parts." — Of course Hamlet means that no one comes back to the state of mortal life; or, as Coleridge says, "no traveller returns to this world as his home or abiding-place."

[13] That is, the pale *complexion of grief*. *Thought* was often used in this way. So in *Twelfth Night*, ii. 4: "She pined *in thought*" ; that is, she wasted away *through grief*. Also in *Julius Cæsar*, ii. 1: "If he love Cæsar, all he can do is to himself; *take thought and die* for Cæsar"; which means *grieve himself to death*.

Ham. I humbly thank you; well, well, well.

Ophe. My lord, I have remembrances of yours,
That I have longèd long to re-deliver;
I pray you, now receive them.

Ham.   No, not I:
I never gave you aught.

Ophe. My honour'd lord, I know right well you did;
And with them words of so sweet breath composed
As made the things more rich: their perfume lost,
Take these again; for to the noble mind
Rich gifts wax poor when givers prove unkind.
There, my lord.

Ham. Ha, ha! are you honest?

Ophe. My lord?

Ham. Are you fair?[14]

Ophe. What means your lordship?

Ham. That if you be honest and fair, your honesty should
admit no discourse to your beauty.[15]

Ophe. Could beauty, my lord, have better commerce than
with honesty?

Ham. Ay, truly; for the power of beauty will sooner

---

[14] Here it is evident that the penetrating Hamlet perceives, from the strange and forced manner of Ophelia, that the sweet girl was not acting a part of her own, but was a decoy: and his after-speeches are not so much directed to her as to the listeners and spies. Such a discovery in a mood so anxious and irritable accounts for a certain harshness in him; and yet a wild up-working of love, sporting with opposites in a wilful, self-tormenting strain of irony, is perceptible throughout. — COLERIDGE.

[15] "Your *chastity* should have no conversation or acquaintance with your beauty." This use of *honesty* for *chastity* is very frequent in Shakespeare. — It should be noted, that in these speeches Hamlet refers, not to Ophelia personally, but to the sex in general. So, especially, when he says, "I have heard of your paintings too," he does not mean that Ophelia paints, but that the use of painting is common with her sex.

transform honesty from what it is to a bawd than the force of honesty can translate beauty into his likeness : this was sometime a paradox, but now the time gives it proof. I did love you once.

Ophe. Indeed, my lord, you made me believe so.

Ham. You should not have believed me ; for virtue cannot so inoculate our old stock but we shall relish of it : [16] I loved you not.

Ophe. I was the more deceived.

Ham. Get thee to a nunnery : why wouldst thou be a breeder of sinners? I am myself indifferent honest : [17] but yet I could accuse me of such things, that it were better my mother had not borne me : I am very proud, revengeful, ambitious ; with more offences at my beck [18] than I have thoughts to put them in, imagination to give them shape, or time to act them in. What should such fellows as I do crawling between earth and heaven? We are arrant knaves all ; believe none of us. Go thy ways to a nunnery. Where's your father?

Ophe. At home, my lord.

Ham. Let the doors be shut upon him, that he may play the fool no where but in's own house. Farewell.

Ophe. [*Aside.*] O, help him, you sweet Heavens !

Ham. If thou dost marry, I'll give thee this plague for thy dowry : Be thou as chaste as ice, as pure as snow, thou shalt not escape calumny. Get thee to a nunnery, go : farewell. Or, if thou wilt needs marry, marry a fool ; for wise men know well enough what monsters you make of them. To a nunnery, go ; and quickly too. Farewell.

[16] " Cannot so penetrate and purify our nature, but that we shall still have a strong taste of our native badness."

[17] " *Indifferent* honest " is *tolerably* honest. See page 105, note 32.

[18] That is, " ready to come about me on a signal of permission."

Ophe. [*Aside.*] O heavenly powers, restore him !

Ham. I have heard of your paintings too, well enough ;
God has given you one face, and you make yourselves another : you jig, you amble, and you lisp, and nickname God's
creatures, and make your wantonness your ignorance.[19] Go
to, I'll no more on't ; it hath made me mad. I say, we will
have no more marriages : those that are married already, all
but one, shall live ; the rest shall keep as they are. To a
nunnery, go.[20]   [*Exit*

Ophe. O, what a noble mind is here o'erthrown !
The courtier's, scholar's, soldier's, eye, tongue, sword :
Th' expectancy and rose of the fair State,
The glass of fashion and the mould of form,[21]
Th' observed of all observers, — quite, quite down !
And I, of ladies most deject and wretched,
That suck'd the honey of his music vows,
Now see that noble and most sovereign reason,
Like sweet bells jangled, out of tune and harsh ;

[19] Johnson explains this, "You mistake by wanton affectation, and pre
tend to mistake by *ignorance*." Moberly, "You use ambiguous words, as
if you did not know their meaning."

[20] Throughout the latter part of this fine scene, Hamlet's disorder runs to
a very high pitch, and he seems to take an insane delight in lacerating the
gentle creature before him. Yet what keenness and volubility of wit ! what
energy and swiftness of discourse ! the intellectual forces in a fiery gallop,
while the social feelings seem totally benumbed. And when Ophelia meets
his question, "Where's your father ?" with the reply, "At home, my lord,"
how quickly he darts upon the true meaning of her presence ! The sweet,
innocent girl, who knows not how to word an untruth, having never tried on
a lie in her life, becomes embarrassed in her part ; and from her manner
Hamlet instantly gathers what is on foot, and forthwith shapes his speech so
as to sting the eavesdroppers.

[21] This is well explained in what Lady Percy says of her lost Hotspur, in
2 *King Henry IV.*, ii. 3 : "By his light did all the chivalry of England move :
he was indeed the glass wherein the noble youth did dress themselves."

That unmatch'd form and feature of blown youth
Blasted with ecstasy.   O, woe is me,
T' have seen what I have seen, see what I see !

Enter the KING *and* POLONIUS.

King. Love ! his affections do not that way tend ;
Nor what he spake, though it lack'd form a little,
Was not like madness.   There's something in his soul,
O'er which his melancholy sits on brood ;
And I do doubt [22] the hatch and the disclose
Will be some danger : which for to prevent,
I have in quick determination
Thus set it down : He shall with speed to England,
For the demand of our neglected tribute :
Haply the seas and countries different,
With variable objects, shall expel
This something-settled matter in his heart ;
Whereon his brains still beating puts him thus
From fashion of himself.   What think you on't ?
Polo. It shall do well : but yet do I believe
The origin and commencement of his grief
Sprung from neglected love. — How now, Ophelia !
You need not tell us what Lord Hamlet said ;
We heard it all. — My lord, do as you please ;
But, if you hold it fit, after the play
Let his Queen mother all alone entreat him
To show his grief : let her be round [23] with him ;
And I'll be placed, so please you, in the ear
Of all their conference.   If she find him not,

[22] *Doubt*, again, in the sense of *fear* or *suspect*.
[23] *Round*, again, for *plain-spoken, downright*.

To England send him ; or confine him where
Your wisdom best shall think.

   King.   It shall be so :
Madness in great ones must not unwatch'd go.   [*Exeunt.*

SCENE II.—*A Hall in the Castle.*

Enter HAMLET *and* Players.[1]

Ham. Speak the speech, I pray you, as I pronounced it
to you, trippingly on the tongue : but if you mouth it, as
many of your players do, I had as lief the town-crier spoke
my lines. Nor do not saw the air too much with your hand,
thus ; but use all gently : for in the very torrent, tempest,
and, as I may say, whirlwind of your passion, you must acquire
and beget a temperance that may give it smoothness. O, it
offends me to the soul to hear a robustious periwig-pated
fellow tear a passion to tatters, to very rags, to split the ears
of the groundlings ;[2] who, for the most part, are capable of
nothing but inexplicable dumb-shows and noise. I would
have such a fellow whipp'd for o'erdoing Termagant ; it out-
herods Herod :[3] pray you, avoid it.

[1] " This dialogue of Hamlet with the players," says Coleridge, "is one of
the happiest instances of Shakespeare's power of diversifying the scene
while he is carrying on the plot."

[2] The ancient theatres were far from the commodious, elegant structures
which later times have seen. The *pit* was, truly, what its name denotes, an
unfloored space in the area of the house, sunk considerably beneath the
level of the stage. Hence this part of the audience were called *groundlings*.

[3] *Termagaunt* is the name given in old romances to the tempestuous god
of the Saracens. He is usually joined with *Mahound*, or Mahomet. John
Florio calls him "*Termigisto*, a great boaster, quarreller, killer, tamer, or
ruler of the universe ; the child of the earthquake and of the thunder, the
brother of death." Hence this personage was introduced into the old Mira-
cle-plays as a demon of outrageous and violent demeanour ; or, as Bale
says, "*Termagauntes* altogether, and very devils incarnate." The murder of

1 Play. I warrant your Honour.

Ham. Be not too tame neither, but let your own discretion be your tutor : suit the action to the word, the word to
the action ; with this special observance, that you o'erstep
not the modesty of nature : for any thing so overdone is from
the purpose of playing, whose end, both at the first and now,
was and is, to hold, as 'twere, the mirror up to Nature ; to
show virtue her own feature, scorn her own image, and the
very age and body of the time his form and pressure.[4] Now,
this overdone, or come tardy of,[5] though it make the unskilful laugh, cannot but make the judicious grieve ; the censure
of the which one must, in your allowance,[6] o'erweigh a whole
theatre of others. O, there be players that I have seen play,
and heard others praise, and that highly, not to speak it pro-
fanely, that, neither having the accent of Christians nor the
gait of Christian, pagan, nor Turk, have so strutted and bel-
lowed, that I have thought some of Nature's journeymen had
made them, and not made them well, they imitated humanity
so abominably.

1 Play. I hope we have reform'd that indifferently[7] with
us, sir.

Ham. O, reform it altogether. And let those that play

the innocents was a favourite subject for a Miracle-play; and wherever
Herod is introduced, he plays the part of a vaunting braggart, a tyrant of
tyrants, and does indeed *outdo Termagant.*

[4] *Pressure* is *impression* here; as when, in i. 5: Hamlet says, " I'll wipe
away all forms, all *pressures* past."

[5] To " come tardy of " a thing is evidently the same as to come short of it.

[6] " The *censure* of the *which one* " means the *judgment* of *one of which,* or
of *whom.* This use of *censure* is very frequent. — *Allowance* is *estimation* or
approval. To *approve* is the more frequent meaning of to *allow,* in Shakespeare. And so in the Bible; as, " The Lord *alloweth* the righteous "; and,
" That which I do I *allow* not."

[7] That is, *tolerably well.* See page 130, note 17.

your Clowns speak no more than is set down for them : for there be of them that will themselves laugh, to set on some quantity of barren spectators to laugh too ; though, in the meantime, some necessary question of the play be then to be considered : that's villainous, and shows a most pitiful ambition in the Fool that uses it.   Go, make you ready.—

[*Exeunt* Players.

Enter POLONIUS, ROSENCRANTZ, *and* GUILDENSTERN.

How now, my lord ! will the King hear this piece of work?

Polo. And the Queen too, and that presently.

Ham. Bid the players make haste.   [*Exit* POLONIUS.]—
Will you two help to hasten them?

Rosen. } We will, my lord.
Guild. }

[*Exeunt* ROSENCRANTZ *and* GUILDENSTERN.

Ham. What ho ! Horatio !

Enter HORATIO.

Hora. Here, sweet lord, at your service.

Ham. Horatio, thou art e'en as just a man
As e'er my conversation coped withal.

Hora. O, my dear lord,—

Ham.   Nay, do not think I flatter ;
For what advancement may I hope from thee
That no revénue[8] hast but thy good spirits,
To feed and clothe thee? Why should the poor be flatter'd?
No, let the candied tongue lick absurd pomp,

---

[8] Here, and generally, though not always, in Shakespeare, *revénue* has the accent on the second syllable. And such is undoubtedly the right pronunciation. I have marked the word in Spenser, Daniel, Dryden, Young, and Thomson, and all have it so. So, too, Daniel Webster, Rufus Choate, and Edward Everett always spoke it.

And crook the pregnant[9] hinges of the knee
Where thrift may follow fawning.   Dost thou hear?
Since my dear soul was mistress of her choice,
And could of men distinguish, her election
Hath seal'd thee for herself : for thou hast been
As one, in suffering all, that suffers nothing ;
A man that Fortune's buffets and rewards
Hath ta'en with equal thanks : and blest are those
Whose blood and judgment are so well commingled,
That they are not a pipe for Fortune's finger
To sound what stop she please.   Give me that man
That is not passion's slave, and I will wear him
In my heart's core, ay, in my heart of heart,
As I do thee. — Something too much of this. —
There is a play to-night before the King :
One scene of it comes near the circumstance
Which I have told thee of my father's death.
I pr'ythee, when thou seest that act a-foot,
Even with the very comment of thy soul
Observe my uncle : if his occulted guilt
Do not itself unkennel in one speech,
It is a damnèd ghost that we have seen ;
And my imaginations are as foul
As Vulcan's stithy.[10]   Give him heedful note :
For I mine eyes will rivet to his face ;
And, after, we will both our judgments join
In censure of his seeming.
    Hora.   Well, my lord ;
If he steal aught the whilst this play is playing,
And 'scape detecting, I will pay the theft.

---

[9] *Pregnant* is *ready, prompt.—Candied* is *sugared;* a tongue steeped in the sweetness of adulation. — *Thrift* is *profit;* the gold that flatterers lie for.
[10] Vulcan's workshop or *smithy; stith* being an *anvil.*

Ham. They're coming to the play; I must be idle :[11]
Get you a place.

Danish march. A flourish. Enter the KING, *the* QUEEN,
POLONIUS, OPHELIA, ROSENCRANTZ, GUILDENSTERN, *and
others.*

King. How fares our cousin Hamlet?

Ham. Excellent, i' faith; of the chameleon's dish: I eat
the air, promise-cramm'd :[12] you cannot feed capons so.

King. I have nothing with this answer, Hamlet; these
words are not mine.

Ham. No, nor mine now. — [*To* POLONIUS.] My lord,
you played once i' the university, you say?

Polo. That did I, my lord; and was accounted a good
actor.

Ham. What did you enact?

Polo. I did enact Julius Cæsar: I was kill'd i' the Capitol; Brutus kill'd me.[13]

Ham. It was a brute part of him to kill so capital a calf
there.[14] — Be the players ready?

Rosen. Ay, my lord; they stay upon your patience.

Queen. Come hither, my dear Hamlet, sit by me.

[11] Must *seem* idle; must behave as if his mind were purposeless, or intent
upon nothing in particular.

[12] Because the chameleon was supposed to live on air. In fact, this and
various other reptiles will live a long time without any visible food. So in
Othello, iii. 3: "I had rather be a toad, and *live upon the vapour* of a dun-
geon," &c. — The King snuffs offence in "I eat the air, promise-cramm'd,"
as implying that he has not kept his promise to Hamlet.

[13] A Latin play on Cæsar's death was performed at Christ's Church, Ox-
ford, in 1582. Malone thinks that there was an English play on the same
subject previous to Shakespeare's. Cæsar was killed in *Pompey's portico,*
and not in the Capitol; but the error is at least as old as Chaucer's time.

[14] He *acted* the part of a brute. — The play on *Capitol* and *capital* is obvious enough.

Ham. No, good mother; here's metal more attractive.

Polo. [*To the* KING.] O ho! do you mark that?

Ham. Lady, shall I lie in your lap?

                   [*Lying down at* OPHELIA'S *feet*

Ophe. No, my lord.

Ham. I mean, my head upon your lap?

Ophe. Ay, my lord. You are merry, my lord.

Ham. Who, I?

Ophe. Ay, my lord.

Ham. O God, your only jig-maker. What should a man do but be merry? for, look you, how cheerfully my mother looks, and my father died within's [15] two hours.

Ophe. Nay, 'tis twice two months, my lord.

Ham. So long? Nay, then let the Devil wear black, for I'll have a suit of sabell.[16] O Heavens! die two months ago, and not forgotten yet? Then there's hope a great man's memory may outlive his life half a year: but, by'r Lady, he must build churches, then; or else shall he suffer not thinking on, with the hobby-horse, whose epitaph is *For O, for O, the hobby-horse is forgot!* [17]

[15] *Within's* is a contraction of *within this.* The Poet has some contractions even harsher than this.

[16] *Sabell* is a *flame*-colour. A writer in *The Critic* for 1854, page 373, remarks that " *sabell* or *sabelle* is properly a fawn-colour a good deal heightened with red, and that the term came from the French *couleur d'isabelle.*" According to the *Dictionary of the French Academy*, *isabelle* is a colour "between white and *yellow*, but with the yellow predominating." It is therefore a very showy, flaring colour; as far as possible from mourning.

[17] The *Hobby-horse* was a part of the old Morris-dance, which was used in the May-games. It was the figure of a horse fastened round a man's waist, the man's legs going through the horse's body, and enabling him to walk, but covered by a long footcloth; while false legs appeared where those of the man's should be, astride the horse. The Puritans waged a furious war against the Morris-dance; which caused the Hobby-horse to be left out of it: hence the burden of a song, which passed into a proverb, The plays of the times have many allusions to it.

Hautboys play.   The Dumb-show enters.

Enter a King *and a* Queen *very lovingly; the* Queen *em-bracing him, and he her.   She kneels, and makes show of protestation unto him.   He takes her up, and declines his head upon her neck; lays him down upon a bank of flowers: she, seeing him asleep, leaves him.   Anon comes in a fellow, takes off his crown, kisses it, and pours poison in the* King's *ears, and exit.   The* Queen *returns, finds the* King *dead, and makes passionate action.   The* Poisoner, *with some two or three* Mutes, *comes in again, seeming to lament with her.   The dead body is carried away.   The* Poisoner *wooes the* Queen *with gifts: she seems loth and unwilling awhile, but in the end accepts his love.*[18]   [*Exeunt.*

Ophe. What means this, my lord?

Ham. Marry, this is miching mallecho;[19] it means mischief.

Ophe. Belike this show imports the argument of the play.

Enter Prologue.

Ham. We shall know by this fellow: the players cannot keep counsel; they'll tell all.[20]

Ophe. Will he tell us what this show meant?

[18] As the King does not take fire at this Dumb-show, we may suppose his attention to be so engaged with some about him, that he does not mark it.

[19] *Miching mallecho* is lurking mischief or evil-doing.   To *mich,* for to skulk, to lurk, was an old English verb in common use in Shakespeare's time; and *mallecho* or *malhecho, misdeed,* he borrowed from the Spanish.

[20] Hamlet is running a high strain of jocularity with Ophelia, in order to hide his purpose.   The wit here turns upon the fact, that an actor's business is speaking; blurting out before the world what would else be unknown; as dramatic personages are always supposed to be speaking, as *without an audience,* what an audience is nevertheless listening to.   Hence, even when keeping counsel, they are *not* keeping it; are telling the very things they are hiding, and blabbing to the public what they are confiding to each other.

Ham. Ay, or any show that you'll show him : be not you ashamed to show, he'll not shame to tell you what it means.

Ophe. You are naught,[21] you are naught ; I'll mark the play.

Prologue.   *For us, and for our tragedy,*
             Here stooping to your clemency,
             We beg your hearing patiently.   [Exit.

Ham. Is this a prologue, or the posy[22] of a ring?
Ophe. 'Tis brief, my lord.
Ham. As woman's love.

Enter two Players, King *and* Queen.

Play. K. *Full thirty times hath Phœbus' cart[23] gone round*
Neptune's salt wash and Tellus' orbèd ground,
And thirty dozen moons with borrow'd sheen
About the world have times twelve thirties been,
Since love our hearts and Hymen did our hands
Unite commutual in most sacred bands.

Play. Q. *So many journeys may the Sun and Moon*
Make us again count o'er ere love be done !
But, woe is me ! you are so sick of late,
So far from cheer and from your former state,
That I distrust you.[24]   Yet, though I distrust,
Discomfort you, my lord, it nothing must :
For women's fear and love hold quantity ;[25]

---

21 That is *naughty, bad* ; not *nothing* or *nought.*

22 The *posy* is the *motto,* that is, words inscribed, and of course **very brief.**

23 *Cart, car,* and *chariot* were used indiscriminately.—"The style," says Coleridge, "of the interlude here is distinguished from the real dialogue by rhyme, as in the first interview with the players by epic verse."

24 "Distrust *your health*"; "am solicitous about you."

25 "Hold quantity " is *have equal strength.*

In neither aught, or in extremity.
Now, what my love is, proof hath made you know;
And as my love is sized, my fear is so:
Where love is great, the littlest doubts are fear;
Where little fears grow great, great love grows there.

  Play. K. *Faith, I must leave thee, love, and shortly too;*
My operant [26] *powers their functions leave to do:*
And thou shalt live in this fair world behind,
Honour'd, beloved; and haply one as kind
For husband shalt thou—

  Play. Q.   *O, confound the rest!*
Such love must needs be treason in my breast:
In second husband let me be accurst!
None wed the second but who kill'd the first.

  Ham. [*Aside.*] Wormwood, wormwood!

  Play. Q. *The instances* [27] *that second marriage move*
Are base respects of thrift, but none of love:
A second time I kill my husband dead,
When second husband kisses me in bed.

  Play. K. *I do believe you think what now you speak;*
But what we do determine oft we break.
Purpose is but the slave to memory,
Of violent birth, but poor validity;
Which now, like fruit unripe, sticks on the tree,
But fall unshaken when they mellow be.
Most necessary [28] *'tis that we forget*

  [26] "*Operant* for *active* or *operative*. So in *Timon of Athens*, iv. 3:
"Sauce his palate with thy most *operant* poison."

  [27] *Instances* for *inducements*. In the next line, *respects* is *considerations*
or *motives*, as usual in Shakespeare.

  [28] *Necessary* here means *natural* simply. So in *Measure for Measure*, ii.
4: "Dispossessing all my other parts of *necessary* fitness."

To pay ourselves what to ourselves is debt:
What to ourselves in passion we propose,
The passion ending, doth the purpose lose.
The violence of either grief or joy
Their own enactures [29] *with themselves destroy:*
Where joy most revels, grief doth most lament;
Grief joys, joy grieves, on slender accident.
This world is not for aye; nor 'tis not strange
That even our loves should with our fortunes change;
For 'tis a question left us yet to prove,
Whether love lead fortune or else fortune love.
The great man down, you mark, his favourite flies;
The poor advanced makes friends of enemies:
And hitherto doth love on fortune tend;
For who not needs shall never lack a friend;
And who in want a hollow friend doth try,
Directly seasons him his enemy.
But, orderly to end where I begun,
Our wills and fates do so contráry run,
That our devices still are overthrown;
Our thoughts are ours, their ends none of our own: [30]
So, think thou wilt no second husband wed;
But die thy thoughts when thy first lord is dead.

    Play. Q. *Nor earth to me give food, nor heaven light!*
Sport and repose lock from me day and night!
To desperation turn my trust and hope!
An anchor's cheer [31] *in prison be my scope!*
Each opposite, that blanks the face of joy, [32]

[29] *Enactures* for *determinations;* what they *enact.*

[30] That is, we can *control* our thoughts, but not their *results.*

[31] A *hermit's fare,* or diet. *Anchor* for *anchoret,* an old word for *hermit.*

[32] To *blank* the face is to make it *white;* to take the blood out of it. The proper colour of joy is *ruddy.*

Meet what I would have well, and it destroy!
Both here and hence pursue me lasting strife,
If, once a widow, ever I be wife!

　Ham. If she should break it now!

　Play. K. *'Tis deeply sworn. Sweet, leave me here awhile:*
My spirits grow dull, and fain I would beguile
The tedious day with sleep.　　　　　　　　[*Sleeps*

　Play. Q.　　　　　*Sleep rock thy brain;*　　2ı8
And never come mischance between us twain!　　[*Exit.*

　Ham. Madam, how like you this play?　　2ı2.

　Queen. The lady protests too much, methinks.

　Ham. O, but she'll keep her word.

　King. Have you heard the argument? Is there no offence in't?

　Ham. No, no, they do but jest, poison in jest; no offence i' the world.

　King. What do you call the play?

　Ham. The Mouse-trap. Marry, how? Tropically.[33] This 2ı0 play is the image of a murder done in Vienna: Gonzago is the King's name; his wife, Baptista: you shall see anon; 'tis a knavish piece of work: but what o' that? your Majesty, and we that have free souls, it touches us not: let the galled jade wince, our withers are unwrung.[34]

Enter LUCIANUS.

This is one Lucianus, nephew to the King.

　Ophe. You are as good as a chorus,[35] my lord.

---

[33] *Tropically* is *figuratively*, or in the way of trope.

[34] The allusion is to a horse wincing as the saddle galls his withers.

[35] The use to which Shakespeare put the *chorus* may be seen in *King Henry V.* Every motion or puppet-show was accompanied by an *interpreter* or showman.

Ham. I could interpret between you and your love,[36] if I could see the puppets dallying.

Ophe. You are keen, my lord, you are keen.

Ham. Begin, murderer; pox! leave thy damnable faces, and begin. Come: *The croaking raven doth bellow for revenge.*[37]

Luci. *Thoughts black, hands apt, drugs fit, and time agreeing;*
Confederate season, else no creature seeing:[38]
Thou mixture rank, of midnight weeds collected,
With Hecate's ban thrice blasted,[39] thrice infected,
Thy natural magic and dire property,
On wholesome life usurp immediately..

              [*Pours the poison into the sleeper's ear.*

Ham. He poisons him i' the garden for's estate. His name's Gonzago: the story is extant, and writ in choice Italian. You shall see anon how the murderer gets the love of Gonzago's wife.

Ophe. The King rises!

Ham. What, frighted with false fire!

Queen. How fares my lord?

Polo. Give o'er the play!

King. Give me some light! — away!

All. Lights, lights, lights!

              [*Exeunt all but* HAMLET *and* HORATIO.

---

36 *Love* for *lover;* a very common usage.

37 "The croaking raven," &c., is probably a quotation from some play then well known. The raven's croak was thought to be ill-boding.

38 No creature but time looking on, and that a confederate in the act, or conspiring with the murderer.

39 Poisonous weeds were supposed to be more poisonous if gathered in the night. *Hecate* was the name given to the Queen of the witches; and her *banning* or cursing brought the poison to the highest intensity.

Ham. Why, let the strucken deer go weep,
  The hart ungallèd play ; [40]
  For some must watch, while some must sleep :
  So runs the world away.
Would not this, sir, and a forest of feathers,[41] — if the rest of
my fortunes turn Turk with me, — with two Provincial roses
on my razed shoes,[42] get me a fellowship in a cry of players,
sir ? [43]

Hora. Half a share.[44]

---

[40] It is said that a deer, when badly wounded, retires from the herd, and goes apart, to weep and die. Of course, *hart* is the same as *deer*, and *ungallèd* the opposite of *strucken*.

[41] Alluding, probably, to a custom which the London players seem to have had in Shakespeare's time, of flaunting it in gaudy apparel, and with *plumes* in their caps, the more the better. So in Chapman's *Monsieur D'Olive*, 1606, iii. 1 : " Three of these *goldfinches* I have entertained for my followers : I am ashamed to train 'em abroad ; they say I carry a whole *forest of feathers* with me." Some one calling himself a Soldier wrote to Secretary Walsingham in 1586, complaining, " It is a woeful sight, to see two hundred *proud players jet in their silks,* where five hundred poor people starve in the streets." — To *turn Turk* with any one was to *desert* or *betray* him, or turn traitor to him. A common phrase of the time.

[42] *Provincial* roses took their name from *Provins*, in Lower Brie, and not from *Provence*. *Razed* shoes are most probably *embroidered* shoes. To *race*, or *raze*, was to *stripe*. So in Markham's *Country Farm*, speaking of wafer cakes : " Baking all together between two irons, having within them many *raced* and checkered draughts after the manner of small squares."

[43] " A *fellowship* in a *cry* of players" is a *partnership* in a *company* of players. The Poet repeatedly uses *cry* thus for *set, pack,* or *troop.* The word was borrowed from the chase, as hounds were selected for a pack according to their barking tones, so as to make a harmonious or musical *cry.*

[44] The players were paid not by salaries, but by *shares* or portions of the profit, according to merit. Perhaps, however, the allusion is rather to the custom, then in vogue, of making the theatrical property a joint-stock affair. Thus Shakespeare himself was a stockholder in the Globe theatre, and so had not only his portion of the profits as one of the players, but also an income from the money invested, or from the shares he held in the stock.

Ham. A whole one, ay.

> For thou dost know, O Damon dear,
>> This realm dismantled was
> Of Jove himself;[45] and now reigns here
>> A very, very — pajock.[46]

Hora. You might have rhymed.[47]

Ham. O good Horatio, I'll take the Ghost's word for a thousand pound. Didst perceive?

Hora. Very well, my lord.

Ham. Upon the talk of the poisoning?

Hora. I did very well note him.

Ham. Ah, ha! Come, some music! come, the recorders![48] —

---

[45] The meaning is, that Denmark was robbed of a king who had the majesty of Jove. — Hamlet calls Horatio Damon, in allusion to the famous friendship of Damon and Pythias.

[46] *Pajock* is probably an old form of *peacock.* Dyce says he has "often heard the lower classes in the north of Scotland call the peacock *peajock.*" Editors have been greatly in the dark as to the reason of the word's being used here. But a writer in *The Edinburgh Review,* October, 1872, shows that in the popular belief of Shakespeare's time the peacock had a very bad character, "being, in fact, the accredited representative of inordinate pride and envy, as well as of unnatural cruelty and lust." And he quotes from what was then the most popular manual of natural history: "The peacocke is a bird that loveth not his young, for the male searcheth out the female, and seeketh out her egges for to break them, that he may so occupy him the more in his lecherie. And he wondereth at the fairenesse of his fethers, and areareth them up as it were a circle about his head, and then he looketh to his feet, and seeth the fouleness of his feet, and lyke as he were ashamed he leteth his fethers fall sodeinlye. And as one sayth, he hath the voice of a feend, the head of a serpent, and the pace of a theefe." The writer adds that "in the whole fauna of the time Hamlet could not have selected the name of bird or beast that expressed with greater emphasis the hateful union of corrupted passion and evil life that now usurped the throne of Denmark."

[47] *Ass* was often used as a rhyme to *was.*

[48] The recorder was a soft-toned instrument, something like the flute

For if the King like not the comedy,
Why then, belike,—he likes it not, perdy.[49]—
Come, some music!

Re-enter ROSENCRANTZ *and* GUILDENSTERN.

Guild. Good my lord, vouchsafe me a word with you.

Ham. Sir, a whole history.

Guild. The King, sir,—

Ham. Ay, sir, what of him?

Guild. —is in his retirement marvellous distemper'd.

Ham. With drink, sir?

Guild. No, my lord, with choler.

Ham. Your wisdom should show itself more richer to sig-nify this to his doctor; for, for me to put him to his purga-tion would perhaps plunge him into more choler.

Guild. Good my lord, put your discourse into some frame, and start not so wildly from my affair.

Ham. I am tame, sir: pronounce.

Guild. The Queen your mother, in most great affliction of spirit, hath sent me to you.

Ham. You are welcome.

Guild. Nay, good my lord, this courtesy is not of the right breed. If it shall please you to make me a wholesome answer, I will do your mother's commandment; if not, your pardon and my return shall be the end of my business.

Ham. Sir, I cannot.

Guild. What, my lord?

So in *Paradise Lost,* i.: "They move in perfect phalanx to the Dorian mood of flutes and soft *recorders.*" To *record* was also used for to *warble* or *sing.* Thus in Drayton's *Eclogues:* "Fair Philomel, night-music of the Spring, sweetly *records* her tuneful harmony."

[49] *Perdy* is a corruption of the French *par Dieu.*

Ham. Make you a wholesome answer; my wit's diseased: but, sir, such answer as I can make, you shall command; or, rather, as you say, my mother: therefore no more, but to the matter: My mother, you say, —

Rosen. Then thus she says: Your behaviour hath struck her into amazement and admiration.[50]

Ham. O wonderful son, that can so astonish a mother! — But is there no sequel at the heels of this mother's admiration? Impart.

Rosen. She desires to speak with you in her closet, ere you go to bed.

Ham. We shall obey, were she ten times our mother. Have you any further trade with us?

Rosen. My lord, you once did love me.

Ham. So I do still, by these pickers and stealers.[51]

Rosen. Good my lord, what is your cause of distemper? you do, surely, bar the door upon your own liberty, if you deny your griefs to your friend.

Ham. Sir, I lack advancement.

Rosen. How can that be, when you have the voice of the King himself for your succession in Denmark?

Ham. Ay, sir, but *While the grass grows*, — the proverb is something musty.[52] —

Re-enter Players *with recorders.*

O, the recorders! let me see one. — To withdraw with you:

[50] *Admiration*, again, in its proper Latin sense of *wonder*.

[51] This is explained by a clause in the Church Catechism: "To keep my *hands* from *picking* and *stealing*." — In "So I do still," *so* is emphatic, and strongly ironical.

[52] "The musty proverb" is, "Whylst grass doth growe, oft sterves the seely steede."

[*Takes* GUILDENSTERN *aside.*] Why do you go about to recover the wind of me, as if you would drive me into a toil?[53]

Guild. O, my lord, if my duty be too bold, my love is too unmannerly.[54]

Ham. I do 'not well understand that. Will you play upon this pipe?

Guild. My lord, I cannot.

Ham. I pray you.

Guild. Believe me, I cannot.

Ham. I do beseech you.

Guild. I know no touch of it, my lord.

Ham. 'Tis as easy as lying : govern these ventages with your fingers and thumb, give it breath with your mouth, and it will discourse most eloquent music. Look you, these are the stops.[55]

Guild. But these cannot I command to any utterance of harmony ; I have not the skill.

Ham. Why, look you now, how unworthy a thing you make of me ! You would play upon me ; you would seem to know my stops ; you would pluck out the heart of my mystery ; you would sound me from my lowest note to the top of my compass : and there is much music, excellent voice, in this little organ ; yet cannot you make it speak. 'Sblood, do you think I am easier to be play'd on than a

---

[53] "To *recover the wind* of me" is a term borrowed from hunting, and means to take advantage of the animal pursued, by getting to the windward of it, that it may not scent its pursuers. — *Toil* is *snare* or *trap*.

[54] Hamlet may well say, "I do not well understand that." The meaning, however, seems to be, "If I am using an unmannerly boldness with you, it is my love that makes me do so."

[55] The *ventages* are the holes of the pipe. *Stops* signifies the mode of stopping the ventages so as to make the notes.

pipe? Call me what instrument you will, though you can
fret me,[56] you cannot play upon me. —

Re-enter POLONIUS.

God bless you, sir !

Polo. My lord, the Queen would speak with you, and
presently.

Ham. Do you see yonder cloud that's almost in shape of
a camel?

Polo. By the Mass, and 'tis like a camel, indeed.

Ham. Methinks it is like a weasel.

Polo. It is backed like a weasel.

Ham. Or like a whale?

Polo. Very like a whale.

Ham. Then will I come to my mother by-and-by. —
[*Aside.*] They fool me to the top of my bent.[57] — I will
come by-and-by.

Polo. I will say so.·   [*Exit* POLONIUS.

Ham. By-and-by is easily said. — Leave me, friends. —
                              [*Exeunt all but* HAMLET.

'Tis now the very witching-time of night,
When churchyards yawn,[58] and Hell itself breathes out
Contagion to this world : now could I drink hot blood,
And do such bitter business as the day
Would quake to look on.   Soft ! now to my mother. —

---

[56] Hamlet keeps up the allusion to a musical instrument.   The *frets* of a
lute or guitar are the ridges crossing the finger-board, upon which the
strings are pressed or *stopped*.   A quibble is intended on *fret*.

[57] They *humour* me to the *full height* of my inclination.   Polonius has
been using the method, common in the treatment of crazy people, of assent-
ing to all that Hamlet says.   This is what Hamlet refers to.

[58] Churchyards *yawn* to let forth the ghosts, who did all their walking in
the night.   And the crimes which darkness so often covers might well be
spoken of as caused by the nocturnal contagion of Hell.

O heart, lose not thy nature ; let not ever
The soul of Nero [59] enter this firm bosom .
Let me be cruel, not unnatural.
I will speak daggers to her, but use none ;
My tongue and soul in this be hypocrites :
How in my words soever she be shent,[60]
To give them seals never, my soul, consent !   [Exit.

SCENE III. — A Room in the Castle.

Enter the KING, ROSENCRANTZ, and GUILDENSTERN.

King. I like him not ; nor stands it safe with us
To let his madness range.   Therefore prepare you :
I your commission will forthwith dispatch,
And he to England shall along with you.
The terms of our estate may not endure
Hazard so dangerous as doth hourly grow
Out of his lunacies.
    Guild.   We will ourselves provide :
Most holy and religious fear it is
To keep those many many bodies safe
That live and feed upon your Majesty.
    Rosen. The single and peculiar life is bound,
With all the strength and armour of the mind,
To keep itself from 'noyance ; but much more
That spirit upon whose weal depend and rest

59 Nero is aptly referred to here, as he was the murderer of his mother,
Agrippina. It may be worth noting that the name of the King in this play
is Claudius; and that, after the death of Domitius her husband, Agrippina
married with her uncle the Emperor Claudius.

60 To shend is to injure, whether by reproof, blows, or otherwise. Shakespeare generally uses shent for reproved, threatened with angry words. "To
give his words seals" is therefore to carry his punishment beyond reproof
The allusion is to the sealing of a deed to render it effective.

The lives of many. The cease of majesty
Dies not alone;[1] but like a gulf doth draw
What's near it with it: 'tis a massy wheel,
Fix'd on the summit of the highest mount,
To whose huge spokes ten thousand lesser things
Are mortised and adjoin'd; which when it falls,
Each small annexment, petty consequence,
Attends the boisterous ruin. Ne'er alone
Did the King sigh, but with a general groan.

 King. Arm you, I pray you, to this speedy voyage;
For we will fetters put upon this fear,
Which now goes too free-footed.

 Rosen. }
 Guild. }   We will haste us.

   [*Exeunt* ROSENCRANTZ *and* GUILDENSTERN.

Enter POLONIUS.

 Polo. My lord, he's going to his mother's closet.
Behind the arras I'll convey myself,
To hear the process; I'll warrant she'll tax him home:[2]
And, as you said, and wisely was it said,
'Tis meet that some more audience than a mother,
Since nature makes them partial, should o'erhear
The speech of vantage.[3] Fare you well, my liege:
I'll call upon you ere you go to bed,
And tell you what I know.

---

[1] Tautological in word, but not in sense. The cease (*decease*) of majesty *comes* not alone.

[2] *Home* as a general intensive, meaning *thoroughly, to the utmost.*

[3] Speech having an advantage in that nature makes the speakers partial to each other. This favours the conclusion that the Queen was not privy and consenting to the murder of Hamlet's father. Both the King and Polonius have some distrust of her.

King.   Thanks, dear my lord. —

                              [*Exit* POLONIUS

O, my offence is rank, it smells to Heaven;
It hath the primal eldest curse upon't,
A brother's murder !   Pray can I not:
Though inclination be as sharp as will,
My stronger guilt defeats my strong intent; [4]
And, like a man to double business bound,
I stand in pause where I shall first begin,
And both [5] neglect.   What if this cursèd hand
Were thicker than itself with brother's blood,
Is there not rain enough in the sweet Heavens
To wash it white as snow?   Whereto serves mercy
But to confront the visage of offence?
And what's in prayer but this twofold force, —
To be forstallèd ere we come to fall,
Or pardon'd being down? [6]   Then I'll look up;
My fault is past.   But, O, what form of prayer
Can serve my turn?   *Forgive me my foul murder ?*
That cannot be ; since I am still possess'd
Of those effects for which I did the murder,
My crown, mine own ambition, and my Queen.
May one be pardon'd, and retain th' offence?
In the corrupted 'currents of this world
Offence's gilded hand may shove-by justice;

---

[4] "Though I were not only willing but strongly inclined to pray, my
guilt would prevent me."   The distinction here implied is philosophically
just.   The inclination is the craving or the impulse to assuage his pangs of
remorse; the will is the determination of the reason or judgment in a question of duty and right.

[5] *Both* refers to the *two matters* of business implied in *double*.

[6] That is, either to be *prevented from falling*, or to be pardoned *after we
have fallen*.   Alluding to a part of the Lord's Prayer.

And oft 'tis seen the wicked prize itself
Buys out the law : but 'tis not so above ;
There is no shuffling, — there the action lies
In his true nature ; and we ourselves compell'd,
Even to the teeth and forehead of our faults,
To give-in evidence.   What then ? what rests ?[7]
Try what repentance can ? what can it not ?
Yet what can it when one cannot repent ?
O wretched state !   O bosom black as death !
O limèd soul,[8] that struggling to be free
Art more engaged !   Help, angels !   Make assay !
Bow, stubborn knees ; and, heart with strings of steel,
Be soft as sinews of a new-born babe !
All may be well.[9]   [*Retires and kneels.*

Enter HAMLET.

Ham. Now might I do it pat, now he is praying ;
And now I'll do't. — And so he goes to Heaven ! —
And so am I revenged ?   That would be scann'd : [10]
A villain kills my father ; and, for that,
I, his sole son, do this same villain send
To Heaven.
Why, this is hire and salary, not revenge.

---

[7] " What *remains* to be done ? " or, " What *else* can I do ? "

[8] Alluding to an old mode of catching birds, by spreading upon the twigs, where they are likely to light, a sticky substance called *bird-lime*. The birds were thus caught and held by the feet, and the more they tried to get away, the more they couldn't.   The thing grew to be a common figure for any sort of snare.   Shakespeare often uses it so.

[9] The final " All may be well " is remarkable ; — the degree of merit attributed by the self-flattering soul to its own struggles, though baffled, and to the indefinite half promise, half command, to persevere in religious duties. — COLERIDGE.

[10] That *should* be *scrutinized*.   See page 48, note II.

He took my father grossly, full of bread ;
With all his crimes [11] broad blown, as flush as May ;
And how his audit stands who knows save Heaven ?
But, in our circumstance and course of thought,[12]
'Tis heavy with him : and am I then revenged,
To take him in the purging of his soul,
When he is fit and season'd for his passage ?
No !
Up, sword, and know thou a more horrid hent : [13]
When he is drunk-asleep, or in his rage ;
At gaming, swearing ; or about some act
That has no relish of salvation in't :
Then trip him, that his heels may kick at Heaven ;
And that his soul may be as damn'd and black
As Hell, whereto it goes.[14]   My mother stays :
This physic but prolongs thy sickly days.[15]   [*Exit.*

[11] *Crimes* in the more general sense of *sins.* So twice before in this play :
" The foul *crimes* done in my days of nature "; and, " Having ever seen in
the prenominate *crimes* the youth you breathe of." — In the preceding line,
grossly goes with *father* as an adjective.   Perhaps it should be printed
grossly-full.

[12] " Circumstance and course of thought " seems to mean the particular
data or circumstantial detail of things from which our thought shapes its
course and draws its conclusions.

[13] *Hent*, both noun and verb, was used in the sense of *seizure, grasp,* or
hold.   Here it has the kindred sense of *purpose.*

[14] Hamlet here flies off to a sort of *ideal* revenge, in order to quiet his
filial feelings without violating his reason.   Yet it is a very mark-worthy
fact, that the King is taken at last in the perpetration of crimes far worse
than any that Hamlet here anticipates.   But that, to be sure, is the Poet's
ordering of the matter, and perhaps should be regarded as expressing *his*
sense of justice in this case; though Hamlet may well be supposed to have
a presentiment, that a man so bad, and so secure in his badness, will not
rest where he is; but will proceed to some further exploiting in crime, in
the midst of which judgment will at last overtake him.

[15] *This physic* refers to the reasons Hamlet has been giving for not strik-

King. [*Rising.*] My words fly up, my thoughts remain
  below :
Words without thoughts never to Heaven go.   [*Exit.*

SCENE IV. — *The Queen's Closet.*

Enter the QUEEN *and* POLONIUS.

Polo. He will come straight.   Look you lay home to him :
Tell him his pranks have been too broad to bear with ;
And that your Grace hath screen'd and stood between
Much heat and him.   I'll sconce me even here.
Pray you, be round with him.
    Ham. [*Within.*] Mother, mother, mother !
    Queen.   I'll warrant you ,
Fear me not.   Withdraw ; I hear him coming.
                    [POLONIUS *hides behind the arras.*

Enter HAMLET.

Ham. Now, mother, what's the matter?
    Queen. Hamlet, thou hast thy father much offended. \ D/ a
    Ham. Mother, you have my father much offended.
    Queen. Come, come ; you answer with an idle tongue.
    Ham. Go, go ; you question with a wicked tongue.
    Queen. Why, how now, Hamlet ! what's the matter now?
Have you forgot me?
    Ham.   No, by the rood,[1] not so :

ing now ; a medicine that prolongs the King's sickness, but does not heal
it ; that is, the purpose is delayed, not abandoned.

[1] *Rood* is an old word for *cross ;* often used for an oath, as here. — In regard to what immediately follows in this scene, Professor Werder has the
following : " Enraged, frantic, he rushes in wildly to his mother, and here,
hearing the voice behind the tapestry, *here, now* supposing the King to be
hidden there, he allows himself to be carried away by his hot blood, by rage

You are the Queen, your husband's brother's wife ;
And — would it were not so ! — you are my mother.

   Queen. Nay, then I'll set those to you that can speak.

   Ham. Come, come, and sit you down ; you shall not
      budge :
You go not till I set you up a glass
Where you may see the inmost part of you.

   Queen. What wilt thou do ? thou wilt not murder me ? —
Help, help, ho !

   Polo. [*Behind.*] What, ho ! help, help, help !

   Ham. [*Drawing.*] How now ! a rat ? Dead, for a ducat,
      dead !   [*Makes a pass through the arras.*

   Polo. [*Behind.*] O, I am slain !   [*Falls and dies.*

   Queen. O me ! what hast thou done ?

   Ham. Nay, I know not : is it the King ?

   Queen. O, what a rash and bloody deed is this !

   Ham. A bloody deed ! almost as bad, good mother,
As kill a king, and marry with his brother.

   Queen. As kill a king !

   Ham.   Ay, lady, 'twas my word. —
      [*Lifts up the arras and discovers* POLONIUS
Thou wretched, rash-intruding fool, farewell !
I took thee for thy better : take thy fortune ;
Thou find'st to be too busy is some danger. —

here, where the worst personal dishonour which has been inflicted upon
him, the living son, by the seducer of his mother, comes so near to him :
here, where the whole air is full of it ; here the voice of the wretch calls up
all his shame ; and, forgetting the strict obligation of his task, he gives full
course to his thirst for vengeance ; he is carried away into the grave error
of plunging his sword through the tapestry. A grave error indeed ! He
has made the thrust at last, — and what is the consequence ? Instead of
being freed from the old burden, he has brought upon his soul a new one.
Thus the error punishes itself." — See, also, the Introduction, page 25.

Leave wringing of your hands : peace ! sit you down,
And let me wring your heart : for so I shall,
If it be made of penetrable stuff ;
If damnèd custom have not brass'd it so,
That it is proof and bulwark against sense.

   Queen. What have I done, that thou darest wag thy tongue
In noise so rude against me?

   Ham.   Such an act
That blurs the grace and blush of modesty ;
Calls virtue hypocrite ;[2] takes off the rose
From the fair forehead of an innocent love,
And sets a blister there ; makes marriage-vows
As false as dicers' oaths : O, such a deed
As from the body of contraction plucks
The very soul ;[3] and sweet religion makes
A rhapsody of words : Heaven's face doth glow ;
Yea, this solidity and compound mass,[4]
With tristful visage, as against the doom,
Is thought-sick at the act.

   Queen.   Ah me, what act,
That roars so loud and thunders in the index ?[5]

---

  [2] A thing is often said to do that which it any way causes to be done.

  [3] *Contraction* here means the *marriage contract ;* of which Hamlet holds religion to be the life and soul, insomuch that without this it is but as a lifeless body, and must soon become a nuisance.

  [4] This solid globe, the Earth. Hamlet in his high-wrought stress of passion, kindling as he goes on, makes the fine climax, that not only the heavenly powers burn with indignation, but even the gross beings of this world are smitten with grief and horror, as if the day of judgment were at hand.

  [5] The *index*, or table of contents, was formerly placed at the beginning of books. In *Othello,* ii. 1, we have, " an *index* and obscure *prologue* to the history of lust and foul thoughts."

Ham. Look here upon this picture, and on this.
The counterfeit presentment [6] of two brothers.
See what a grace was seated on this brow ;
Hyperion's curls ; the front of Jove himself ; [7]
An eye like Mars, to threaten and command :
A station [8] like the herald Mercury
New-lighted on a heaven-kissing hill ;
A combination and a form indeed,
Where every god did seem to set his seal,
To give the world assurance of a man :
This was your husband.   Look you now what follows :
Here is your husband ; like a mildew'd ear,
Blasting his wholesome brother.[9]   Have you eyes?
Could you on this fair mountain leave to feed,
And batten [10] on this moor?   Ha ! have you eyes?
You cannot call it love ; for at your age
The hey-day in the blood is tame, it's humble,
And waits upon the judgment : and what judgment
Would step from this to this?   Sense, sure, you have,
Else could you not have motion ; but, sure, that sense
Is apoplex'd : [11] for madness would not err,

[3] *Counterfeit presentment*, or *counterfeit* simply, was used for *likeness*.   It is to be supposed that Hamlet wears a miniature of his father, while his mother wears one of the present King.

[7] The statues of Jupiter represented him as the most intellectual of all the gods, as Apollo was the most beautiful ; while in Mercury we have the ideal of swiftness and despatch.

[8] *Station* does not here mean the spot where any one is placed, but the *act of standing*, the *attitude*.   So in *Antony and Cleopatra*, iii. 3 : " Her motion and her *station* are as one."

[9] The allusion is to the blasted ears of corn that destroyed the full and good ears, in Pharaoh's dream ; *Genesis*, xli. 5–7.

[10] To *batten* is to *feed rankly* or *grossly ;* it is usually applied to the fattening of animals.

[11] There is some confusion here, owing to the different meanings with

Nor sense to ecstasy was ne'er so thrall'd,
But it reserved some quantity of choice,[12]
To serve in such a difference.   What devil was't,
That thus hath cozen'd you at hoodman-blind?[13]
Eyes without feeling, feeling without sight,
Ears without hands or eyes, smelling sans all,
Or but a sickly part of one true sense
Could not so mope.[14]
O shame! where is thy blush?   Rebellious Hell,
If thou canst mutine[15] in a matron's bones,
To flaming youth let virtue be as wax,
And melt in her own fire:[16] proclaim no shame,
When the compulsive ardour gives the charge,
Since frost itself as actively doth burn,
And reason panders will.

which *sense* is used. The first *sense* is *sensation* as necessary to bodily motion; the second refers to the mind, and comes pretty near meaning *reason*. The idea seems to be, that her reason must be not merely unseated, as in madness, but absolutely quenched.—In "madness would not err," the meaning is, "madness would not *so* err."

[12] Sense was never so *dominated* by the delusions of *insanity*, but that it still retained some *power* of choice. We have before had *quantity* in much the same sense. See page 140, note 25.

[13] *Hoodman-blind* is the old game of *blindman's-buff*.

[14] To *mope* is to be *dull and stupid*.

[15] *Mutine* for *mutiny*. This is the old form of the verb. Shakespeare calls *mutineers mutines* in a subsequent scene.

[16] The views here set forth by Hamlet are very different from those of Polonius in his advice to Laertes, as remarked upon in note 22, page 72. Hamlet seems to think that generous passions are the proper safety of youth, and he would keep the soul sweet by setting it on fire with moral beauty. The author of *Ecce Homo* has an apt passage in point: "How can warmth cleanse? The answer is, that *moral* warmth does cleanse. No heart is pure that is not passionate; no virtue is safe that is not enthusiastic." The case is well-nigh desperate indeed, when the ardour of youth, which is the proper life of virtue, becomes itself the death of virtue.

Queen.   O Hamlet, speak no more !
Thou turn'st mine eyes into my very soul ;
And there I see such black and grainèd [17] spots
As will not leave their tint.

Ham.   Nay, but to live
Stew'd in corruption, —

Queen.   O, speak to me no more !
These words like daggers enter in mine ears :
No more, sweet Hamlet !

Ham.   A murderer and a villain ;
A slave that is not twentieth part the tithe
Of your precedent lord ; a Vice of kings ; [18]
A cutpurse of the empire and the rule,
That from a shelf the precious diadem stole, [19]
And put it in his pocket !

Queen.   No more !

Ham. A king of shreds and patches, —

Enter the GHOST.

Save me and hover o'er me with your wings,
You heavenly guards ! — What would your gracious figure ?

Queen. Alas, he's mad !

Ham. Do you not come your tardy son to chide,

---

[17] " *Grained* spots " are spots *ingrained*, or *dyed in the grain*, so that they
will not part with their colour, or lose their tint.

[18] An allusion to the old Vice or jester, a stereotyped character in the
Moral-plays, which were going out of use in the Poet's time. The Vice
wore a motley or patchwork dress ; hence the *shreds and patches* applied in
this instance.

[19] This should not be taken as meaning that Claudius is not the lawful
King of Denmark. He " stole the diadem," not by an act of usurpation
but by murdering the rightful holder of it.

That, lapsed in time and passion,[20] lets go by
Th' important acting of your dread command?
O, say!

    Ghost. Do not forget. This visitation
Is but to whet thy almost-blunted purpose.
But, look, amazement on thy mother sits:
O, step between her and her fighting soul!
Conceit in weakest bodies [21] strongest works.
Speak to her, Hamlet.

    Ham.   How is't with you, lady?

    Queen. Alas, how is't with you,
That you do bend your eye on vacancy,
And with th' incorporal air do hold discourse?
Forth at your eyes your spirits wildly peep;
And, as the sleeping soldiers in th' alarm,
Your bedded hairs, like life in excrements,[22]
Start up, and stand on end. O gentle son,
Upon the heat and flame of thy distemper
Sprinkle cool patience. Whereon do you look?

    Ham. On him, on him! Look you, how pale he glares!
His form and cause conjoin'd, preaching to stones,
Would make them capable.[23] — Do not look upon me;
Lest with this piteous action you convert
My stern affects: [24] then what I have to do

---

[20] The sense appears to be, having failed *in respect* both of time and of purpose. Or it may be, having allowed passion to cool by lapse of time.

[21] *Conceit*, again, for *conception, imagination. Bodies* is here put for *minds*, or *persons;* as *corpora* also is in classical Latin.

[22] That is, like excrements *alive*, or having *life in them. Hair*, nails, feathers, &c., were called *excrements*, as being without life.

[23] Would put sense and understanding into them. The use of *capable* for *susceptible, intelligent*, is not peculiar to Shakespeare.

[24] *Affects* is repeatedly used by Shakespeare for *affections* or *passions*

Will want true colour ; tears, perchance, for blood.

 Queen. To whom do you speak this?

 Ham.   Do you see nothing there?

 Queen. Nothing at all ; yet all that is I see.

 Ham. Nor did you nothing hear?

 Queen.   No, nothing but ourselves.

 Ham. Why, look you there ! look, how it steals away !

My father, in his habit as he lived !

Look, where he goes, even now, out at the portal !

             [*Exit* GHOST.

 Queen. This is the very coinage of your brain :

This bodiless creation ecstasy

Is very cunning in.[25]

 Ham.   Ecstasy !

My pulse, as yours, doth temperately keep time,

And makes as healthful music : 'tis not madness

That I have utter'd : bring me to the test,

And I the matter will re-word ; which madness

Would gambol from.[26]   Mother, for love of grace,

and may signify any mood or temper of mind looking to action.   Hamlet is afraid lest the " piteous action " of the Ghost should make his stern mood or temper of revenge give place to tenderness, so that he will see the ministry enjoined upon him in a false light, and go to shedding tears instead of blood.

[25] The Ghost in this scene, as also in the banquet-scene of *Macbeth*, is plainly what we should call a *subjective* ghost ; that is, existing only in the heated imagination of the beholder.   As the Queen says, insanity is very fertile in such " bodiless creations."   It is not so with the apparition in the former scenes, as the Ghost is there seen by other persons.   To be sure, it was part of the old belief, that ghosts could, if they chose, make themselves visible only to those with whom they were to deal ; but this is just what we mean by *subjective*.   The ancients could not take the idea of subjective visions, as we use the term.   So that the words here put into the Ghost's mouth are to be regarded as merely the echo of Hamlet's own thoughts.

[26] Mad people, if asked to repeat a thing that they have just said, are apt

Lay not that flattering unction to your soul,
That not your trespass but my madness speaks:
It will but skin and film the ulcerous place,
Whilst rank corruption, mining all within,
Infects unseen.   Confess yourself to Heaven;
Repent what's past, avoid what is to come;
And do not spread the compost on the weeds,
To make them ranker.   Forgive me this my virtue;
For in the fatness of these pursy times
Virtue itself of vice must pardon beg,
Yea, courb [27] and woo for leave to do him good.

    Queen. O Hamlet, thou hast cleft my heart in twain.

    Ham. O, throw away the worser part of it,
And live the purer with the other half.
Good night: but go not to my uncle's bed;
Assume a virtue, if you have it not.
That monster, custom, who all sense doth eat
Of habits evil, is angel yet in this,[28]
That to the use of actions fair and good
He likewise gives a frock or livery,
That aptly is put on.   Refrain to-night,
And that shall lend a kind of easiness
To the next abstinence: the next more easy;
For use almost can change the stamp of nature,

to go on and say something else without knowing it; thus *gamboling* from
the matter which they undertake to re-word.   But the test is far from being
a sure one; madmen being sometimes as firm and steady in the intellectual
faculties as the sanest are.

   [27] To *courb* is to *bend, curve,* or *truckle;* from the French *courber.*

   [28] The meaning appears to be, that, though custom is a monster that *eats
out* all *sensibility* or *consciousness* of evil habits; yet, on the other hand, it is
an angel in this respect, that it works in a manner equally favourable to
good actions. — In this passage *custom, habit,* and *use* all have about the
same meaning; I mean the second *use,* — "For use almost," &c.

And either shame the Devil or throw him out [29]
With wondrous potency.　Once more, good night:
And when you are desirous to be blest,
I'll blessing beg of you.[30]　For this same lord,　　*170*

　　　　　　　　　[*Pointing to* POLONIUS.

I do repent: but Heaven hath pleased it so,
To punish me with this and this with me,
That I must be their [31] scourge and minister.
I will bestow him, and will answer well
The death I gave him.　So, again, good night. —
[*Aside.*]　I must be cruel, only to be kind:
Thus bad begins, and worse remains behind. —
One word more, good lady.

　　Queen.　　　　　　　What shall I do?

　　Ham.　Not this, by no means, that I bid you do: *180*
Let the bloat [32] King tempt you again to bed;
Pinch wanton on your cheek; call you his mouse; [33]
And let him, for a pair of reechy [34] kisses,
Or paddling in your neck with his damn'd fingers,
Make you to ravel all this matter out,
That I essentially am not in madness,

　　[29] The sense of *out* extends back over *shame* as well as over *throw;* the
meaning being, "And either shame the Devil *out* or *force* him out." See
Critical Notes.

　　[30] How beautiful this is! Of course Hamlet means that, when he finds
his mother on her knees to God, he will be on his knees to her.

　　[31] The pronoun *their* refers to *Heaven,* which is here used as a collective
noun, and put for *heavenly powers.*

　　[32] *Bloat* for *bloated.*　Many preterites were formed so.　See page 56,
note 7.

　　[33] *Mouse* was a term of endearment.　Thus Burton, in his *Anatomy of
Melancholy :* "Pleasant names may be invented, bird, *mouse*, lamb, puss,
pigeon."

　　[34] *Reeky* and *reechy* are the same word, and applied to any vaporous
exhalation.

But mad in craft. 'Twere good you let him know;
For who, that's but a queen, fair, sober, wise,
Would from a paddock, from a bat, a gib,[35]
Such dear concernings hide? who would do so!
No, in despite of sense and secrecy,
Unpeg the basket on the house's top,
Let the birds fly, and, like the famous ape,
To try conclusions,[36] in the basket creep,
And break your own neck down.

    Queen. Be thou assured, if words be made of breath,
And breath of life, I have no life to breathe
What thou hast said to me.

    Ham. I must to England; you know that?

    Queen.   Alack,
I had forgot: 'tis so concluded on.

    Ham. There's letters seal'd; and my two schoolfellows, —
Whom I will trust as I will adders fang'd, —
They bear the mandate; they must sweep my way,
And marshal me to knavery. Let it work;
For 'tis the sport to have the engineer
Hoist with his own petar:[37] and't shall go hard
But I will delve one yard below their mines,
And blow them at the Moon. O, 'tis most sweet
When in one line two crafts directly meet!
This man shall set me packing:

---

[35] *A paddock* is a *toad;* a *gib*, a *cat*.

[36] To *try conclusions* is the old phrase for *trying experiments*, or putting a thing to the proof. — The passage alludes, apparently, to some fable or story now quite forgotten. Sir John Suckling, in one of his letters, refers to "the story of the jackanapes and the partridges."

[37] *Hoist* for *hoisted*, as in note 32. — *Petar*, now spelt *petard*, is a kind of mortar used for blowing open gates and doors. — "It shall go hard" means "I will try hard." Repeatedly used so by the Poet.

I'll lug the corse into the neighbour roon .

Mother, good night.　Indeed this counsellor

Is now most still, most secret, and most grave,

Who was in life a foolish-prating knave. —

Come, sir, to draw toward an end with you. —

Good night, mother.

[Exeunt severally; HAMLET *dragging in* POLONIUS.

SCENE V. — *Another Room in the Castle.*

Enter the KING, *the* QUEEN, ROSENCRANTZ, *and* GUILDEN-
STERN.

King. There's matter in these sighs : these profound
heaves

You must translate ; 'tis fit we understand them.

Where is your son?

Queen. Bestow this place on us a little while. —

[Exeunt ROSENCRANTZ *and* GUILDENSTERN.

Ah, my good lord, what have I seen to-night !

King. What, Gertrude?　How does Hamlet?

Queen. Mad as the sea and wind, when both contend

Which is the mightier : in his lawless fit,

Behind the arras hearing something stir,

He whips his rapier out, and cries *A rat, a rat !*

And in this brainish[1] apprehension kills

The unseen good old man.

King.　　　　　　　O heavy deed !

It had been so with us, had we been there :

His liberty is full of threats to all,

To you yourself, to us, to every one.

Alas, how shall this bloody deed be answer'd?

---

[1] *Brainish* for *brainsick;* that is, *crazy.*

It will be laid to us, whose providence
Should have kept short, restrain'd, and out of haunt,[2]
This mad young man : but so much was our love,
We would not understand what was most fit ;   20
But, like the owner of a foul disease,
To keep it from divulging, let it feed
Even on the pith of life.[3]   Where is he gone?

   Queen. To draw apart the body he hath kill'd ;
O'er whom his very madness, like fine ore
Among a mineral [4] of metals base,
Shows itself pure : he weeps for what is done.

   King. O Gertrude, come away !
The Sun no sooner shall the mountains touch,
But we will ship him hence ; and this vile deed
We must, with all our majesty and skill,
Both countenance and excuse. — Ho, Guildenstern !

Re-enter ROSENCRANTZ *and* GUILDENSTERN.

Friends both, go join you with some further aid :
Hamlet in madness hath Polonius slain,
And from his mother's closet hath he dragg'd him :
Go seek him out ; speak fair, and bring the body
Into the chapel.   I pray you, haste in this. —
            [*Exeunt* ROSENCRANTZ *and* GUILDENSTERN.
Come, Gertrude, we'll call up our wisest friends ;

---

   2 Out of *haunt* means out of *company.*

   3 Certain diseases appear to be attended with an instinct of concealment.
I have heard of persons dying of external cancer; yet they had kept so secret
about it that their nearest friends had not suspected it.

   4 *Mineral* for *mine;* in accordance with old usage. So Hooker, in
Ecclesiastical Polity, i. 4, 3, speaks of the fallen Angels as "being dispersed,
some on the earth, some in the water, some amongst the *minerals,* dens,
and caves, that are under the earth."

And let them know both what we mean to do
And what's untimely done : so, haply, slander —
Whose whisper o'er the world's diameter,
As level as the cannon to his blank,[5]
Transports his poison'd shot — may miss our name,
And hit the woundless air.   O, come away !
My soul is full of discord and dismay.   [*Exeunt.*

SCENE VI.— *Another Room in the Castle.*

Enter HAMLET.

Ham. Safely stowed.

Rosen. ⎫
Guild. ⎬ [*Within.*] Hamlet ! Lord Hamlet !

Ham. What noise? who calls on Hamlet?   O, here they
come.

Enter ROSENCRANTZ *and* GUILDENSTERN.

Rosen. What have you done, my lord, with the dead
        body?

Ham. Compounded it with dust, whereto 'tis kin.

Rosen. Tell us where 'tis, that we may take it thence
And bear it to the chapel.

Ham. Do not believe it.

Rosen. Believe what?

Ham. That I can keep your counsel and not mine own.
Besides, to be demanded of a sponge,[1] what replication should
be made by the son of a king?

---

[5] As *direct,* or as *sure-aimed,* as the cannon to its *mark.*   *Direct* is one of
the old meanings of *level.*   The *blank* was the *white* spot at which aim was
taken in target-shooting.

[1] That is, *on being* demanded *by* a sponge.   An instance of the infinitive
used *gerundively,* or like the Latin *Gerund,* and equivalent, in English, to a

Rosen. Take you me for a sponge, my lord?

Ham. Ay, sir; that soaks up the King's countenance, his rewards, his authorities.   But such officers do the King best service in the end : he keeps them, as an ape doth nuts, in the corner of his jaw; first mouth'd, to be last swallowed : [2] when he needs what you have glean'd, it is but squeezing you, and, sponge, you shall [3] be dry again.

Rosen. I understand you not, my lord.

Ham. I am glad of it : a knavish speech sleeps in a fool- ish ear. [4]

Rosen. My lord, you must tell us where the body is, and go with us to the King.

Ham. The body is with the King, but the King is not with the body. [5]   The King is a thing —

Guild. A thing, my lord !

Ham. — of nothing : bring me to him.   Hide fox, and all after. [6]   *Exeunt.*

participle and a preposition.   The usage is very frequent in Shakespeare, and sometimes renders his meaning rather obscure. — *Replication* is the same as *reply.*

[2] Apes are provided with a pouch on each side of the jaw, in which they stow away the food first taken, and there keep it till they have eaten the rest.

[3] *Shall* for *will;* the two being often used indiscriminately.

[4] Perhaps this is best explained by a passage in *Love's Labour's Lost,* v. 2: "A jest's prosperity lies in the ear of him that hears it, never in the tongue of him that makes it."

[5] Hamlet is talking riddles, in order to tease and puzzle his questioners. The meaning of this riddle, to the best of my guessing, is, that the King's body is with the King, but not the King's soul : he's a king without kingli- ness.   Perhaps, however, the passage should be regarded simply as a piece of intentional downright nonsense.

[6] " Hide fox, and all after," was a juvenile sport, most probably what is now called *hide and seek.*

SCENE VII. — *Another Room in the Castle.*

Enter the KING, *attended.*

King. I have sent to seek him, and to find the body.
How dangerous is it that this man goes loose !
Yet must not we put the strong law on him :
He's loved of the distracted [1] multitude,
Who like not in their judgment, but their eyes ;
And where 'tis so, th' offender's scourge is weigh'd,
But never the offence.[2]　To bear all smooth and even,
This sudden sending him away must seem
Deliberate pause : [3] diseases desperate grown
By desperate appliance are relieved,
Or not at all. —

Enter ROSENCRANTZ.

　　　　　　How now ! what hath befall'n ?
Rosen. Where the dead body is bestow'd, my lord,
We cannot get from him.
King.　　　　　　But where is he ?
Rosen. Without, my lord ; guarded, to know your pleasure.
King. Bring him before us.
Rosen. Ho, Guildenstern ! bring in my lord.

Enter HAMLET *and* GUILDENSTERN.

King. Now, Hamlet, where's Polonius ?
Ham. At supper.

[1] *Distracted* in the sense of *discordant,* or *disagreeing;* sometimes called *many-headed.* Perhaps the sense of *fickle, inconstant,* is also intended.

[2] Who like not what their judgment approves, for they have none, but what pleases their eyes; and in this case the criminal's punishment is considered, but not his crime.

[3] "To keep all things quiet and in order, this sudden act must seem a thing that we *have paused and deliberated upon.*" See page 99, note 11.

King. At supper ! where?

Ham. Not where he eats, but where he is eaten : a certain convocation of politic worms are e'en at him.[4] Your
worm is your only emperor for diet : we fat all creatures else
to fat us, and we fat ourselves for maggots. Your fat king
and your lean beggar is but variable service, — two dishes,
but to one table : that's the end.

King. Alas, alas !

Ham. A man may fish with the worm that hath eat of a
king, and eat of the fish that hath fed of that worm.

King. What dost thou mean by this?

Ham. Nothing but to show you how a king may go a
progress through a beggar.[5]

King. Where is Polonius?

Ham. In Heaven ; send thither to see : if your messenger find him not there, seek him i' the other place yourself.
But indeed, if you find him not within this month, you shall
nose him as you go up the stairs into the lobby.

King. [*To some* Attendants.] Go seek him there.

Ham. He will stay till ye come.   [*Exeunt* Attendants.

King. Hamlet, this deed, for thine especial safety, —
Which we do tender,[6] as we dearly grieve
For that which thou hast done, — must send thee hence
With fiery quickness : therefore prepare thyself ;

---

[4] Alluding, probably, to the Diet of Worms, which Protestants regarded
as a convocation of *politicians*. Here, again, I am indebted to Mr. Joseph
Crosby, who aptly prompts me, that there is a further allusion to the character of Polonius ; meaning such worms as might naturally be bred in the
carcass of a defunct old political wire-puller. And he remarks, " Had the
old gentleman been conspicuous for his ambition, it would have been just
like Shakespeare to call the worms bred from him *aspiring* worms."

[5] Alluding to the *royal* journeys of state, called *progresses*.

[6] To *tender* a thing is to *be careful* of it. See page 73, note *27*.

The bark is ready, and the wind at help,
Th' associates tend,[7] and every thing is bent
For England.

Ham. For England !

King. Ay, Hamlet.

Ham. Good.

King. So is it, if thou knew'st our purposes.

Ham. I see a cherub that sees them.[8] — But, come ; for
England ! — Farewell, dear mother.

King. Thy loving father, Hamlet.

Ham. My mother : father and mother is man and wife ;
man and wife is one flesh ; and so, my mother. — Come, for
England !   [*Exit.*

King. Follow him at foot ; tempt him with speed aboard ;
Delay it not ; I'll have him hence to-night :
Away ! for every thing is seal'd and done
That else leans on th' affair ; pray you, make haste. —

[*Exeunt* ROSENCRANTZ *and* GUILDENSTERN.

And, England, if my love thou hold'st at aught, —
As my great power thereof may give thee sense,
Since yet thy cicatrice looks raw and red
After the Danish sword, and thy free awe
Pays homage to us, — thou may'st not coldly set [9]
Our sovereign process ; which imports at full,
By letters cónjuring [10] to that effect,

---

[7] The associates of your voyage *are waiting.* — " The wind *at help* " means
the wind *serves*, or is right, to forward you.

[8] Hamlet means that he divines them, or has an inkling of them.

[9] To *set* formerly meant to *estimate.* To *set* much or little by a thing, is
to *estimate* it much or little.

[10] In Shakespeare's time the two senses of *conjure* had not acquired each
its peculiar way of pronouncing the word. Here *conjuring* has the *first*
syllable long, with the sense of *earnestly entreating.*

The present death of Hamlet.   Do it, England ;
For like the hectic in my blood he rages,
And thou must cure me : till I know 'tis done,
Howe'er my haps, my joys were ne'er begun.[11]   [*Exit.*

ACT IV.

SCENE I. — *A Plain in Denmark.*

Enter FORTINBRAS, *a* Captain, *and* Soldiers, *marching.*

Fortin. Go, captain, from me greet the Danish King ;
Tell him that by his license Fortinbras
Claims the conveyance of a promised march
Over his kingdom.   You know the rendezvous.[1]
If that his Majesty would aught with us,
We shall express our duty in his eye ;[2]
And let him know so.

Capt.   I will do't, my lord.

Fortin. Go softly on.

            [*Exeunt* FORTINBRAS *and* Soldiers.

Enter HAMLET, ROSENCRANTZ, GUILDENSTERN, *and others.*

Ham. Good sir, whose powers are these ?

Capt. They are of Norway, sir.

---

[11] Of course strict grammar would here require "*will* ne'er *begin*"; the tense being changed for the rhyme.   See page 96, note 26.

[1] The rendezvous here meant is the place where Fortinbras is to wait for the Captain after the latter has done his message to the King.

[2] In the *Regulations for the Establishment of the Queen's Household,* 1627 : "All such as doe service *in the queen's eye.*"   And in *The Establishment of Prince Henry's Household,* 1610 : "All such as doe service *in the prince's eye.*"   Fortinbras means, "I will wait upon his presence, and pay my respects to him in person."

Ham. How purposed, sir, I pray you?

Capt. Against some part of Poland.

Ham. Who commands them, sir?

Capt. The nephew to old Norway, Fortinbras.

Ham. Goes it against the main of Poland, sir,
Or for some frontier?

Capt. Truly to speak, sir, and with no addition,
We go to gain a little patch of ground
That hath in it no profit but the name.
To pay five ducats, five, I would not farm it;[3]
Nor will it yield to Norway or the Pole
A ranker rate, should it be sold in fee.

Ham. Why, then the Polack never will defend it.

Capt. Yes, 'tis already garrison'd.

Ham. Two thousand souls and twenty thousand ducats
Will not debate the question of this straw:
This is th' imposthume[4] of much wealth and peace,
That inward breaks, and shows no cause without
Why the man dies. — I humbly thank you, sir.

Capt. God b' wi' you, sir.   [*Exit.*

Rosen.   Will't please you go, my lord?

Ham. I'll be with you straight.   Go a little before. —

                         [*Exeunt all but* HAMLET.

---

[3] The meaning is, "I would not pay five ducats for the exclusive privilege of collecting all the revenue it will yield to the State.   To *farm* or *farm out* taxes is to sell commissions for collecting them, the buyers to have the privilege of making what they can by the process.   Burke uses the word in a like sense in his *Articles of Charge against Hastings:* "The *farming* of the defence of a country, being wholly unprecedented and evidently abused, could have no real object but to enrich the contractors at the Company's expense." — *To pay* has the force of *by paying*.   The infinitive again used *gerundively*.   See page 169, note 1.

[4] *Imposthume* was in common use for *abscess* in Shakespeare's time.   It is a corruption of *apostem*.

How all occasions do inform against me,
And spur my dull revenge !   What is a man,
If his chief good and market of his time
Be but to sleep and feed? a beast, no more.
Sure, He that made us with such large discourse,
Looking before and after, gave us not
That capability and godlike reason
To fust [5] in us unused.   Now, whether it be
Bestial oblivion, or some craven scruple
Of thinking too precisely on th' event,—
A thought which, quarter'd, hath but one part wisdom
And ever three parts coward,—I do not know
Why yet I live to say *This thing's to do,*
Sith [6] I have cause and will and strength and means
To do't.   Examples gross as earth exhort me :
Witness this army of such mass and charge,
Led by a delicate and tender prince ;
Whose spirit, with divine ambition puff'd,[7]
Makes mouths at the invisible event ;
Exposing what is mortal and unsure
To all that fortune, death, and danger dare,
Even for a egg-shell.   Rightly to be great
Is not to stir without great argument,
But greatly to find quarrel in a straw
When honour's at the stake.   How stand I, then,
That have a father kill'd, a mother stain'd,
Excitements of my reason and my blood,[8]

---

[5] To *fust* is to *become mouldy;* an old word now quite obsolete.

[6] *Sith* is merely an old form of *since;* now quite out of use.

[7] *Puff'd*, here, is *inspired* or *animated.*—To *make mouths* at a thing is to *scorn* it, or *hold it in contempt.*

[8] Provocations which excite both my reason and my passions.

And let all sleep? while, to my shame, I see
The imminent death of twenty thousand men,   60
That for a fantasy and trick of fame
Go to their graves like beds; fight for a plot
Whereon the numbers cannot try the cause;
Which is not tomb enough and continent[9]
To hide the slain?   O, from this time forth,
My thoughts be bloody, or be nothing worth![10]   [*Exit.*

SCENE II.—*Elsinore.   A Room in the Castle.*

Enter the QUEEN *and* HORATIO.

Queen. I will not speak with her.

Hora. She is impórtunate, indeed distract;[1]
Her mood will needs be pitied.

Queen.   What would she have?

Hora. She speaks much of her father; says she hears

[9] *Continent* means that which contains or encloses. " If there be no ful-
nesse, then is the *continent* greater than the content."—Bacon's *Advancement of Learning.*

[10] Weary is Hamlet, weary under his burden.   Now, when he is shipped
off to England, the charge of murder resting on him through his own fault,
— comparing *his* lot, chained as he is to his task, with that of Fortinbras
who is so free in all his movements,—now comes the fear that, notwith
standing all his trouble, all his patient endurance, his task has at last be
come impossible.   This horrible dread penetrates him to the quick, and
weighs down his soul.   How,—considering the character of his task,—how
he is to satisfy the *reason* of the thing, he cannot conceive; but he can at
least content his blood, should he strike the decisive blow.   And how it
shrieks in his ear, how it surges over his soul!   This horrible doubt, which
has for its background the remorse he feels for the error he has made,—
the doubt whether he shall throw all the dictates of reason to the winds,—
this is the demon that rules in this soliloquy, and runs wild therein; and
therefore I have said it is the shriek of Hamlet's agony which here relieves
itself.—WERDER.

[1] *Distract* for *distracted;* just as *bloat* and *hoist* before.

There's tricks i' the world ; and hems, and beats her heart ;
Spurns enviously at straws ;[2] speaks things in doubt,
That carry but half sense : her speech is nothing,
Yet the unshapèd use of it doth move
The hearers to collection ;[3] they aim at it,
And botch the words up fit to their own thoughts ;   10
Which, as her winks and nods and gestures yield them,
Indeed would make one think there might be thought,
Though nothing sure, yet much unhappily.[4]
'Twere good she were spoken with ; for she may strew
Dangerous conjectures in ill-breeding minds.

    Queen. Let her come in. —   [*Exit* HORATIO.
To my sick soul, as sin's true nature is,
Each toy seems prologue to some great amiss :[5]
So full of artless jealousy is guilt,
It spills itself in fearing to be spilt.   20

    Re-enter HORATIO, *with* OPHELIA.[6]

    Ophe. Where is the beauteous Majesty of Denmark?
    Queen. How now, Ophelia !

---

  2 *Kicks spitefully* at straws. Such was the common use of *spurn* in the
Poet's time. So in *The Merchant,* i. 3 : "And foot me as you *spurn* a stranger cur over your threshold." And in *Julius Cæsar,* iii. 1 : " I *spurn* thee
like a cur out of my way." — *Envy* and its derivatives were commonly used
in the sense of *malice.*

  3 *Collection* is *inference* or *conjecture.* — *Aim* is *guess.*

  4 *Unhappily* is here used in the sense of *mischievously.*

  5 Shakespeare is not singular in the use of *amiss* as a substantive. "Each
toy" is each *trifle.*

  6 There is no part of this play in its representation on the stage more
pathetic than this scene; which, I suppose, proceeds from the utter insensi-
bility Ophelia has to her own misfortunes. A great sensibility, or none at
all, seems to produce the same effects. In the latter case the audience supply what is wanting, and with the former they sympathize. — Sir J. REY-
NOLDS.

Ophe. [Sings.] *How should I your true love know*
    From another one ?
    By his cockle hat and staff,
    And his sandle shoon.[7]

Queen. Alas, sweet lady, what imports this song?
Ophe. Say you? nay, pray you, mark.

  [Sings.] *He is dead and gone, lady,*
    He is dead and gone ;
    At his head a grass-green turf,
    At his heels a stone.

Queen. Nay, but, Ophelia, —
Ophe. Pray you, mark.

  [Sings.] *White his shroud as the mountain snow, —*

     Enter the KING.

Queen. Alas, look here, my lord.

Ophe. [Sings.] *— Larded* [8] *with sweet flowers ;*
    Which bewept to the grave did go,
    With true-love showers.

King. How do you, pretty lady?
Ophe. Well, God 'ield you ![9] They say the owl was a
baker's daughter.[10] Lord, we know what we are, but know
not what we may be.   God be at your table !

---

[7] These were the badges of pilgrims. The *cockle shell* was an emblem
of their intention to go beyond sea. The habit, being held sacred, was often
assumed as a disguise in love-adventures.

[8] *Larded* is *garnished.*

[9] God *yield* or *reward* you.

[10] There was a tradition that the Saviour went into a baker's shop and
asked for some bread. The baker put some dough in the oven to bake for
Him, and was rebuked by his daughter for doing so. For this wickedness
the daughter was transformed into an owl.

King. Conceit upon her father.

Ophe. Pray you, let's have no words of this ; but when they ask you what it means, say you this : —

[Sings.] *To-morrow is Saint Valentine's day,*
  All in the morning betime,
  And I a maid at your window,
  To be your Valentine.[11]

King. How long hath she been thus?

Ophe. I hope all will be well. We must be patient ; but I cannot choose but weep, to think they should lay him i' the cold ground. My brother shall know of it ; and so I thank you for your good counsel. — Come, my coach ! — Good night, ladies ; good night, sweet ladies ; good night, good night.   [*Exit.*

King. Follow her close ; give her good watch, I pray you. —   [*Exit* HORATIO.

O, this is the poison of deep grief ; it springs
All from her father's death. O, Gertrude, Gertrude,
When sorrows come, they come not single spies,
But in battalias.[12]   First, her father slain :
Next, your son gone ; and he most violent author
Of his own just remove : the people mudded,
Thick and unwholesome in their thoughts and whispers,

---

[11] Of course *Valentine* stands for a person here; and it means much the same as *lover* or *sweet-heart*. The old use of the name is well shown in Scott's *Fair Maid of Perth*, where Simon Glover wishes to make a match between his daughter Catharine and Henry Smith, the hero of the tale. He therefore so arranges matters, that Smith shall be the first person whom Catharine sees on the morning of St. Valentine's day. This makes him her Valentine for the year : as such, he may claim a kiss of her on the spot, and also as often as they meet during the year.

[12] Men go out *singly*, or one by one, to act as spies; when they go forth to *fight*, they go in armies.

For good Polonius' death ; and we have done but greenly,
In hugger-mugger [13] to inter him : poor Ophelia
Divided from herself and her fair judgment,
Without the which we're pictures, or mere beasts :
Last, and as much containing as all these,
Her brother is in secret come from France ;
Feeds on his wonder, keeps himself in clouds,
And wants not buzzers to infect his ear
With pestilent speeches of his father's death ;
Wherein necessity, of matter beggar'd,
Will nothing stick our person to arraign
In ear and ear.[14]   O my dear Gertrude, this,
Like to a murdering-piece,[15] in many places
Gives me superfluous death.   [*A noise within.*

   Queen.   Alack, what noise is this?
   King.   Where are my Switzers?[16]   Let them guard the
     door.—

            Enter a Gentleman.

What is the matter?
   Gent.   Save yourself, my lord :
The ocean, overpeering of his list,[17]
Eats not the flats with more impetuous haste

---

[13] This phrase was much used, before and in the Poet's time, for any thing done hurriedly and by stealth. Thus Florio explains *clandestinare*, "to hide or conceal by stealth, or *in hugger-mugger*." And in North's Plutarch Antony urges that Cæsar's "body should be honourably buried, and not in *hugger-mugger*."

[14] " In *ear* and *ear*" is used, apparently, to give a plural sense.

[15] A murdering-piece, or *murderer*, was a small piece of artillery. Case-shot, filled with small bullets, nails, old iron, &c., was often used in these *murderers*. This accounts for the raking fire attributed to them in the text.

[16] *Switzers*, for royal guards. The Swiss were then, as since, mercenary soldiers of any nation that could afford to pay them.

[17] *Overflowing* his *bounds*, or *limits*.

Than young Laertes, in a riotous head,
O'erbears your officers. The rabble call him lord ;
And — as [18] the world were now but to begin,
Antiquity forgot, custom not known,
The ratifiers and props of every word —
They cry, *Choose we ; Laertes shall be king !*
Caps, hands, and tongues applaud it to the clouds,
Laertes shall be king, Laertes king !

　Queen. How cheerfully on the false trail they cry ! —
O, this is counter,[19] you false Danish dogs !

　King. The doors are broke.　　　　　　*[Noise within.*

　　　　Enter LAERTES, *armed ;* Danes *following.*

　Laer. Where is this King ? — Sirs, stand you all without.

　Danes. No, let's come in.

　Laer.　　　　　　　　I pray you, give me leave.

　Danes. We will, we will.　*[They retire without the door.*

　Laer. I thank you : keep the door. — O thou vile King,
Give me my father !

　Queen.　　　　　Calmly, good Laertes.

　Laer. That drop of blood that's calm proclaims me bas-
　　tard,
And brands the harlot even here, between
The chaste unsmirchèd [20] brows of my true mother.

　King. What is the cause, Laertes,

---

[18] *As* has here the force of *as if.* The explanation sometimes given of
the passage is, that the rabble are the ratifiers and props of every *idle* word.
The plain sense is, that antiquity and custom are the ratifiers and props of
every *sound* word touching the matter in hand, the ordering of human
society, and the State.

[19] Hounds are said to run *counter* when they are upon a false scent, or
hunt by the heel, running backward and mistaking the course of the game.

[20] *Unsmirched* is *unsullied, spotless.*

That thy rebellion looks so giant-like ? —
Let him go, Gertrude ; do not fear our person :
There's such divinity doth hedge a king,
That treason can but peep to what it would,
Acts little of his will. — Tell me, Laertes,
Why thou art thus incensed. — Let him go, Gertrude. —
Speak, man.

   Laer. Where is my father?

   King.   Dead.

   Queen.   But not by him.

   King. Let him demand his fill.

   Laer. How came he dead?   I'll not be juggled with :
To Hell, allegiance ! vows, to the blackest devil !
Conscience and grace, to the profoundest pit !
I dare damnation : to this point I stand, —
That both the worlds I give to negligence,
Let come what comes ; only I'll be revenged
Most throughly [21] for my father.

   King.   Who shall stay you?

   Laer. My will, not all the world :
And for my means, I'll husband them so well,
They shall go far with little.

   King.   Good Laertes,
If you desire to know the certainty
Of your dear father's death, is't writ in your revenge,
That, swoopstake, [22] you will draw both friend and foe,
Winner and loser?

---

21 *Throughly* and *thoroughly*, as also *through* and *thorough*, were used indifferently in the Poet's time.   They are, in fact, only different forms of the
same word ; as to be *thorough* in a thing is to *go through* it.

22 *Swoopstake* here means *indiscriminately*.   A sweepstake is one who
wins or *sweeps in all the stakes*, whether on the race-grounds or at the gam-
ing-table.

Laer. None but his enemies.

King.   Will you know them, then?

Laer. To his good friends thus wide I'll ope my arms,
And, like the kind life-rendering pelican,
Repast them with my blood.[23]

King.   Why, now you speak
Like a good child and a true gentleman.
That I am guiltless of your father's death,
And am most sensibly in grief for it,
It shall as level to your judgment pierce[24]
As day does to your eye.

Danes. [*Within.*]   Let her come in.

Laer. How now! what noise is that?—

Re-enter OPHELIA.

O heat, dry up my brains! tears seven-times salt,
Burn out the sense and virtue of mine eye!—
By Heaven, thy madness shall be paid by weight,
Till our scale turn the beam.   O rose of May!
Dear maid, kind sister, sweet Ophelia!—
O Heavens! is't possible, a young maid's wits
Should be as mortal as an old man's life?
Nature is fine in love; and where 'tis fine
It sends some precious instance of itself
After the thing it loves.[25]

---

[23] The pelican is a fabulous bird, often referred to by the old poets for illustration.   An old book entitled *A Choice of Emblems and other Devices*, by Geffrey Whitney, 1586, contains a picture of an eagle on her nest, tearing open her breast to feed her young.

[24] *Level*, again, for *direct.* — *Pierce*, here, has the sense of *penetrate*, that is, *go through* or *reach*.

[25] Here, as often, *instance* is *proof, example, specimen, assurance.*   The precious thing which Ophelia's fineness of nature has sent after her father is " her fair judgment," that is, her sanity.

Ophe. [Sings.] *They bore him barefaced on the bier;*
                Hey non nonny, nonny, hey nonny;
                And on his grave rain'd many a tear. —

Fare you well, my dove !

Laer. Hadst thou thy wits, and didst persuade revenge,
It could not move me thus.

Ophe. You must sing, *Down a-down, an you call him
a-down-a.* O, how the wheel[26] becomes it ! It is the false
steward, that stole his master's daughter.[27]

Laer. This nothing's more than matter.[28]

Ophe. There's rosemary, that's for remembrance ; pray
you, love, remember : and there is pansies, that's for
thoughts.[29]

Laer. A document[30] in madness ; thoughts and remembrance fitted.

[26] The *wheel* is the *burden* of a ballad; from the Latin *rota*, a *round*,
which is usually accompanied with a burden frequently repeated.

[27] Meaning, probably, some old ballad, of which no traces have come to
light.

[28] He means that Ophelia's nonsense tells more, as to her condition,
than speaking sense would.

[29] The language of flowers is very ancient, and the old poets have many
instances of it. In *The Winter's Tale,* iv. 3, Perdita makes herself delectable in the use of it, distributing her flowers much as Ophelia does here.
Rosemary, being supposed to strengthen the memory, was held emblematic
of remembrance, and in that thought was distributed at weddings and funerals. — Pansies, from the French *pensees*, were emblems of pensiveness,
thought being here again used for *grief*, the same as in page 128, note 13.
The next speech, "*thoughts* and remembrance fitted," is another instance
of the same usage.

[30] *Document*, from the Latin *doceo*, was often used in the original sense
of *lesson*, or *something taught.* So in *The Faerie Queene,* i. 10, 19, where
Fidelia takes the Redcross Knight under her tuition, and draws upon " her
sacred booke," –

    And heavenly *documents* thereout did preach,
    That weaker witt of man could never reach.

Ophe. There's fennel for you, and columbines : [31]—there's rue for you ; and here's some for me : we may call it herb of grace o' Sundays : — O, you must wear your rue with a difference.[32] There's a daisy : — I would give you some violets,[33] but they wither'd all when my father died : they say he made a good end, —

[Sings.] *For bonny sweet Robin is all my joy.*[34]

Laer. Thought and affliction, passion,[35] Hell itself, She turns to favour and to prettiness.

Ophe. [Sings.] *And will he not come again ?*
              And will he not come again ?
                 No, no, he is dead,
                 Gone to his death-bed;
            He never will come again.

           His beard was white as snow,
            All flaxen was his poll :

---

[31] Fennel and columbine were significant of cajolery and ingratitude ; so that Ophelia might fitly give them to the guileful and faithless King.

[32] Rue was emblematic of sorrow or *ruth*, and was called *herb-grace* from the moral and medicinal virtues ascribed to it. — There may be some uncertainty as to Ophelia's meaning, when she says to the Queen, "you must wear your rue with a *difference."* *Bearing a difference* is an old heraldic phrase ; and the difference here intended is probably best explained in Cogan's *Haven of Health :* "The second property is that *rue abateth carnal lust,* which is also confirmed by Galen." So that the difference in the Queen's case would be emblematic of her "hasty return to the nuptial state, and a severe reflection on her indecent marriage."

[33] The daisy was an emblem of dissembling ; the violet, of faithfulness, and is so set down in *The Lover's Nosegay.*

[34] Poor Ophelia in her madness remembers fragments of many old popular ballads. *Bonny Robin* appears to have been a favourite, for there were many others written to that tune.

[35] *Thought*, again, for *grief.* — *Passion* for *suffering ;* the classical sense,

> *He is gone, he is gone,*
> *And we cast away moan :*
> *God ha' mercy on his soul !*

And of [36] all Christian souls, I pray God. — God b' wi' ye.

[*Exit.*

Laer. Do you see this, O God ?

King. Laertes, I must cómmune [37] with your grief,
Or you deny me right.   Go but apart ;
Make choice of whom your wisest friends you will,
And they shall hear and judge 'twixt you and me :
If by direct or by collateral hand
They find us touch'd, we will our kingdom give,
Our crown, our life, and all that we call ours,
To you in satisfaction ; but, if not,
Be you content to lend your patience to us,
And we shall jointly labour with your soul
To give it due content.

Laer.   Let this be so :
His means of death, his obscure burial, —
No trophy, sword, nor hatchment o'er his bones,
No noble rite nor formal ostentation, [38] —
Cry to be heard, as 'twere from Heaven to Earth,
That [39] I must call't in question.

King.   So you shall ;
And where th' offence is let the great axe fall.
I pray you, go with me.   [*Exeunt.*

---

[36] *Of*, again, for *on*. See page 108, note 38.

[37] *Commune* has the accent on the first syllable. Generally used so by the English poets ; at least I have noted it so in Milton and Wordsworth.

[38] The funerals of knights and persons of rank were made with great ceremony and ostentation formerly. Sir John Hawkins observes that "the sword, the helmet, the gauntlet, spurs, and tabard are still hung over the grave of every knight."

[39] *That* is continually used by the old poets with the force of *so that*, or *insomuch that*.

SCENE III. — *Another Room in the Castle.*

Enter HORATIO *and a* Servant.

Hora. What are they that would speak with me?

Serv. Sailors, sir : they say they have letters for you.

Hora. Let them come in. —   [*Exit* Servant.
I do not know from what part of the world
I should be greeted, if not from Lord Hamlet.

Enter Sailors.

1 Sail. God bless you, sir.

Hora. Let Him bless thee too.

1 Sail. He shall, sir, an't please Him. There's a letter
for you, sir, — it comes from the ambassador that was bound
for England, — if your name be Horatio, as I am let to know
it is.

Hora. [Reads.] *Horatio, when thou shalt have over-*
look'd this, give these fellows some means to the King : they
have letters for him. Ere we were two days old at sea, a
pirate of very warlike appointment[1] gave us chase. Finding
ourselves too slow of sail, we put on a compelled valour ; in
the grapple I boarded them : on the instant they got clear of
our ship ; so I alone became their prisoner. They have
dealt with me like thieves of mercy : but they knew what they
did ; I am to do a good turn for them. Let the King have
the letters I have sent ; and repair thou to me with as much
speed as thou wouldst fly death. I have words to speak in
thine ear will make thee dumb ; yet are they much too light for

---

[1] *Appointment*, here, is *armament*, or *equipment.* Still used thus in military language. Also in "a *well-appointed* house"; meaning, of course
well-furnished, or *well-ordered*.

*the bore [2] of the matter.   These good fellows will bring thee
where I am.   Rosencrantz and Guildenstern hold their course
for England : of them I have much to tell thee.   Farewell.*
                    He that thou knowest thine, HAMLET.

Come, I will make you way for these your letters ;
And do't the speedier, that you may direct me
To him from whom you brought them.   [*Exeunt.*

SCENE IV.—*Another Room in the Castle.*

Enter the KING *and* LAERTES.

King. Now must your conscience my acquittance seal,
And you must put me in your heart for friend,
Sith you have heard, and with a knowing ear,
That he which hath your noble father slain
Pursued my life.

Laer.   It well appears : but tell me
Why you proceeded not against these feats,
So crimeful and so capital in nature,
As by your safety, wisdom, all things else,
You mainly [1] were stirr'd up.

King.   O, for two special reasons ;
Which may to you perhaps seem much unsinew'd,
But yet to me they're strong.   The Queen his mother
Lives almost by his looks ; and for myself, —
My virtue or my plague, be't either-which, —
She's so conjunctive to my life and soul,

---

[2] The *bore* is the *caliber* or *capacity* of a gun ; as a ten-pounder, or a
seventy-four pounder.

[1] The Poet sometimes uses *mainly* for *greatly* or *strongly.* So in *Troilus
and Cressida,* iv. 4 : " I do not call your faith in question so *mainly* as my
merit."

That, as the star moves not but in his sphere,
I could not but by her.   The other motive,
Why to a public count I might not go,
Is the great love the general gender [2] bear him ;
Who, dipping all his faults in their affection,
Would, like the spring that turneth wood to stone,
Convert his gyves to graces : [3] so that my arrows,
Too slightly timber'd for so loud a wind, [4]
Would have reverted to my bow again,
And not where I had aim'd them. [5]

    Laer.   And so have I a noble father lost ;
A sister driven into desperate terms,
Whose worth, if praises may go back again, [6]
Stood challenger on mount of all the age [7]
For her perfections.   But my revenge will come.

    King.   Break not your sleeps for that : you must not think
That we are made of stuff so flat and dull,
That we can let our beard be shook with danger,
And think it pastime.   You shortly shall hear more :
I loved your father, and we love ourself ;
And that, I hope, will teach you to imagine —

              Enter a Messenger.

How now ! what news ?

    2 " The general *gender*" is the common *race* or *sort* of people ; the multi-
tude.   Shakespeare has the like phrase, " one *gender* of herbs."

    3 Punishment would invest him with more grace in the people's eye ; his
fetters would make him appear the lovelier to them.

    4 So in Roger Ascham's *Toxophilus :* " Weake bowes and lyghte shaftes
cannot stande in a *rough* wynde."

    5 Elliptical.   "And *would not have gone* where I had aim'd them," is the
meaning.

    6 The meaning probably is, " If I may praise her for what she was, but
has now ceased to be."

    7 That is, " stood challenger of all the age."

Mess.   Letters, my lord, from Hamlet ·
This to your Majesty ; this to the Queen.
  King.   From Hamlet ! who brought them ?
  Mess.   Sailors, my lord, they say ; I saw them not :
They were given me by Claudio ; he received them
Of him that brought them.
  King.   Laertes, you shall hear them. —
Leave us.   [*Exit* Messenger.

  [Reads.] *High and mighty : You shall know I am set
naked* [8] *on your kingdom. To-morrow shall I beg leave to
see your kingly eyes ; when I shall, first asking your pardon
thereunto, recount the occasion of my sudden and more
strange return.*   HAMLET.

What should this mean ?   Are all the rest come back ?
Or is it some abuse,[9] and no such thing ?
  Laer.   Know you the hand ?
  King.   'Tis Hamlet's character.   *Naked !*
And in a postscript here, he says *alone.*
Can you advise me ?
  Laer. I'm lost in it, my lord.   But let him come :
It warms the very sickness in my heart,
That I shall live and tell him to his teeth,
Thus diddest thou.
  King.   If it be so, Laertes, —
As how should it be so, how otherwise ? [10] —
Will you be ruled by me ?

---

  [8] *Naked*, here, means destitute of attendants ; *alone.*
  [9] *Abuse* for *cheat, deception,* or *delusion.*
  [10] That is, " how should it be either true or not true ? " The thing seems
incredible either way ; incredible that Hamlet should have returned ; incredible that the letter should not be in Hamlet's *character*, or *hand-writing.*

Laer.   I will, my lord,
So you will not o'errule me to a peace.

King. To thine own peace.   If he be now return'd,
As checking[11] at his voyage, and that he means
No more to undertake it, I will work him
To an exploit now ripe in my device,
Under the which he shall not choose but fall:
And for his death no wind of blame shall breathe;
But even his mother shall uncharge the practice,[12]
And call it accident.

Laer.   My lord, I will be ruled;
The rather, if you could devise it so,
That I might be the organ.

King.   It falls right.
You have been talk'd of since your travel much,
And that in Hamlet's hearing, for a quality
Wherein they say you shine: your sum of parts
Did not together pluck such envy from him
As did that one; and that, in my regard,
Of the unworthiest siege.[13]

Laer.   What part is that, my lord?

King. A very[14] riband in the cap of youth,
Yet needful too; for youth no less becomes
The light and careless livery that it wears

---

11 To *check at* is a term in falconry, meaning to start away or fly off from the lure. So in Hinde's *Eliosto Libidinoso*, 1606: "For who knows not, quoth she, that this hawk, which comes now so fair to the fist, may to-morrow *check at* the lure?"

12 *Acquit* the proceeding or the *contrivance* of all *design*.

13 The Poet again uses *siege* for *seat*, that is, *place or rank*, in *Othello*, i. 2: "I fetch my life and being from men of royal *siege*." The usage was not uncommon.

14 The Poet repeatedly has *very* in the sense of *mere*.

Than settled age his sables and his weeds,
Importing health and graveness.[15]   Two months since
Here was a gentleman of Normandy:
I've seen, myself, and served against, the French,
And they can [16] well on horseback: but this gallant
Had witchcraft in't; he grew unto his seat;
And to such wondrous doing brought his horse,
As he had been incorpsed and demi-natured
With the brave beast.   So far he topp'd my thought,
That I, in forgery of shapes and tricks,[17]
Come short of what he did.

   Laer.   A Norman was't?

   King. A Norman.

   Laer. Upon my life, Lamond.

   King.   The very same.

   Laer. I know him well: he is the brooch,[18] indeed,
And gem of all the nation.

   King. He made confession of you;
And gave you such a masterly report
For art and exercise in your defence,[19]
And for your rapier most especially,

---

[15] The sense of *health* goes with the preceding clause; the "light and careless livery" denoting health, as the black dress denotes gravity. Shakespeare has many instances of like construction. — *Weeds* was often used for *clothes* or *dress* in general.   Here the sense of *settled* continues over *weeds*: *staid* or *sober* dress.

[16] *Can* is here used in its original sense of *ability* or *skill*.

[17] That is, in *the imagination* of shapes and tricks, or *feats*. This use of *forge* and *forgery* was not unfrequent. — To *top* is to *surpass*.

[18] *Brooch* was used for any conspicuous ornament in general.   So in *The World runnes on Wheeles*, 1630: "These sonnes of Mars, who in their times were the glorious *Brooches* of our nation, and admirable terrour to our enemies."

[19] *Defence* here means *fencing* or *sword-practice*.

That he cried out, 'twould be a sight indeed,
If one could match you : the scrimers [20] of their nation,
He swore, had neither motion, guard, nor eye,
If you opposed them.   Sir, this report of his
Did Hamlet so envenom with your envy,[21]
That he could nothing do but wish and beg
Your sudden coming o'er, to play with him.
Now, out of this, —

    Laer.   What out of this, my lord?
    King.   Laertes, was your father dear to you?
Or are you like the painting of a sorrow,
A face without a heart?

    Laer.   Why ask you this?
    King. Not that I think you did not love your father ;
But that I know love is begun by time,[22]
And that I see, in passages of proof,[23]
Time qualifies the spark and fire of it.
There lives within the very flame of love
A kind of wick or snuff that will abate it ;
And nothing is at a like goodness still ;
For goodness, growing to a plurisy,[24]
Dies in his own too-much.   That we would do,
We should do when we would ; for this *would* changes,
And hath abatements and delays as many

[20] *Scrimer* is from the French *escrimeur,* which means *fencer.*

[21] "With envy *of you.*" The objective genitive, as it is called. Shake-speare often has both the objective and the subjective genitive in cases where present usage does not admit them.

[22] As love is begun by *time,* and has its gradual increase, so *time* quali-fies and abates it.

[23] *Passages of proof* means *instances of trial,* or *experience.*

[24] *Plurisy* is from the Latin *plus, pluris,* and must not be confounded with *pleurisy.*   It means *excess,* much the same as Burns's " *unco* guid." So in Massinger's *Unnatural Combat :* " *Plurisy* of goodness is thy ill."

As there are tongues, are hands, are accidents;
And then this *should* is like a spendthrift sigh,
That hurts by easing.[25]   But, to th' quick o' the ulcer:
Hamlet comes back: what would you undertake,
To show yourself your father's son in deed
More than in words?

   Laer.   To cut his throat i' the church.

   King. No place, indeed, should murder sanctuarize;[26]
Revenge should have no bounds.   But, good Laertes,
Will you do this,[27] keep close within your chamber.
Hamlet return'd shall know you are come home:
We'll put on[28] those shall praise your excellence,
And set a double varnish on the fame
The Frenchman gave you; bring you, in fine, together,
And wager on your heads.   He, being remiss,
Most generous, and free from all contriving,
Will not peruse[29] the foils; so that, with ease
Or with a little shuffling, you may choose
A sword unbated,[30] and in a pass of practice
Requite him for your father.

[25] It was anciently believed that sighing consumed the blood.   The Poet has several allusions to this, as in *A Midsummer-Night's Dream*, iii. 2: "Sighs of love that cost the fresh blood dear."   There is also a fine moral meaning in the figure.   Jeremy Taylor speaks of certain people who take to a sentimental penitence, as "cozening themselves with their own tears," as if these would absolve them from "doing works meet for repentance." Such tears may be fitly said to "hurt by easing."

[26] Murder should not have the protection or privilege of sanctuary in any place.   The allusion is to the rights of sanctuary with which certain religious places were formerly invested, so that criminals resorting to them were shielded not only from private revenge, but from the arm of the law.

[27] That is, "*If* you will do this"; or, "It you *would* do this."

[28] *Put on*, here, is *stir up*, *incite*, or, as we say, *set on*.

[29] *Peruse*, for *observe closely* or *scrutinize*.

[30] *Unbated* is *unblunted*: a foil without the cap, or button, which was

Laer.   I will do't;
And, for that purpose, I'll annoint my sword.
I bought an unction of a mountebank,[31]
So mortal that, but dip a knife in it,
Where it draws blood no cataplasm so rare,
Collected from all simples[32] that have virtue
Under the Moon, can save the thing from death
That is but scratch'd withal: I'll touch my point
With this contagion, that, if I gall him slightly,
It may be death.
    King.   Let's further think of this;
Weigh what convenience both of time and means
May fit us to our shape.   If this should fail,
And that our drift look through our bad performance,[33]
'Twere better not assay'd: therefore this project
Should have a back or second, that might hold,
If this should blast in proof.[34]   Soft! — let me see:—
We'll make a solemn wager on your cunnings,—
I ha't:
When in your motion you are hot and dry,—

put upon the point, when fencers were to play or practise their art. — *A pass of practice* is a *thrust* made as in exercise of skill, and without any purpose of harm; the thruster pretending to be ignorant of the button's being off the foil.

[31] *Mountebank* commonly meant a *quack*, but is here put, apparently, for *druggist* or *apothecary*. The word seems to have been used originally of a pedlar or pretender who mounted a bench, or a bank by the wayside, and hawked off his wares or his skill. — Here, as generally in Shakespeare, *mortal* is *deadly;* that which *kills*.

[32] *Cataplasm* is a *soft plaster*, or a *poultice.* — *Simples* is, properly, *herbs;* but was used of any *medicine.* See page 144, note 39.

[33] "If our purpose should expose or betray itself through lack of skill in the execution."

[34] Should break down in the trial. The image is of proving guns, which of course sometimes burst in the testing.

As make your bouts more violent to that end, —
And that he calls for drink, I'll have prepar'd him
A chalice for the nonce;[35] whereon but sipping,
If he by chance escape your venom'd stuck,[36]
Our purpose may hold there. —

Enter the QUEEN.

How now, sweet Queen!

Queen. One woe doth tread upon another's heel,
So fast they follow. — Your sister's drown'd, Laertes.

Laer. Drown'd! O, where?[37]

Queen. There is a willow grows aslant a brook,
That shows his hoar leaves in the glassy stream:
There with fantastic garlands did she come
Of crow-flowers, nettles, daisies, and long purples,
That liberal[38] shepherds give a grosser name,
But our cold maids do dead-men's fingers call them:
There, on the pendent boughs her coronet weeds
Clambering to hang, an envious sliver broke;
When down her weedy trophies and herself
Fell in the weeping brook. Her clothes spread wide,
And, mermaid-like, awhile they bore her up;

[35] " For the *nonce*" is for the *occasion;* literally, for the *once.* — In the line before, instead of "And *that*," we should say "And *when*." See page 55, note 1.

[36] *Stuck,* a fencing-term, is *thrust;* the same as the Italian and Spanish *stoccata* and *staccado.* So in *Twelfth Night,* iii. 4: " He gives me the *stuck-in* with such mortal motion, that it is inevitable."

[37] That Laertes might be excused in some degree for not cooling, the Act concludes with the affecting death of Ophelia; who in the beginning lay like a little projection of land into a lake or stream, covered with spray-flowers, quietly reflected in the quiet waters; but at length is undermined or loosened, and becomes a fairy isle, and after a brief vagrancy sinks almost without an eddy. — COLERIDGE.

[38] *Liberal* is repeatedly used by Shakespeare for *loose-tongued.*

Which time she chanted snatches of old tunes,
As one incapable [39] of her own distress,
Or like a creature native and indued
Unto that element : but long it could not be
Till that her garments, heavy with their drink,
Pull'd the poor wretch [40] from her melodious lay
To muddy death.

    Laer.   Alas, then is she drown'd !

    Queen. Drown'd, drown'd.

    Laer. Too much of water hast thou, poor Ophelia,
And therefore I forbid my tears : but yet
It is our trick ; nature her custom holds,
Let shame say what it will : when these are gone,
The woman will be out.[41] — Adieu, my lord ;
I have a speech of fire, that fain would blaze,
But that this folly drowns it.   [*Exit.*

    King.   Let's follow, Gertrude :
How much I had to do to calm his rage !
Now fear I this will give it start again ;
Therefore let's follow.   [*Exeunt.*

---

[39] *Incapable* for *insensible* or *unconscious.* The Poet has it so in one or two other places. So in *As You Like It*, iii. 5, we have *capable* in the opposite sense : " Lean but upon a rush, the cicatrice and *capable* impressure thy palm some moment keeps."

[40] *Wretch*, again, as a strong term of endearment. See page 103, note 24.

[41] " I shall have wept the woman's tenderness all out of me, and shall be again ready for a man's work."

ACT V.

SCENE I. — *A Churchyard.*

Enter two Clowns, *with spades, &c.*

1 Clown. Is she to be buried in Christian burial that wil·fully seeks her own salvation?

2 Clown. I tell thee she is; and therefore make her grave straight:[1] the crowner hath sat on her, and finds it Christian burial.

1 Clown. How can that be, unless she drown'd herself in her own defence?

2 Clown. Why, 'tis found so.

1 Clown. It must be *se offendendo*;[2] it cannot be else. For here lies the point: If I drown myself wittingly, it argues an act; and an act hath three branches; it is, to act, to do, and to perform: argal[3] she drown'd herself wittingly.

2 Clown. Nay, but hear you, goodman delver, —

1 Clown. Give me leave. Here lies the water; good: here stands the man; good: if the man go to this water, and drown himself, it is, will he, nill he,[4] he goes, — mark you that; but if the water come to him and drown him, he drowns not himself: argal he that is not guilty of his own death shortens not his own life.

2 Clown. But is this law?

---

1 *Straight* for *straightway;* a common usage.

2 The Clown, in undertaking to show off his legal learning, blunders *offendendo* for *defendendo.*

3 *Argal* is an old vulgar corruption of the Latin *ergo, therefore.*

4 " Will he, *nill* he," is will he, *or will* he *not.*

1 Clown. Ay, marry, is't; crowner's-quest law.[5]

2 Clown. Will you ha' the truth on't? If this had not been a gentlewoman, she should have been buried out o' Christian burial.

1 Clown. Why, there thou say'st; and the more pity that great folk should have countenance in this world to drown or hang themselves, more than their even-Christian.[6] — Come, my spade. There is no ancient gentlemen but gardeners, ditchers, and grave-makers; they hold up Adam's profession.

2 Clown. Was he a gentleman?

1 Clown. He was the first that ever bore arms.

2 Clown. Why, he had none.

1 Clown. What, art a heathen? How dost thou understand the Scripture? The Scripture says Adam digg'd: could he dig without arms? I'll put another question to thee: if thou answerest me not to the purpose, confess thyself —

2 Clown. Go to.

1 Clown. What is he that builds stronger than either the mason, the shipwright, or the carpenter?

---

[5] Sir John Hawkins thinks the Poet here meant to ridicule a case reported by Plowden. Sir James Hales had drowned himself in a fit of insanity, and the legal question was whether his lease was thereby forfeited to the Crown. Much subtilty was expended in finding out whether Sir James was the *agent* or the *patient;* that is, whether *he went to the water* or *the water came to him.* The following is part of the argument: "Sir James Hales was dead, and how came he to his death? It may be answered, by drowning; and who drowned him? Sir James Hales; and when did he drown him? In his lifetime. So that Sir James Hales being alive caused Sir James Hales to die, and the act of the living man was the death of the dead man."

[6] *Even-Christian* for *fellow-Christian* was the old mode of expression and is to be found in *Chaucer* and the *Chroniclers.* Wicliffe has *even-servant* for *fellow-servant.*

2 Clown. The gallows-maker; for that frame outlives a thousand tenants.

1 Clown. I like thy wit well, in good faith: the gallows does well: but how does it well? it does well to those that do ill: now, thou dost ill to say the gallows is built stronger than the church: argal the gallows may do well to thee. To't again; come.

2 Clown. Who builds stronger than a mason, a shipwright, or a carpenter?

1 Clown. Ay, tell me that, and unyoke.[7]

2 Clown. Marry, now I can tell.

1 Clown. To't.

2 Clown. Mass, I cannot tell.

Enter HAMLET *and* HORATIO, *at a distance.*

1 Clown. Cudgel thy brains no more about it, for your dull ass will not mend his pace with beating; and when you are asked this question next, say *a grave-maker:* the houses that he makes last till doomsday. Go, get thee to Yaughan; fetch me a stoup of liquor.   [*Exit* 2 Clown.

[He digs, and sings.]

In youth, when I did love, did love,
    Methought it was very sweet,
To contract—O—the time, for—ah—my behove—
    O—Methought there was nothing meet.[8]

---

[7] This was a common phrase for giving over or ceasing to do a thing, a metaphor derived from the *unyoking* of oxen at the end of their labour.

[8] The original ballad from whence these stanzas are taken is printed in Tottel's *Miscellany, or Songes and Sonnettes by Lord Surrey and others,* 1575. The ballad is attributed to Lord Vaux, and is printed by Dr. Percy in his *Reliques of Ancient Poetry.* The *O's* and *ahs* are meant to express the Clown's gruntings as he digs.

Ham. Has this fellow no feeling of his business, that he sings at grave-making?

Hora. Custom hath made it in him a property of easiness.

Ham. 'Tis e'en so : the hand of little employment hath the daintier sense.

1 Clown. [Sings.] *But age, with his stealing steps,*
           Hath claw'd me in his clutch,
           And hath shipp'd me intil the land,
           As if I had never been such.

                        [Throws up a skull.

Ham. That skull had a tongue in it, and could sing once : how the knave jowls it to the ground, as if it were Cain's jaw-bone, that did the first murder ! It might be the pate of a politician, which this ass now o'erreaches ; one that would circumvent God, might it not?[9]

Hora. It might, my lord.

Ham. Or of a courtier ; which could say *Good morrow, sweet lord ! How dost thou, good lord ?* This might be my lord such-a-one, that praised my lord such-a-one's horse, when he meant to beg it, might it not?[9]

Hora. Ay, my lord.

Ham. Why, e'en so ; and now my Lady Worm's ;[10] chapless, and knock'd about the mazzard with a sexton's spade : here's fine revolution, an we had the trick to see't. Did these bones cost no more the breeding, but to play at loggats[11] with 'em? mine ache to think on't.

---

[9] Shakespeare uses *politician* for a *plotter* or *schemer;* one who is ever trying to out-craft and overreach his neighbour, and even Providence, and to intrigue his way to popularity or profit. The equivoque in *o'erreaches* is obvious enough.

[10] The skull that was *my Lord Such-a-one's* is now *my Lady Worm's,*

[11] *Loggats* are small logs or pieces of wood. Hence *loggats* was the

1 Clown. [Sings.]

> *A pick-axe, and a spade, a spade,*
> *For and* [12] *a shrouding sheet; — O —*
> *A pit of clay for to be made*
> *For such a guest is meet.*

> [Throws up another skull.

Ham. There's another: why may not that be the skull of a lawyer? Where be his quiddits now, his quillets, [13] his cases, his tenures, and his tricks? why does he suffer this rude knave now to knock him about the sconce [14] with a dirty shovel, and will not tell him of his action of battery? Hum! This fellow might be in's time a great buyer of land, with his statutes, his recognizances, his fines, his double vouchers, his recoveries: [15] is this the fine of his fines, and the recovery of his recoveries, to have his fine pate full of

name of an ancient rustic game, wherein a stake was fixed in the ground at which *loggats* were thrown; in short, a ruder kind of quoit-play.

12 "*For and,*" says Dyce, "in the present version of the stanza, answers to *And eke* in that given by Percy." So in Beaumont and Fletcher's *Knight of the Burning Pestle:* "Your squire doth come, and with him comes the lady, *for and* the Squire of Damsels, as I take it."

13 *Quiddits* are quirks, or subtle questions; and *quillets* are nice and frivolous distinctions. The etymology of this last word has plagued many learned heads. Blount, in his *Glossography,* clearly points out *quodlibet* as the origin of it. Bishop Wilkins calls a *quillet* "a frivolousness."

14 *Sconce* was not unfrequently used for *head.*

15 Shakespeare here is profuse of his legal learning. Ritson, a lawyer, shall interpret for him: "A recovery with *double voucher* is so called from *two* persons being successively *voucher,* or called upon to warrant the tenant's title. Both *fines* and *recoveries* are fictions of law, used to convert an estate tail into a fee-simple. Statutes are (not acts of parliament but) statutes *merchant* and staple, particular modes of *recognizance* or acknowledgment for securing *debts,* which thereby become a charge upon the party's land. *Statutes* and *recognizances* are constantly mentioned together in the covenants of a purchase deed."

fine dirt?[16] will his vouchers vouch him no more of his pur-
chases, and double ones too, than the length and breadth of
a pair of indentures?[17]   The very conveyances of his lands
will hardly lie in this box; and must the inheritor himself
have no more, ha?

Hora. Not a jot more, my lord.

Ham. Is not parchment made of sheep-skins?

Hora. Ay, my lord, and of calf-skins too.

Ham. They are sheep and calves which seek out assurance in that.[18]   I will speak to this fellow. — Whose grave's
this, sirrah?

1 Clown. Mine, sir. —

> [Sings.]   O — *A pit of clay for to be made*
> *For such a guest is meet.*

Ham. I think it be thine indeed, for thou liest in't.

1 Clown. You lie out on't, sir, and therefore it is not
yours: for my part, I do not lie in't and yet it is mine.

Ham. Thou dost lie in't, to be in't and say it is thine:
'tis for the dead, not for the quick; therefore thou liest.

1 Clown. 'Tis a quick lie, sir; 'twill away again, from me
to you.

[16] Here we have *fine* used in four different senses: first, in the proper
Latin sense, *end;* second, in the legal sense, to denote certain processes in
law; third, in the sense of *proud, elegant,* or *refined;* fourth, in the ordinary
sense of *small.*

[17] *Indenture, conveyance,* and *assurance* are all used here as equivalent
terms, and mean what we call *deeds;* instruments relating to the tenure and
transfer of property.   They were called *indentures,* because two copies were
written on the same sheet of parchment, which was cut in two in a toothed
or *indented* line, to guard against counterfeits, and to prove genuineness in
case of controversy. — *Inheritor,* in the next line, is *possessor* or *owner.*   The
Poet often uses the verb to *inherit* in the same sense.

[18] A quibble is here implied upon *parchment;* deeds, which were always
written on parchment, being in legal language "common assurances."

Ham. What man dost thou dig it for?

1 Clown. For no man, sir.

Ham. What woman, then?

1 Clown. For none, neither.

Ham. Who is to be buried in't?

1 Clown. One that was a woman, sir; but, rest her soul! she's dead.

Ham. How absolute the knave is! we must speak by the card,[19] or equivocation will undo us. By the Lord, Horatio, these three years I have taken a note of it; the age is grown so pickèd,[20] that the toe of the peasant comes so near the heel of the courtier, he galls his kibe.[21] — How long hast thou been a grave-maker?

1 Clown. Of all the days i' the year, I came to't that day that our last King Hamlet overcame Fortinbras.

Ham. How long is that since?

1 Clown. Cannot you tell that? every fool can tell that: it was the very day that young Hamlet was born; he that is mad, and sent into England.

Ham. Ay, marry; why was he sent into England?

1 Clown. Why, because he was mad: he shall recover his wits there; or, if he do not, it's no great matter there.

Ham. Why?

1 Clown. 'Twill not be seen in him there; there the men are as mad as he.

Ham. How came he mad?

1 Clown. Very strangely, they say.

---

[19] To speak by the card, is to speak precisely, by rule, or according to a prescribed course. It is a metaphor from the seaman's *card* or chart by which he guides his course.

[20] *Picked* is *curious, over-nice.*

[21] *Kibe* is an old word for *chilblain.* The Poet has it several times.

Ham. How strangely?

1 Clown. Faith, e'en with losing his wits.

Ham. Upon what ground?

1 Clown. Why, here in Denmark. I have been sexton here, man and boy, thirty years.

Ham. How long will a man lie i' the earth ere he rot?

1 Clown. I' faith, if he be not rotten before he die, — as we have many pocky corses now-a-days, that will scarce hold the laying in, — he will last you some eight year or nine year : a tanner will last you nine year.

Ham. Why he more than another?

1 Clown. Why, sir, his hide is so tann'd with his trade, that he will keep out water a great while : and your water is a sore decayer of your whoreson dead body. Here's a skull now ; this skull has lain in the earth three-and-twenty years.

Ham. Whose was it?

1 Clown. A whoreson mad fellow's it was : whose do you think it was?

Ham. Nay, I know not.

1 Clown. A pestilence on him for a mad rogue ! 'a pour'd a flagon of Rhenish on my head once. This same skull, sir, was Yorick's skull, the King's jester.

Ham. This?

1 Clown. E'en that.

Ham. Let me see. [*Takes the skull.*] — Alas, poor Yorick ! — I knew him, Horatio ; a fellow of infinite jest, of most excellent fancy : he hath borne me on his back a thousand times ; and now how abhorred in my imagination it is ! my gorge rises at it. Here hung those lips that I have kissed I know not how oft. — Where be your gibes now? your gambols? your songs? your flashes of merriment, that were wont to set the table on a roar? Not one now, to mock your own grinning? quite chap-fallen? Now get you to my lady's chamber, and tell her, let her paint an inch thick, to this favour she must come : make her laugh at that !—Pr'y-thee, Horatio, tell me one thing.

Hora. What's that, my lord?

Ham. Dost thou think Alexander look'd o' this fashion i' the earth?

Hora. E'en so.

Ham. And smelt so? pah !   [*Puts down the skull.*

Hora. E'en so, my lord.

Ham. To what base uses we may return, Horatio ! Why may not imagination trace the noble dust of Alexander till he find it stopping a bung-hole?

Hora. 'Twere to consider too curiously, to consider so.

Ham. No, faith, not a jot ; but to follow him thither with modesty enough, and likelihood to lead it ; as thus : Alexander died, Alexander was buried, Alexander returneth into dust ; the dust is earth ; of earth we make loam : and why of that loam whereto he was converted might they not stop a beer-barrel?

> Imperial Cæsar, dead and turn'd to clay,
> Might stop a hole to keep the wind away :
> O, that that earth which kept the world in awe
> Should patch a wall t' expel the Winter's flaw ![22]

But soft ! but soft ! aside ! here comes the King,
The Queen, the courtiers : —

Enter Priests, *&c., in procession ; the Corpse of* OPHELIA,
    LAERTES *and* Mourners *following ; the* KING, *the* QUEEN,
    their Trains, &c.

                            Who is that they follow?

---

[22] A *flaw* is a violent gust or blast of wind.

And with such maimèd rites?   This doth betoken,
The corse they follow did with desperate hand
Fordo its own life : 'twas of some estate.[23]
Couch we awhile, and mark.   [*Retiring with* HORATIO.

   Laer. What ceremony else?

   Ham. That is Laertes, a very noble youth : mark.

   Laer. What ceremony else?

   1 Priest. Her obsequies have been as far enlarged
As we have warrantise : her death was doubtful ;
And, but that great command o'ersways the order,
She should in ground unsanctified have lodged
Till the last trumpet ; for charitable prayers,
Shards,[24] flints, and pebbles should be thrown on her :
Yet here she is allow'd her virgin crants,[25]
Her maiden strewments, and the bringing home
Of [26] bell and burial.

   Laer. Must there no more be done?

   1 Priest.   No more be done :
We should profane the service of the dead,
To sing a requiem and such rest to her
As to peace-parted souls.[27]

---

[23] *Estate* was a common term for persons of *rank.* — To *fordo* is to *undo* or *destroy.* See page 95, note 21.

[24] *Shards* not only means fragments of pots and tiles, but rubbish of any kind. Our version of the Bible has preserved to us *pot-sherds ;* and bricklayers, in Surrey and Sussex, use the compounds *tile-sherds, slate-sherds.* — *For,* in the preceding line, has the force of *instead of.*

[25] *Crants* is an old word for *garlands ;* very rare, and not used again by Shakespeare. It was customary in some parts of England to have a garland of flowers and sweet herbs carried before a maiden's coffin. Johnson says it was the custom in rural parishes in his time.

[26] *Of* has here the force of *with.*

[27] A *requiem* is a mass sung for the rest of the soul. So called from the words, *Requiem æternam dona eis, Domine.* — "Peace-parted souls" is souls

Laer.   Lay her i' the earth ;
And from her fair and unpolluted flesh
May violets spring ! — I tell thee, churlish priest,
A ministering angel shall my sister be,
When thou liest howling.

Ham.   What, the fair Ophelia !

Queen. Sweets to the sweet : farewell ! [*Scattering flowers.*
I hoped thou shouldst have been my Hamlet's wife ;
I thought thy bride-bed to have deck'd, sweet maid,
And not have strew'd thy grave.

Laer.   O, treble woe
Fall ten times treble on that cursèd head
Whose wicked deed thy most ingenious [28] sense
Deprived thee of ! — Hold off the earth awhile,
Till I have caught her once more in mine arms.

                    [*Leaps into the grave.*

Now pile your dust upon the quick and dead,
Till of this flat a mountain you have made
T' o'ertop old Pelion or the skyish head
Of blue Olympus.

Ham. [*Advancing.*] What is he whose grief
Bears such an emphasis? whose phrase of sorrow
Conjures the wandering stars, and makes them stand
Like wonder-wounded hearers?   This is I,
Hamlet the Dane !   [*Leaps into the grave*

Laer.   The Devil take thy soul !

                    [*Grappling with him.*

that have *departed in peace;* or, as the Prayer-book has it, "in favour with
Thee our God, and in perfect charity with the world."

[28] *Ingenious* for *ingenuous, guileless.*   Even Defoe has it so in his *Colonel
Jack,* 1738 : "But 'tis contrary to an *ingenuous* spirit to delight in such service."

Ham. Thou pray'st not well.

I pr'ythee, take thy fingers from my throat ;

For, though I am not splenitive and rash,

Yet have I something in me dangerous,

Which let thy wisdom fear : hold off thy hand !

King. Pluck them asunder.

Queen.   Hamlet, Hamlet !

All. Gentlemen, —

Hora.   Good my lord, be quiet.

[*The* Attendants *part them, and they come out of the grave.*

Ham. Why, I will fight with him upon this theme

Until my eyelids will no longer wag.

Queen. O my son, what theme ?

Ham. I loved Ophelia : forty thousand brothers

Could not, with all their quantity of love,

Make up my sum. — What wilt thou do for her ?

King. O, he is mad, Laertes.

Queen. For love of God, forbear him.

Ham. 'Swounds, show me what thou'lt do :

Woo't weep ? woo't fight ? woo't fast ? woo't tear thyself ?

Woo't drink up Esill ? [29] eat a crocodile ?

I'll do't.   Dost thou come here to whine ?

To outface me with leaping in her grave ?

---

[29] What particular lake, river, frith, or gulf was meant by the Poet, is something uncertain.   The more common opinion is, that he had in mind the river *Yesel*, which, of the larger branches of the Rhine, is the one nearest to Denmark.   In the maps of our time, *Isef* is the name of a gulf almost surrounded by land, in the Island of Zealand, not many miles west of Elsinore.   Either of these names might naturally enough have been spelt and pronounced *Esill* or *Isell* by an Englishman in Shakespeare's time.   In strains of hyperbole, such figures of speech were often used by the old poets. — *Woo't* is a contraction of *wouldst thou*, said to be common in the northern counties of England.

Be buried quick with her, and so will I ;
And, if thou prate of mountains, let them throw
Millions of acres on us, till our ground,
Singeing his pate against the burning zone,[30]
Make Ossa like a wart !   Nay, an thou'lt mouth,
I'll rant as well as thou.

    Queen.   This is mere[31] madness :
And thus awhile the fit will work on him ;
Anon, as patient as the female dove,
When that her golden couplets are disclosed,[32]
His silence will sit drooping.

    Ham.   Hear you, sir :
What is the reason that you use me thus ?
I loved you ever : but it is no matter ;
Let Hercules himself do what he may,
The cat will mew, and dog will have his day.   *[Exit.*

    King. I pray you, good Horatio, wait upon him. —
                          [Exit HORATIO.

[To LAERTES.] Strengthen your patience in our last night's
      speech ;
We'll put the matter to the present push. —
Good Gertrude, set some watch over your son. —
This grave shall have a living monument :
An hour of quiet shortly shall we see ;
Till then, in patience our proceeding be.   *[Exeunt.*

---

    [30] " The burning zone " is no doubt the path, or seeming path, of the Sun
in the celestial sphere ; the Sun's diurnal orbit.

    [31] Here, as often, *mere* is *absolute* or *downright.*

    [32] The " golden couplets " are the two chicks of the dove ; which, when
first hatched, are covered with a *yellow* down ; and in her patient tenderness
the mother rarely leaves the nest, till her little ones attain to some degree of
dove-discretion. — *Disclose* was often used for *hatch.*

SCENE II. — *A Hall in the Castle.*

Enter HAMLET *and* HORATIO.

Ham. So much for this, sir; now shall you see the other:
You do remember all the circumstance?[1]

Hora. Remember it, my lord!

Ham. Sir, in my heart there was a kind of fighting,
That would not let me sleep:[2] methought I lay
Worse than the mutines in the bilboes.[3]   Rashly, —
And praised be rashness for it; let us know,
Our indiscretion sometimes serves us well,
When our deep plots do pall;[4] and that should teach us
There's a divinity that shapes our ends,
Rough-hew them how we will, —   10

---

[1] *Circumstance* probably means the *circumstantial account* given by Hamlet in his letter to Horatio. — *The other* refers, no doubt, to the further matter intimated in that letter: "I have words to speak in thine ear will make thee dumb."

[2] Hamlet has from the first divined the King's purpose in sending him to England. Since the close of the interlude, when the King was "frighted with false fire," Hamlet *knows* that the King did indeed murder his father, and he also knows that the King *suspects* him of knowing it. Hence, on shipboard, he naturally has a vague, general apprehension of mischief, and this as naturally fills him with nervous curiosity as to the particular shape of danger which he is to encounter.

[3] The *bilboes* were bars of iron with fetters annexed to them, by which mutinous or disorderly sailors were linked together. The word is derived from *Bilboa*, in Spain, where the things were made. To understand the allusion, it should be known that, as these fetters connected the legs of the offenders very closely together, their attempts to rest must be as fruitless as those of Hamlet, in whose mind *there was a kind of fighting that would not let him sleep.* — *Mutines* is for *mutineers.*

[4] *Pall* is from the old French *palser*, to *fade* or *fall away.* So in *Antony and Cleopatra:* "I'll never follow thy *pall'd* fortunes more." — Note that all after *rashly*, down to the beginning of Hamlet's next speech, is parenthetical.

Hora.   That is most certain.

Ham. — Up from my cabin,
My sea-gown scarf'd about me,[5] in the dark
Groped I to find out them ; had my desire ;
Finger'd their packet ; and, in fine, withdrew
To mine own room again : making so bold,
My fears forgetting manners, to unseal
Their grand commission ; where I found, Horatio, —
O royal knavery ! — an exact command,
Larded with many several sorts of reasons, —
Importing Denmark's health, and England's too,
With, ho ! such bugs and goblins in my life,[6] —
That, on the supervise, no leisure bated,[7]
No, not to stay the grinding of the axe,
My head should be struck off.

Hora.   Is't possible ?

Ham. Here's the commission : read it at more leisure.
But wilt thou hear me how I did proceed ?

Hora. I beseech you.

Ham. Being thus be-netted round with villainies, —
Ere I could make a prologue to my brains,
They had begun the play,[8] — I sat me down,

---

5 *Thrown*, or *gathered, loosely* about me.

6 Such *bugbears* and *fantastic dangers growing out of* my life. The Poet
has *bug* several times in that sense. So in *The Winter's Tale*, iii. 2: "Sir,
spare your threats: the *bug*, which you would fright me with, I seek." —
Goblins were a knavish sort of fairies, perhaps *ignes fatui*, and so belonged
to the genus Humbug.

7 The language is obscure, though the general sense is plain enough. I
suspect *batea* is an instance of the passive form with the active sense ; no
leisure *abating* the speed ; or the haste not being lessened by any pause. —
Supervise is *looking over, perusal*.

8 An allusion to the stage, where a play was commonly introduced by a
prologue. Hamlet means that his thoughts were so fiery-footed as to start

Devised a new commission ; wrote it fair :
I once did hold it, as our statists do,
A baseness to write fair,[9] and labour'd much
How to forget that learning ; but, sir, now
It did me yeoman's service.[10]　Wilt thou know
Th' effect of what I wrote ?

    Hora.　　　　　　　　　Ay, good my lord.

    Ham. An earnest conjuration from the King, —
As England was his faithful tributary ;
As love between them like the palm might flourish ;
As peace should still her wheaten garland wear,
And stand a cement 'tween their amities ;
And many such-like *ases* of great charge,[11] —
That, on the view and knowing of these contents,
Without debatement further, more or less,
He should the bearers put to sudden death,
Not shriving-time [12] allow'd.

    Hora.　　　　　　　　How was this seal'd ?

    Ham. Why, even in that was Heaven ordinant.
I had my father's signet in my purse,

---

off in the play itself before he could get through with the introduction
to it.

  [9] *Statist* is the old word for *statesman.* Blackstone says that "most of
our great men of Shakespeare's time wrote very bad hands; their secreta-
ries, very neat ones." It was accounted a mechanical and vulgar accom-
plishment to write a fair hand.

  [10] In the days of archery, the English yeomanry, with their huge bows
and long arrows, were the most terrible fighters in Europe.

  [11] Of course "*ases*" refers to the use of *As* three times in the preceding
lines. In Shakespeare's time *as* and *that* were often used interchangeably.
So here; and, according to present usage, the second *As* and also the third
should be *That.* — *Great charge* is great *importance; charged* with great *import.*

  [12] "*Shriving-*time" is time for confession and absolution.

50

Which was the model of that Danish seal ;
Folded the writ up in form of th' other ;
Subscribed it ; gave't th' impression ; placed it safely,
The changeling never known. Now, the next day
Was our sea-fight ; and what to this was sequent
Thou know'st already.

    Hora. So Guildenstern and Rosencrantz go to't.

    Ham. Why, man, they did make love to this employment :
They are not near my conscience ; their defeat
Does by their own insinuation grow : [13]

60

'Tis dangerous when the baser nature comes
Between the pass and fell-incensèd points
Of mighty opposites.[14]

[13] Horatio seems to regret, as he well may, the fate of Guildenstern and Rosencrantz, who, of course, did not distinctly know the purpose of their commission, else they would have turned back, after the separation of Hamlet from them. Of course, too, Hamlet expected, at the time, to go to England with them ; and it has been suggested that, had he done so, he would have arrested the effect of the substituted commission. But I prefer the view taken by Professor Werder : "As surely as Rosencrantz and Guildenstern deliver their letter, his head falls. *That* letter, then, they *must not be allowed* to deliver ; they *must* deliver a different one. But do you say he could have spared them ? he could have written something that would endanger neither him nor them ? Does he know or can he discover from them so that he may depend upon their word, how far they are cognizant of the purport of their errand ? whether they are not charged with some oral message ? What if they should contradict what he might write of a harmless character ? What if the King of England, being in doubt, should send back to Denmark for further directions, detain all three, and then, as surely was to be expected, put Hamlet to death ? No, there is no expedient possible, no evasion, no choice between *thus* or otherwise. He *must* sacrifice them, *and* even without allowing them time to confess, — *must* do this even. For, if only they are allowed time for confession, after they are seized and made sensible of their position, there is no foreseeing what turn things may take for him."

[14] When men of lower rank come between the thrusts and sword-points of great men engaged in fierce and mortal duel, or bent on fighting it out to

Hora.   Why, what a king is this !

Ham. Does it not, think'st thou, stand me now upon ?[15]
He that hath kill'd my King, and stain'd my mother ;
Popp'd in between th' election and my hopes ;
Thrown out his angle for my proper life,
And with such cozenage, — is't not perfect conscience
To quit [16] him with this arm? and is't not to be damn'd,
To let this canker of our nature come
In further evil ?[17]

Hora. It must be shortly known to him from England
What is the issue of the business there.

---

the death. — Here, as usual in Shakespeare, *opposites* is *opponents*. — I
quote again from Professor Werder: "Whoever, from his position, or from
his zeal and officiousness, undertakes the office of carrying the letter and
Hamlet to England, must suffer whatever of harm to himself may be connected with such an errand.   The business is dangerous; such affairs
always are.   The baseness of Rosencrantz and Guildenstern is their ruin:
they promenade, so to speak, in the sphere of a fate which involves damnation, without scenting or wishing to scent the sulphur.   Where such a king
bears rule, his servants are always exposed to the very worst that can befall;
and at any moment their ruin may come through circumstances and causes,
from which nothing may seem more remote than the catastrophe: for the
main thing is overlooked, because it is *always* present, even the *ground* on
which all concerned live and move, upon which all rests, and which is itself
Destruction.   Whoever serves such a king, and, without any misgiving of
his crime, serves him with ready zeal; upon him Hell has a claim; and, if
that claim be made good, he has no right to complain. — These are things
in which Shakespeare knows no jesting, because he is so great an ex-
pounder of the Law, the Divine Law; and he holds to it as no second poet
has done."

[15] " It stands me upon " is an old phrase for "it is incumbent upon me,"
or, " it is my bounden duty."   Shakespeare has it repeatedly.   So in *King
Richard II.,* ii. 3 : " It stands your Grace upon, to do him right."

[16] Here, as in many other places, to *quit* is to *requite.*

[17] " Is it not a damnable sin to let this *cancer* of humanity proceed further
in mischief and villainy ? "   *Canker,* in one of its senses, means an eating,
malignant sore, like a *cancer;* which word is from the same original.

Ham. It will be short : the interim is mine ; [18]
And a man's life's no more than to say *One.*
But I am very sorry, good Horatio,
That to Laertes I forgot myself ;
For by the image of my cause I see
The portraiture of his.[19] I'll court his favours ; [20]
But; sure, the bravery of his grief did put me
Into a towering passion.

 Hora.   Peace ! who comes here?

Enter OSRIC.

Osric. Your lordship is right welcome back to Denmark.

Ham. I humbly thank you, sir. — [*Aside to* HORATIO.]
Dost know this water-fly ? [21]

Hora. [*Aside to* HAMLET.] No, my good lord.

Ham. [*Aside to* HORATIO.] Thy state is the more gracious ; for 'tis a vice to know him. He hath much land,
and fertile : let a beast be lord of beasts, and his crib shall
stand at the King's mess.[22] 'Tis a chough ; but, as I say,
spacious in the possession of dirt.

[18] Hamlet justly looks forward to the coming of that news as the crisis
of his task : it will bring things to a head, and give him a practicable twist
on the King : he can then meet both him and the publie with *justifying
proof* of his guilt.

[19] Hamlet and Laertes have lost each his father, and both have perhaps
lost equally in Ophelia ; so that their cause of sorrow is much the same.

[20] Hamlet means "I'll solicit his *good will;*" the general meaning of
favours in the Poet's time.

[21] In *Troilus and Cressida,* v. 1, Thersites says of Patroclus : "How the
poor world is pestered with such *water-flies ;* diminutives of nature." As
Johnson says, "A water-fly skips up and down upon the surface of the
water without any apparent purpose or reason, and is thence the proper
emblem of a busy trifler."

[22] This is meant as a sarcastic stroke at the King for keeping such a fin-
ical sap-head near his person. Let even a biped puppy be rich, the lord or

Osric. Sweet lord, if your lordship were at leisure, I should impart a thing to you from his Majesty.

Ham. I will receive it, sir, with all diligence of spirit. Put your bonnet to his right use ; 'tis for the head.

Osric. I thank your lordship, it is very hot.

Ham. No, believe me, 'tis very cold ; the wind is north erly.

Osric. It is indifferent cold, my lord, indeed.

Ham. But yet methinks it is very sultry and hot for my complexion.

Osric. Exceedingly, my lord ; it is very sultry,—as 'twere, — I cannot tell how. But, my lord, his Majesty bade me signify to you that he has laid a great wager on your head. Sir, this is the matter, —

Ham. I beseech you, remember [24] —

[HAMLET *moves him to put on his hat.*

Osric. Nay, in good faith ; for mine ease, in good faith. Sir, here is newly come to Court Laertes ; believe me, an absolute gentleman, full of most excellent differences,[25] of very soft society and great showing : indeed, to speak feel-ingly of him, he is the card or calendar of gentry ; for you

owner of large herds of cattle, and he shall be the King's bosom friend, and feed at his table. — In what follows, *chough* is a bird of the jackdaw sort; and Osric is aptly so called because he chatters euphuistic jargon *by rote.*

[24] The full phrase occurs in *Love's Labour's Lost,* v. 1 : "I do beseech thee, remember *thy courtesy;* I beseech thee, apparel thy head." Aptly ex-plained by Dr. Ingleby : "If any one, from ill-breeding or over politeness, stood uncovered a longer time than was necessary to perform the simple act of courtesy, the person saluted reminded him of the fact, that the re-moval of the hat was a courtesy; and this was expressed by the euphemism, 'Remember thy courtesy,' which thus implied, 'Complete your courtesy and replace your hat.'"

[25] In the affected phrase-making of this euphuist, *excellent differences* probably means *distinctive excellences.*

shall find in him the continent of what part a gentlemen
would see.   110

Ham. Sir, his definement suffers no perdition in you ;[26]
though, I know, to divide him inventorially would dizzy the
arithmetic of memory,[27] and yet but yaw[28] neither, in respect of his quick sail.[29]   But, in the verity of extolment, I
take him to be a soul of great article ; and his infusion of
such dearth and rareness, as, to make true diction of him,
his semblable is his mirror ; and who else would trace him,
his umbrage,[30] nothing more.

Osric. Your lordship speaks most infallibly of him.

Ham. The concernancy,[31] sir ? why do we wrap the gentleman in our more rawer breath ?   121

26 " He suffers no *loss* in your *description* of him."

27 " To *distinguish* all his good parts, and make a schedule or *inventory*
of them, would be too much for the most mathematical head."

28 This word occurs as a substantive in Massinger's *Very Woman :* " O,
the *yaws* that she will make !   Look to your stern, dear mistress, and steer
right."   Where Gifford notes " A *yaw* is that unsteady motion which a ship
makes in a great swell, when, in steering, she inclines to the right or left of
her course."   Scott also has the word in the *The Antiquary,* " Thus escorted,
the Antiquary moved along full of his learning, like a lordly man-of-war,
and every now and then *yawing* to starboard and larboard to discharge a
broadside upon his followers." — In the text, *yaw* is a verb, and is in the
same construction with *dizzy ;* " and yet would do nothing but yaw "; that
is, *vacillate,* or *reel hither and thither,* instead of going straight ahead.

29 *In respect of* is equivalent to *in comparison with.*   Such is the common meaning of the phrase in old writers.   So that the sense of the passage
comes thus : " To discriminate the good parts of Laertes, and make a full
catalogue of them, would dizzy the head of an arithmetician, and yet would
be but a slow and staggering process, *compared to* his swift sailing."   Hamlet is running Osric's hyperbolical euphuism into the ground, and is purposely obscure, in order to bewilder the poor fop.

30 To *trace* is to *track,* or *keep pace* with.   *Umbrage,* from the Latin
umbra, is *shadow.*   So that the meaning here is, " The only resemblance to
him is in his mirror ; and nothing but his shadow can keep up with him."

31 That is, " How does this concern us ? "

Osric. Sir?

Hora. Is't not possible to understand in another tongue?[32]
You will do't, sir, really.

Ham. What imports the nomination of this gentleman?

Osric. Of Laertes?

Hora. [*Aside to* HAMLET.] His purse is empty already;
all's golden words are spent.

Ham. Of him, sir.

Osric. I know you are not ignorant —

Ham. I would you did, sir; yet, in faith, if you did, it
would not much approve me. Well, sir?

Osric. You are not ignorant of what excellence Laertes
is —

Ham. I dare not confess that, lest I should compare with
him in excellence : but to know a man well, were to know
himself.[33]

Osric. I mean, sir, for his weapon ; but in the imputation
laid on him by them, in his meed he's unfellow'd.[34]

Ham. What's his weapon?

Osric. Rapier and dagger.

Ham. That's two of his weapons ; but, well?

[32] Horatio means to imply, that what with Osric's euphuism, and what
with Hamlet's catching of Osric's style, they are not speaking in a tongue
that can be understood ; and he hints that they try *another* tongue, that is
the common one.

[33] The meaning is, that he will not claim to appreciate the excellence of
Laertes, as this would imply equal excellence in himself; on the principle
that a man cannot understand that which exceeds his own measure. Hamlet goes into these subtilties on purpose to maze Osric. — The words, "*but*
to know," mean "*only* to know."

[34] *Unfellow'd* is *unequalled*. *Fellow* for *equal* is very frequent. — *Meed*
for *merit;* also a frequent usage. — *Imputation*, also, for *reputation*. So in
Troilus and Cressida, i. 3 : "Our *imputation* shall be oddly poised in this
wild action."

Osric. The King, sir, hath wager'd with him six Barbary horses; against the which he has imponed,[35] as I take it, six French rapiers and poniards, with their assigns, as girdle, hangers, and so. Three of the carriages, in faith, are very dear to fancy, very responsive to the hilts, most delicate carriages, and of very liberal conceit.

Ham. What call you the carriages?

Hora. [*Aside to* HAMLET.] I knew you must be edified by the margent[36] ere you had done.

Osric. The carriages, sir, are the hangers.

Ham. The phrase would be more germane[37] to the matter, if we could carry cannon by our sides: I would it might be hangers till then. But, on: Six Barbary horses against six French swords, their assigns, and three liberal-conceited carriages; that's the French bet against the Danish. Why is this *imponed*, as you call it?

Osric. The King, sir, hath laid, that in a dozen passes between yourself and him he shall not exceed you three hits: he hath laid, on twelve for nine; and it would come to immediate trial, if your lordship would vouchsafe the answer.[38]

Ham. How, if I answer no?

Osric. I mean, my lord, the opposition of your person in trial.

[35] *Imponed* is probably meant as an Osrician form of *impawned*. To *impawn* is to *put in pledge*, to *stake* or *wager*.

[36] "I knew you *would have to be* instructed by a *marginal commentary*." The allusion is to the printing of comments in the margin of books. So in *Romeo and Juliet*, i. 3:—

> And what obscured in this fair volume lies,
> Find written in the margent of his eyes.

[37] *Germane* is *kindred* or *akin*; hence, *appropriate*.

[38] That is, vouchsafe to *accept the proposition*. Hamlet chooses to take it in another sense, because he likes to quiz Osric.

Ham. Sir, I will walk here in the hall : if it please his Majesty, 'tis the breathing-time [39] of day with me ; let the foils be brought, the gentleman willing, and the King hold his purpose, I will win for him if I can ; if not, I will gain nothing but my shame and the odd hits.

Osric. Shall I re-deliver you e'en so ?

Ham. To this effect, sir ; after what flourish your nature will.

Osric. I commend my duty to your lordship.

Ham. Yours, yours. [*Exit* Osric.] — He does well to commend it himself ; there are no tongues else for's turn.

Hora. This lapwing runs away with the shell on his head. [40]

Ham. He did comply with his dug, [41] before he suck'd it. Thus has he — and many more of the same bevy that I know the drossy age dotes on — only got the tune of the time and outward habit of encounter ; a kind of yesty collection, [42] which carries them through and through the most fond and winnowed opinions ; [43] and do but blow them to their trial, the bubbles are out. *Enter a* Lord.

Lord. My lord, his Majesty commended him to you by

[39] " The *breathing*-time " is the time for *exercise*. The use of to *breathe* for to *exercise* occurs repeatedly in Shakespeare. It was common.

[40] Meaning that Osric is a raw, unfledged, foolish fellow. It was a common comparison for a forward fool. Thus in Meres's *Wits Treasury*, 1598 : " As the lapwing runneth away with the shell on her head, as soon as she is hatched."

[41] *Comply* is used in the same sense here as in note 59, page 113. In Fulwel's *Art of Flattery*, 1579, the same idea occurs : " The very sucking babes hath a kind of adulation towards their nurses for the dug."

[42] *Yesty* is *frothy*. A *gathering* of mental and lingual froth.

[43] Here, *fond* is *affected*. The passage is well explained in the Clarendon edition : " Osric, and others like him, are compared to the chaff which mounts higher than the sifted wheat, and to the bubbles which rise to the surface through the deeper water."

young Osric, who brings back to him, that you attend him in
the hall : he sends to know if your pleasure hold to play with
Laertes, or that you will take longer time.

Ham. I am constant to my purposes ; they follow the
King's pleasure : if his fitness speaks, mine is ready ; now or
whensoever, provided I be so able as now.

Lord. The King and Queen and all are coming down.

Ham. In happy time.[44]

Lord. The Queen desires you to use some gentle entertainment to Laertes before you fall to play.

Ham. She well instructs me.   [*Exit* Lord.

Hora. You will lose this wager, my lord.

Ham. I do not think so : since he went into France, I
have been in continual practice ; I shall win at the odds.
But thou wouldst not think how ill all's here about my heart ;
but it is no matter.

Hora. Nay, good my lord, —

Ham. It is but foolery ; but it is such a kind of gaingiving[45] as would perhaps trouble a woman.

Hora. If your mind dislike any thing, obey it : I will forestall their repair hither, and say you are not fit.

Ham. Not a whit ; we defy[46] augury : there is a special
providence in the fall of a sparrow. If it be now, 'tis not to
come ; if it be not to come, it will be now ; if it be not now,
yet it will come : the readiness is all. Since no man knows
aught of what he leaves, what is't to leave betimes?[47]

---

[44] That is, in *fitting* time ; like the French *a la bonne heure.*

[45] *Gain-giving* probably means *misgiving ;* formed in the same way as
gainsay and *gainstrive.*

[46] To *defy*, here, is to *renounce* or *disclaim.* Often so.

[47] Johnson interprets the passage thus: "Since *no man knows aught* of
the state which *he leaves ;* since he cannot judge what other years may produce ; why should we be afraid of *leaving* life betimes ? "

Enter the KING, *the* QUEEN, LAERTES, Lords, OSRIC, *and*
Attendants *with foils, &c.*

   King. Come, Hamlet, come, and take this hand from me.
            [*The* KING *puts* LAERTES'S *hand into* HAMLET'S
   Ham. Give me your pardon, sir : I've done you wrong ;
But pardon't, as you are a gentleman.
This presence knows,
And you must needs have heard, how I am punish'd
With sore distraction. What I have done,
That might your nature, honour, and exception
Roughly awake, I here proclaim was madness.
Was't Hamlet wrong'd Laertes ? Never Hamlet :
If Hamlet from himself be ta'en away,
And when he's not himself does wrong Laertes,
Then Hamlet does it not ; Hamlet denies it.
Who does it, then ? His madness. If't be so,
Hamlet is of the faction that is wrong'd ;
His madness is poor Hamlet's enemy.
Sir, in this audience,
Let my disclaiming from a purposed evil
Free me so far in your most generous thoughts,
That I have shot mine arrow o'er the house,
And hurt my brother.
   Laer.   I am satisfied in nature,
Whose motive, in this case, should stir me most
To my revenge : but in my terms of honour
I stand aloof ; and will no reconcilement
Till by some elder masters, of known honour,
I have a voice and precedent of peace,[48]

---

   [48] The meaning probably is, "till some experts in the code of honour
give me the warrant of custom and usage for standing on peaceful terms

To keep my name ungored.   But, till that time,
I do receive your offer'd love like love,
And will not wrong it.

    Ham.   I embrace it freely;
And will this brother's wager frankly play. —
Give us the foils. — Come on.

    Laer.   Come, one for me.

    Ham. I'll be your foil, Laertes:[49] in mine ignorance
Your skill shall, like a star i' the darkest night,
Stick fiery off indeed.

    Laer.   You mock me, sir.

    Ham. No, by this hand.

    King. Give them the foils, young Osric. — Cousin Hamlet,
You know the wager?

    Ham.   Very well, my lord;
Your Grace hath laid the odds[50] o' the weaker side.

    King. I do not fear it; I have seen you both:
But, since he's better'd, we have therefore odds.[51]

    Laer. This is too heavy; let me see another.

    Ham. This likes me well. —These foils have all a length?

with you." Laertes thinks, or pretends to think, that the laws of honour require him to insist on a stern vindication of his manhood. Hamlet has before spoken of Laertes as "a very noble youth." In this part of the scene, he has his faculties keenly on the alert against Claudius; but it were a sin in him even to suspect Laertes of any thing so unfathomably base as the treachery now on foot.

49 Hamlet plays on the word *foil*; which here has the sense of *contrast*, or that which *sets off* a thing, and makes it show to advantage; as a dark night sets off a star, "when only one is shining in the sky."

50 The *odds* here referred to is the value of the stakes, the King having wagered six Barbary horses against a few rapiers, poniards, &c.; which was about as twenty to one.

51 Here the reference is to the *three odd hits* in Hamlet's favour, the numbers being nine and twelve. The King affects to regard this as a fair offset for Laertes's improved skill in the handling of his weapon.

Osric. Ay, my good lord.   [*They prepare to play.*

King. Set me the stoups of wine upon that table.—
If Hamlet give the first or second hit,
Or quit [52] in answer of the third exchange,
Let all the battlements their ordnance fire :
The King shall drink to Hamlet's better breath ;
And in the cup an union [53] shall he throw,
Richer than that which four successive kings
In Denmark's crown have worn.   Give me the cups ;
And let the kettle to the trumpet speak,
The trumpet to the cannoneer without,
The cannons to the heavens, the heavens to earth,
Now the King drinks to Hamlet ! — Come, begin ; —
And you, the judges, [54] bear a wary eye.

Ham. Come on, sir.

Laer. Come, my lord.   [*They play*

Ham. One.

Laer. No.

Ham. Judgment.

Osric. A hit, a very palpable hit.

Laer. Well ; — again.

King. Stay ; give me drink.—Hamlet, this pearl is thine ;
Here's to thy health. —

                    [*Trumpets sound, and cannon shot off within.*
                         Give him the cup.

---

[52] *Quit*, again, for *requite*, or *retaliate.*   See page 216, note 16.

[53] *Union* was a name for the largest and finest pearls, such as were worn in crowns and coronets. So in Florio's *Italian Dictionary*, 1598 : "Also a faire, great, orient pearle, called an *union.*" A rich gem thus put into a cup of wine was meant as present to the drinker of the wine. Of course the *union* in this case was a preparation of poison.

[54] These *judges* were the umpires appointed beforehand, with Osric at their head, to decide in case of any dispute arising between the fencers.

Ham. I'll play this bout first; set it by awhile. —
Come. [*They play.*]   Another hit; what say you?

Laer. A touch, a touch, I do confess.

King. Our son shall win.

Queen.   He's hot, and scant of breath. —
Here, Hamlet, take my napkin,[55] rub thy brows:
The Queen carouses to thy fortune, Hamlet.

Ham. Good madam![56]

King.   Gertrude, do not drink.

Queen. I will, my lord; I pray you, pardon me.

King. [*Aside.*] It is the poison'd cup; it is too late.

Ham. I dare not drink yet, madam; by-and-by.[57]

Queen. Come, let me wipe thy face.

Laer. My lord, I'll hit him now.

King.   I do not think't.

Laer. [*Aside.*] And yet 'tis almost 'gainst my conscience.

Ham. Come, for the third, Laertes: you but dally:
I pray you, pass with your best violence;
I am afeard you make a wanton of me.[58]

Laer. Say you so? come on.   [*They play.*

Osric. Nothing, neither way.

---

[55] *Napkin* was continually used for *handkerchief.*

[56] This exclamation is probably meant to hint that Hamlet suspects, or more than suspects, the contents of that cup. The same appears more clearly just after in "I dare not drink yet."

[57] Hamlet now sees, or judges, that his time has come: the playing done, he will attend to that cup, and *invite Claudius to drink it.* Such is evidently his purpose.

[58] To make a wanton of a man, as the phrase is here used, is to treat him as a child, to avoid playing your best with him, or rather to play the game into his hands. — This is a quiet, but very significant stroke of delineation. Laertes is not playing his best, and it is the conscience of what is at the point of his foil that keeps him from doing so; and the effects are perceptible to Hamlet, though he dreams not of the reason.

Laer. **Have at you now !**

     [LAERTES *wounds* HAMLET ; *then, in scuffling, they*
        change rapiers, and HAMLET *wounds* LAERTES.[59]

King.   Part them ; they are incensed.

Ham. Nay, come, again.   [*The* QUEEN *falls.*

Osric.   Look to the Queen there, ho !

Hora. They bleed on both sides. — **How is it, my lord?**

Osric. How is't, Laertes?

Laer. Why, as a woodcock to mine own springe, Osric ;
I 'm justly kill'd with mine own treachery.

Ham. How does the Queen?

King.   She swoons to see them bleed.

Queen. **No, no, the drink, the drink, —** O my dear Hamlet, —
The drink, the drink !   I am poison'd !   [*Dies.*

Ham. O villainy ! — Ho ! let the door be lock'd ! —
Treachery ! seek it out !

Laer. It is here, Hamlet.   Hamlet, thou art slain ;
No medicine in the world can do thee good ;
In thee there is not half an hour of life :
The treacherous instrument is in thy hand,
Unbated and envenom'd. The foul practice
Hath turn'd itself on me : lo, here I lie,
Never to rise again. Thy mother's poison'd ; —
I can no more. The King, — the King's to blame.

---

[59] Up to this moment Hamlet has not put forth his strength; he has
been *merely* playing: now, on being unexpectedly pierced, he is instantly
stung into fiery action; and he is a terrible man with the sword, when his
blood is up. — The exchanging of foils takes place well in Mr. Edwin
Booth's ordering of the matter on the stage. There Hamlet, in a rapture
of energy and adroitness, strikes the foil out of Laertes's hand, picks it up,
and throws down his own, which, again, is presently picked up by
Laertes.

Ham. The point envenom'd too ! —
Then, venom, to thy work !   [*Stabs the* KING.

All. Treason ! treason !

King. O, yet defend me, friends ! I am but hurt.

Ham. Here, thou incestuous, murderous, damnèd Dane,
Drink off this potion !   Is thy union here?
Follow my mother !   [KING *dies.*[60]

Laer.   He is justly served ;
It is a poison temper'd by himself. —
Exchange forgiveness with me, noble Hamlet ;
Mine and my father's death come not upon thee,
Nor thine on me !   [*Dies.*[61]

Ham. Heaven make thee free of it !   I follow thee. —
I'm dead, Horatio. —Wretched Queen, adieu ! —
You that look pale and tremble at this chance,
That are but mutes or audience to this act,
Had I but time, — as this fell sergeant,[62] Death,
Is strict in his arrest, — O, I could tell you, —
But let it be. — Horatio, I am dead ;
Thou livest : report me and my cause aright
To the unsatisfied.

Hora.   Never believe it :
I am more an antique Roman than a Dane :
Here's yet some liquor left.

Ham.   As thou'rt a man,
Give me the cup : let go ; by Heaven, I'll have't.

---

[60] Of course the King dies of the wound, — dies without drinking the
poison. Hamlet, instantly seeing the way clear for the avenging stroke,
and having a free thrust at Claudius, can hardly be supposed to leave any
thing for poison to do.

[61] Laertes also dies of the *wound*, not of the *venom*.

[62] *Sergeant* was the title of a sheriff's officer, whose business it was to
make arrests and execute warrants.

O God, Horatio ! what a wounded name,
Things standing thus unknown, shall live behind me !
If thou didst ever hold me in thy heart,
Absent thee from felicity awhile,
And in this harsh world draw thy breath in pain,
To tell my story. —   [*March afar off, and shot within.*
                    What warlike noise is this?

   Osric. Young Fortinbras, with conquest come from Po-
          land,
To the ambassadors of England gives
This warlike volley.

   Ham.   O, I die, Horatio ;
The potent poison quite o'er-crows [63] my spirit :
I cannot live to hear the news from England ;
But I do prophesy th' election lights
On Fortinbras : he has my dying voice ;
So tell him, with th' occurrents, more and less,
Which have solicited [64] —   [*Dies.*

   Hora.   The rest is silence :
Now cracks a noble heart. — Good night, sweet Prince ;
And flights of angels sing thee to thy rest ! —
Why does the drum come hither.   [*March within.*

   Enter FORTINBRAS, *the* English Ambassadors, *and others.*

   Fortin. Where is this sight?

   Hora.   What is it ye would see?
If aught of woe or wonder, cease your search.

---

   [63] To *overcrow* is to *overcome*, to *subdue*. The word was borrowed from
the cock-pit ; the victorious cock crowing in triumph over the vanquished.
   [64] *Occurrents* was much used in the Poet's time for *events* or *occurrences.*
— *Solicited* is *prompted* or *excited;* as "this supernatural *soliciting*" in
Macbeth. — "*More* and *less*" is *greater* and *smaller;* a common usage with
the old writers.

Fortin. This quarry cries on havoc.[65] — O proud Death,
What feast is toward [66] in thine eternal cell,
That thou so many princes at a shot
So bloodily hast struck?

   1 Ambas.   The sight is dismal;
And our affairs from England come too late:
The ears are senseless that should give us hearing,
To tell him his commandment is fulfill'd;
That Rosencrantz and Guildenstern are dead.
Where should we have our thanks?

   Hora.   Not from his mouth,
Had it th' ability of life to thank you;
He never gave commandment for their death.
But since, so jump [67] upon this bloody question,
You from the Polack wars, and you from England,
Are here arrived, give order that these bodies
High on a stage be placed to the view;
And let me speak to th' [68] yet unknowing world
How these things came about: so shall you hear
Of carnal,[69] bloody, and unnatural acts;
Of accidental judgments, casual slaughters;
Of deaths put on by cunning and forced cause; [70]

---

   65 *Quarry*, a term of the chase, was used for a *heap of dead game*. To *cry on*, as before noted, is to *exclaim*, or *cry out, against. Havoc* here means *indiscriminate slaughter.* To shout *havoc!* in a battle, was a signal for giving no quarter to the enemy. So that the meaning in the text is, " This pile of corpses cries out against indiscriminate slaughter."

   66 *Toward*, again, for *forthcoming*, or *at hand.* See page 50, note 19.

   67 As before noted, *jump* was used for *just* or *exactly.*

   68 The Poet often thus elides *the*, so as to make it coalesce with the preceding word into one syllable. So he has *for th'*, *by th'*, *from th'*, *on th'*, &c.

   69 *Carnal*, here, probably means *sanguinary, cruel*, or *inhuman;* referring to the murder of Hamlet's father.

   70 The phrase *put on* here means *instigated* or *set on foot. Cunning*, re-

And, in this upshot, purposes mistook
Fall'n on th' inventors' heads : all this can I
Truly deliver.

    Fortin.   Let us haste to hear it,
And call the noblest to the audience.
For me, with sorrow I embrace my fortune :
I have some rights of memory [71] in this kingdom,
Which now to claim my vantage doth invite me.

    Hora. Of that I shall have also cause to speak,
And from his mouth whose voice will draw on more : [72]
But let this same be presently perform'd,
Even while men's minds are wild, lest more mischance,
On plots and errors, happen.

    Fortin.   Let four captains
Bear Hamlet, like a soldier, to the stage ;
For he was likely, had he been put on,
T' have proved most royally : and, for his passage,
The soldiers' music and the rites of war
Speak loudly for him. —
Take up the bodies. — Such a sight as this
Becomes the field, but here shows much amiss. —
Go, bid the soldiers shoot.

    [*A dead march. Exeunt, bearing off the dead bodies,
              after which a peal of ordnance is shot off.*

---

ers, apparently, to Hamlet's action touching " the packet," and *forced cause*,
to the " compelling occasion," which moved him to that piece of practice.

    [71] *Rights of memory* appears to mean rights founded in prescription or
the order of inheritance.

    [72] Whose vote will induce others to vote the same way. Horatio refers
to Hamlet saying of Fortinbras, " he has my dying voice."

CRITICAL NOTES ON HAMLET.

Page 51.   " As, by the same *co-mart*,
        And carriage of the article *design'd*,
        His fell to Hamlet."

In the first of these lines, the folio has *cov'nant* instead of *co-mart*, which is the reading of the quartos. Shakespeare elsewhere uses to *mart* for to *trade* or to *bargain*. — In the second line, I give the reading of the second folio; the earlier editions having, with various spelling, *designe* instead of *design'd*. The confounding of final *d* and final *e* is among the commonest of misprints.

P. 52. " The graves stood tenantless, and the sheeted dead
        Did squeak and gibber in the Roman streets :
        So, stars with trains of fire ; and dews of blo d ;
        Disasters in the Sun ; and the moist star," &c.

This passage is not in the folio. The quartos have no point after *streets*, and they have " *As* starres with trains of fire," &c. The passage has troubled the commentators vastly, and a great many changes have been proposed, all quite unsatisfactory. Dyce pronounces i . hope lessly mutilated," and I once thought so too. But it rather seems to me now that a just and fitting sense may be got by merely changing *As* to *So*. See foot-note 33.

P. 52. " Unto our *climature* and countrymen."

So Dyce. The quartos have *climatures*. Not in the folio.

ACT I., SCENE II.

P 56. " Yet so far hath discretion fought with nature,
       That we with *wiser* sorrow think on him," &c.

The old copies have *wisest* instead of *wiser*, which I think the con
text fairly requires.

P. 60. " Together with all forms, *modes*, shows of grief," &c.

The old copies have *moodes* and *moods*, which appear to be only old
ways of spelling *modes*. At all events, *moods*, in its present meaning,
does not suit the context, as Hamlet here refers entirely to the outward
marks of sadness.

P. 61. " You are the most immediate to our throne ;
       And with *no less nobility* of love
       Than that which dearest father bears his son
       Do I impart toward you."

Dr. Badham would read " And with *nobility no less* of love," &c.
This would give a definite object to *impart*, which now has no object
expressed. So that the change is at least plausible. On the other
hand, with this reading, *nobility* would have to be understood as meaning the honour of being heir-presumptive. But it may well be doubted
whether Shakespeare would have used *nobility* with this meaning ; and
nobility, in the proper sense of the term, Hamlet has already by birth.
If we could read " With *this* nobility no less of love," &c., the sense
would come right, but that would perhaps be an unwarrantable .hange
See foot-note 24.

P. 64. " I would not *hear* your enemy say so."

So the quartos after that of 1603. Instead of *hear*, the folio has
have, which some editors prefer. But surely *hear* accords much better
with what follows.

P. 65. ' Season your admiration for a while
       With an *attentive* ear, till I deliver," &c.

The second and third quartos, and the folio, have " an *atient* eare ";
the first, fourth, and fifth quartos have *attentive*. All the old copies
read " till I *may* deliver." Pope omits *may*.

P. 65. "In the dead *vast* and middle of the night."

So the first quarto, and the fifth. The other quartos and the folio have *wast* and *waste* instead of *vast*.

P. 65.
"Whilst they, *distill'd*
Almost to jelly with the act of fear," &c.

So the quartos. Instead of *distill'd*, the folio has *bestil'd*, which Collier's second folio alters to *bechill'd*. In support of *distill'd*, Dyce aptly quotes from Sylvester's *Du Bartas*, 1641: "Melt thee, *distill* thee, turne to wax or snow." See foot-note 42.

P. 66. "But answer made it none ; yet once methought
It lifted up *its* head," &c.

The old copies have "lifted up *it* head." So, again, in v. i, of this play: "The corse they follow did with desperate hand fordo *it* own life." The Poet has as many as fourteen other instances of *it* thus used possessively; which is at least curious, as showing his reluctance to admit *its*, which was then just creeping into use. Some insist on keeping strictly to the old letter in all such cases ; but this, it seems to me, is conservatism in *it* dotage.

P. 67. "Let it be *tenable* in your silence still."

So the quartos. The folio has *treble* instead of *tenable*.

ACT I., SCENE III.

P. 69.
"For on his choice depends
The safety and *the* health of the whole State."

The quartos read "The safety and health" ; the folio, "The *sanctity* and health." Probably, as Malone thought, *safety* was altered to *sanctity* merely because a trisyllable was wanted to complete the verse; the editor not perceiving that the article had dropped out before *health.* Hanmer reads, "The *sanity* and health." The reading in the text is Warburton's.

P. 69. "As he in his *particular act* and *place*
May give his saying deed."

So the quartos. The folio reads " in his *peculiar Sect* and *force.*"

P. 70.   " *Th' unchariest* maid is prodigal enough,
          If she unmask her beauty to the Moon."

The old copies read " *The chariest* maid." This gives a very weak
sense, and one, it seems to me, not at all suited to the occasion or the
character. "The *chary* maid" would be far better ; but Laertes is apt
to be superlative in thought and speech; and surely nothing less than
unchariest would be intense enough for him here.

P. 71.   " And they in France of the best rank and station
          Are most select and generous, chief in that."

The first quarto reads " Are *of a* most select and *generall* chiefe in
that." The other quartos have " Are of a most select and *generous*,
chiefe in that "; the folio, " generous *cheff* in that." A great variety
of changes has been made or proposed. The reading in the text is
Rowe's, and is adopted by many of the best editors.

P. 73.   " Or — not to crack the wind of the poor phrase,
          Running it thus — you'll tender me a fool."

Instead of *Running*, the quartos have *Wrong*, and the folio *Roam-
ing*. *Running* was conjectured by both Dyce and Collier independ-
ently, and is also the reading of Collier's second folio.

P. 74.   " For they are brokers, —
          Not of *that dye* which their investments show,
          But mere implorators of unholy suits,
          Breathing like sanctified and pious *bawds*,
          The better to beguile."

In the second of these lines, the quartos, after 1603, have "Not of
that die"; the folio, "Not of *the eye*." Some editors have strongly
insisted on *eye;* whereupon Dyce asks, — "though our early writers
talk of ' an *eye of green*,' ' an *eye of red*,' ' an *eye of blue*,' &c., do they
ever use *eye* by itself to denote colour ? " — In the fourth line, again,
the old copies have *bonds* instead of *bawds*, which is the reading of
Theobald, Pope, and Collier's second folio. The context, and especially
the word *brokers*, is decisive that a noun signifying persons, and not
things, is required. *Broker* was often used as a synonym of *bawd*, and
so it is here.

ACT I., SCENE IV.

P. 77. " By *the* o'ergrowth of some complexion."

All this speech, after " More honour'd in the breach than the observance," is wanting in the quarto of 1603 and the folio. The other quartos have " By *their* ore-grow'th " ; an error which the context readily corrects.

P. 77. " *Their* virtues else — be they as pure as grace,

As infinite as man may undergo —

Shall in the general censure take corruption

From that particular fault ; the dram of *leav'n*

Doth all the noble substance of *'em sour*,

To his own scandal."

Not in the first quarto or the folio. In the first of these lines, the other quartos have *His* instead of *Their ;* another error which the context readily corrects. In the fourth and fifth lines, the quartos of 1604 and 1605 read " the dram of *eale* Doth all the noble substance of *a doubt*." The later quartos have the same, except that they substitute *ease* for *eale*. This dreadful passage may, I think, be fairly said to have baffled all the editors and commentators. The Cambridge edition notes upwards of forty different readings which have been printed or proposed, all of them so unsatisfactory that the editors reject them, and give the old text, apparently regarding the corruption as hopeless. There is surely no possibility of making any sense out of it as it stands; and so far, I believe, all are agreed. Lettsom, I think, was the first to perceive the reference to St. Paul's proverbial saying : " Shakespeare's meaning," says he, " evidently is, that a little leaven leavens the whole lump " ; and the same thought occurred to me before I lighted on his remark. This clew was not long in guiding me to the two other changes I have made : in fact, the present reading was suggested to me by the passage from Bacon quoted in foot-note 11, which see. It gives *a* sense, I hope a natural and fitting one. And the language is in just accordance with what Hamlet says a little before, — " that too much o'er-*leavens* the form of plausive manners." Nor was *leaven*, especially if written in the shortened form *lev'n*, unlikely to be corrupted into

eale : at all events, we have many undoubted misprints much more emphatic than that. I was at one time minded to substitute *yeast* for *eale* ;
but I doubt whether *yeast* was ever used for *leaven* in Shakespeare's
time : certainly he does not use it so anywhere else.

P. 81. "And each particular hair to stand *on* end."

So the first quarto. The other old copies have " stand *an* end."

P. 81. " List, list, O list ! "

So the quartos, after 1603. The folio reads " List *Hamlet,* oh list."

P. 82. "That *roots* itself in ease on Lethe wharf."

So the quartos. The folio has *rots* instead of *roots.*

P. 82. "With witchcraft of his *wit,* with traitorous gifts," &c.

The old copies have *wits* instead of *wit.* Corrected by Pope.

P. 84. "Cut off even in the *blossom* of my *sins.*"

The old copies read " the *Blossomes* of my *sinne.*" Dyce conjectured *blossom :* the reading in the text is Mr. P. A. Daniel's. The mis-
printing of plurals and singulars for each other occurs very often.

P. 84. "With all my imperfections on my head.
         Ham. O, horrible ! O, horrible ! most horrible !
         Ghost. If thou hast nature in thee, bear it not ; " &c.

The old copies, except the first quarto, give nothing to Hamlet
here, but print all three of these lines as spoken by the Ghost. The
first quarto makes Hamlet exclaim "O God ! " It was suggested to
Johnson, by " a very learned lady," that the second line should be given
to Hamlet ; and Garrick is said to have adopted that arrangement on
the stage. Rann first printed as in the text. And surely so it ought
to be.

P. 85. "And shall I couple Hell? O, fie ! — Hold, *hold,*
         my heart ; " &c.

So the second and third quartos. The fourth and fifth quartos and
the folio omit the second *hold.*

P. 89.　"There are more things in Heaven and Earth,
Horatio,
Than are dreamt of in *your* philosophy."

So all the quartos. The folio has *our* instead of *your*. The latter
has at least as good authority, and is, I think, the better reading of the
two, inasmuch as it conveys a mild sneer, which is well in keeping
with Hamlet's temper and cast of mind. Of course the stress is on
philosophy, not on *your*.

ACT II., SCENE I.

P. 91.　　　　　　　　　　　　"And finding,
By this encompassment and drift of question,
That they do know my son, come you more nearer
Than your particular demands will touch it."

There is some doubt whether, in the last of these lines, we ought to
print *Than* or *Then*. The old copies have *Then ;* but this determines
nothing, as that form was continually used in both senses. It seemed
to me very clear, at one time, that we ought to read "come you more
nearer ; *Then* your particular demands," &c.; on the ground that particular inquiries would come to the point faster than general ones. If
this notion be wrong, as it probably is, I am indebted to Mr. H. H.
Furness for having set me right. See foot-note 3.

P. 91.　"You must not put another scandal on him
Than he is open to incontinency."

The old copies have *That* instead of *Than*. This is nowise recon-
cilable with the context, and involves a contradiction too palpable,
surely, to be put into the mouth of Polonius. Yet "another scandal
than he is open," &c., sounds rather harsh : perhaps we should read
"Than *that* he's open," &c. And it appears that, where two consecu-
tive words begin with the same letters, as *than* and *that*, one of them
is apt to drop out in the printing or transcribing. The reading in the
text is Keightley's.

P. 94. " He falls to such perusal of my face
        As he would draw it. Long *time* stay'd he so."

So Pope. The old copies are without *time,* thus untuning the rhythm.

ACT II., SCENE II.

P. 102. " You know, sometimes he walks *for* hours together
        Here in the lobby."

So Hanmer and Collier's second folio. The old copies read " walkes *foure* houres together."

P. 104. " For if the Sun breed maggots in a dead dog, being
        a *good* kissing carrion," &c.

So all the old copies, and rightly, I have no doubt. Warburton substituted *god* for *good,* and the change was most extravagantly praised by Johnson. I not only believe the old text to be right, but can get no fitting sense out of the modern reading. The latter, however, has been adopted by nearly all the leading editors: even the Cambridge editors adopt it. I understand the meaning of the old text to be, " a dead dog, which is a good carrion for the Sun to kiss, and thus impregnate with new life." " A good kissing person " for a person good to kiss, or good for kissing, is a very common form of speech, and one often used by Shakespeare. See foot-note 27.

P. 107. " And sure, dear friends, my thanks are too dear at
        a halfpenny."

So Hanmer. The old copies read " too deare a halfpenny."

P. 108. " What a piece of work is man ! "

So the quarto of 1637. The earlier quartos have the *a* misplaced: " What peece of worke is *a* man." The folios have the *a* in both places : " What a piece of work is *a* man ! "

P. 109. " The clown shall make those laugh whose lungs
        are *tickle* o' the sear."

This is not in the quartos, and the folio has *tickled* instead of *tickle.* The correction (and it is of the first class) was proposed by Staunton.

P. 110. "I think their *innovation* comes by the means of the late *inhibition*."

In the old text, *innovation* and *inhibition* change places with each other. Johnson notes upon the passage as follows: "Hamlet inquires not about an 'inhibition,' but an 'innovation': the answer probably was, — 'I think their innovation,' that is, their new practice of strolling, 'comes by means of the late inhibition.'" See foot-note 47.

P. 111. "These are now the fashion; and so *berattle* the common stages," &c.

So the second folio. The first has *be-ratted* instead of *berattle.* — Of this and the six following speeches there are no traces in any of the quartos, except the first, and but slight traces there.

P. 111. "If they should grow themselves to common players, — as it is *most like*," &c.

The folio reads "as it is *like most.*" See preceding note.

P. 114. "O Jephtha, what a treasure hadst thou !
Polo. What treasure had he, my lord?"

So Walker. The old copies read "What *a* treasure had he." Probably the *a* got repeated accidentally from the line above. Walker says, "*What treasure*, surely, for grammar's sake."

P. 115. "For look where my *abridgements come.*"

So the folio. The quartos, "my *abridgement comes.*'

P. 115. "You are welcome, masters; welcome, all. I am glad to see *ye* well; welcome, good friends."

The old copies read "I am glad to see *thee* well." An error which the context rectifies.

P. 117. "Nor no matter in the phrase that might indict the author of *affectation*."

So the folio. Instead of *affectation*, the quartos have *affection*, which was sometimes used for *affectation*.

P. 123. "That I, the son of a dear *father* murder'd," &c.

So the fourth, fifth, and sixth quartos. The other quartos and the
folio omit *father*.

ACT III.; SCENE I.

P. 125.   "*Most free* of question, but of our demands
             Niggard in his reply."

The old text has *Most free* and *Niggard* transposed; which nowise
accords with the course of the dialogue referred to, nor with the first
speech of Guildenstern in this scene. The correction is Warburton's,
who notes upon the old reading thus: "This is given as the description
of the conversation of a man whom the speaker *found not forward
to be sounded;* and who *kept aloof* when they would *bring him to confession.* Shakespeare certainly wrote it just the other way." It has
been suggested that perhaps "a correct account of the interview" was
not intended. But I can see no reason why Rosencrantz should wish
to misrepresent it. See foot-note 2.

P. 126.   "And, for your part, Ophelia, I do wish
             That your good *beauty* be the happy cause," &c.

So Walker. Instead of *beauty*, the old copies have *Beauties;* an
easy misprint when the word was written *beautie*.

P. 127.   "The *slings* and arrows of outrageous fortune."

Walker says that "*stings* is undoubtedly the true reading." Perhaps
he is right; but *slings* and arrows were often spoken of together in the
language of ancient warfare. And the line, as it stands, is so much a
household word, that it seems hardly well to make any change.

P. 127.   "The pangs of *disprized* love, the law's delay," &c.

So the folio. The quartos have *despiz'd* instead of *disprized*. The
folio reading is the stronger; for if a love *unprized* be hard to bear, a
love *scorned* must be much harder.

P. 128.   "When he himself might his quietus make
             With a bare bodkin? *who'd these* fardels bear," &c.

The quartos read "who *would fardels* beare"; the folio, "who *would these* fardles beare." The contraction of *who would* to *who'd* is Walker's. I prefer the folio reading, because it makes what follows more continuous with what precedes; and it seems more natural that Hamlet should still keep his mind on the crosses already mentioned.

P. 129. "My honour'd lord, *I* know right well you did."

So the folio. The quartos have "*you* know." The folio reading has, I think, more delicacy, and at least equal feeling.

P. 130. "With more offences at my *beck* than I have thoughts to put them in," &c.

Collier's second folio changes *beck* to *back*, and Walker would make the same change.

P. 131. "The courtier's, *scholar's*, *soldier's*, eye, tongue, sword."

Such is the order of the words in the first quarto. The other old copies transpose *scholar's* and *soldier's*. This naturally connects *tongue* with *soldier*, and *sword* with *scholar;* which is certainly not the meaning.

ACT III., SCENE II.

P. 134. "Now, this overdone, or come tardy *of*, though it make the unskilful laugh," &c.

So the sixth quarto. The other old copies read "*tardy off*." Mason conjectured "*tardy of*"; and Walker proposed the same. See footnote 5.

P. 134. "Nor the gait of Christian, Pagan, nor *Turk*."

So the first quarto. Instead of *Turk*, the other quartos have *man*, and the folio *Norman*.

P. 134. "That I have thought some of Nature's journeymen had made *them*, and not made them well," &c.

The old copies read "had made *men*." Theobald conjectured *them*, and so Rann printed. Farmer proposed *the men*, which may be bet ter, but gives the same sense. Surely, at all events, *men* cannot be right; for that must mean *all* men, or men *in general;* whereas the context fairly requires the meaning to be limited to *the* men that "imi-tated humanity so abominably."

P. 138. "Nay, then let the Devil wear black, for I'll have a suit of *sabell*."

The old copies read "a suite of *Sables*." As sable is itself a mourn-ing colour, the oppugnancy of the two clauses is evident. Warburton saw the discrepancy, and changed *for* to *'fore*. This makes the mean-ing to be, "let the Devil put on mourning before I will." The reading in the text was proposed by a writer in *The Critic*, 1854, page 317. It seems to me to give just the sense wanted. See foot-note 16.

P. 143. "Gonzago is the *King's* name."

Here, instead of *King*, the old copies have *Duke*. But in the stage-directions for the dumb-show the same person is repeatedly called *King*, as he also is a little after: "This is one Lucianus, nephew to the *King*." Probably the error crept in somehow from the first quarto, where the King and Queen of the interlude are called *Duke* and *Duchess*.

P. 148. "*Rosen.* My lord, you once did love me.
       Ham. So *I* do still, by these pickers and stealers."

So the folio. The quartos have "*And* do still." I think the former gives a characteristic shade of meaning which is lost in the latter. See foot-note 51.

P. 150. "And do such *bitter business* as the day
          Would quake to look on."

So the folio. The quartos read "such business as the *bitter day*."

ACT III., SCENE IV.

P. 156.   " I'll *sconce* me even here.
                    Pray you be round with him."

So Hanmer and Collier's second folio. The old copies, after 1603, have *silence* instead of *sconce*. The corresponding passage of the first quarto reads " I'll *shrowde* myselfe behinde the Arras." In *The Merry Wives*, iii., 3, Falstaff says, " I will *ensconce* me behind the arras."

P. 156. *Queen.* " Why, how now, Hamlet ! what's the matter now ?
                    Have you forgot me ? "

The old copies print these clauses as so many distinct speeches, assigning the second, " what's the matter now ? " to Hamlet. Walker says " Perhaps all this belongs to the Queen "; whereupon Dyce notes, " I do not think so." Nevertheless I am satisfied that Walker's conjecture is right.

P. 162. " Your bedded *hairs*, like life in excrements,
                    Start up and *stand* on end."

The second and third quartos and the folio have " *start* up and *stand* "; the later quartos, " *starts* up and *stands* "; while all the old copies, except the first, where the passage is not found, have *haire*, instead of *hairs*, which is Rowe's reading.

P. 162. " Lest with this piteous action you convert
                    My stern *affects*."

Instead of *affects*, the old copies have *effects*. The correction is Singer's ; who justly observes that " the ' piteous action ' of the Ghost could not alter things *effected*, but might move Hamlet to a less stern mood of mind." The same error occurs elsewhere.

P. 164. " That monster, custom, who all sense doth eat
                    Of habits *evil*, is angel yet in this," &c.

So Thirlby proposed, and Theobald printed. The quartos have

devill instead of *evil*. The passage is not in the folio. With *devil*, the text seems to me quite insusceptible of any fair or fitting explanation; and the hard shifts that have been resorted to for the purpose of making sense out of it, are to me strong argument of corruption. See foot-note 28.

P. 165.   " For use almost can change the stamp of nature,
                And either *shame* the Devil or throw him out
                With wondrous potency."

Not in the folio. The second and third quartos read "And *either* the devil"; the later quartos, "And *master* the devil"; thus leaving both sense and metre defective. Some editors combine the two readings,—"And *either master* the devil"; but this, again, makes the line unmetrical. Pope and Capell read "And master *even* the devil"; Malone, "And either *curb* the devil." But the Poet seems to have intended the alternative sense of either making the Devil glad to leave or compelling him to leave. And the phrase, "*shame* the Devil," was part of an old proverb, which Shakespeare quotes elsewhere. So in *1 Henry IV.*, iii., 1 : —

> "And I can teach thee, coz, to shame the Devil
> By telling truth; tell truth, and shame the Devil:
> If thou have power to raise him, bring him hither,
> And I'll be sworn I've power to shame him hence."

ACT III., SCENE V.

P. 167.   Scene V. — *Another Room in the Castle.*

Modern editions, generally, make the fourth Act begin here. None of the old copies have any marking of the Acts and Scenes, after the second Scene of the second Act ; and it seems very clear that there is no sufficient interval or pause in the action to warrant the beginning of a new Act in this place. I therefore agree with Caldecott and Elze that Act IV., ought to begin with the fourth Scene after.

P. 168. "O'er whom his very madness, like *fine* ore
        Among a mineral of metals base," &c.

So Walker. The old text has *some* instead of *fine*. As *some* would naturally be written with the long *s*, such a misprint might easily occur.

P. 168. "But we will ship him hence; and this *vile* deed
        We must, with all our majesty and skill,
        Both countenance and excuse."

The quartos have "this *vile* deed," the folio, "this *vilde* deed." I strongly suspect it ought to be "this *wild* deed"; that is, *mad* or *crazy*. The epithet *wild* just suits the case: and, as the King knows that the Queen fully believes Hamlet to be mad, is it likely that in speaking to her of the act he would use the epithet *vile?* And the King himself says, a little after, "Hamlet *in madness* hath Polonius slain." The two words *vilde* and *wilde* were often confounded.

P. 169. "And let them know both what we mean to do
        And what's untimely done: *so, haply, slander* —
        Whose whisper o'er the world's diameter," &c.

So Capell. The words *so, haply, slander* are wanting in all the old copies. This leaves the sentence without any subject; and some insertion is imperatively required. Theobald reads "*for*, haply, slander." Malone reads "So viperous slander," as the Poet has, in *Cymbeline* iii., 4, "the secrets of the grave this *viperous slander* enters." But in the present passage the sense of *viperous* is given in "*poison'd* shot."

ACT III., SCENE VI.

P. 170. "He keeps them, *as an ape doth nuts* in the corner of his jaw."

The words *as an ape doth nuts* are from the corresponding passage of the first quarto. The other quartos read "he keepes them like an apple in the corner," &c.; the folio, "He keepes them like an Ape in the corner."

ACT III., SCENE VII.

P. 174.   " And thou must cure me : till I know 'tis done,
              Howe'er my haps, my joys *were* ne'er *begun*."

So the folio.   The quartos read " my joyes *will* nere *begin*."   The
change was doubtless made in the folio in order to have the scene end
with a rhyme.   But is the rhyme worth the breach of grammar which
it costs?   I should certainly read with the quartos, but that Walker,
Dyce, the Cambridge editors, Singer, Staunton, and White all prefer
the folio reading.

ACT IV., SCENE I.

P. 175.   " Truly to speak, *sir*, and with no addition,
              We go to gain a little patch of ground," &c.

So Capell.   The old copies lack *sir* in the first line.   Pope reads
" Truly to speak *it*," &c.

ACT IV., SCENE II.

P. 178.   " 'Twere good she were spoken with ; for she may
              strew
              Dangerous conjectures in ill-breeding minds.
          Queen. Let her come in."

The quartos assign all this to Horatio ; the folio gives it all to the
Queen.   The first two lines clearly ought not to be spoken by the
Queen ; and there can be little doubt that, as Hanmer judged, her
speech ought to begin with " Let her come in " ; which of course marks
her final yielding to Horatio's urgent request.

P. 179.   " *Which bewept to the grave did go*
              With true-love showers."

So Pope, and most editors since.   The old copies all read " to the
grave did *not* go" ; which is manifestly against all reason both of
metre and of sense.

P. 182. "Even here, between the chaste unsmirchèd *brows*
      Of my true mother."

Instead of *brows*, the old copies have *browe* and *brow*.

P. 184. "It shall as level to your judgment *pierce*
      As day does to your eye."

So the folio. Instead of *pierce*, the quartos have *peare*, which Dyce
strangely prefers, printing it *'pear*.

P. 185. "Hadst thou thy wits, and didst persuade revenge,
      It could not move *me* thus."

So Walker. The old copies are without *me*.

P. 186. "*No, no, he is dead,*
    Gone to his death-bed;
    He never will come again."

So Collier's second folio. The old copies have "*go* to *thy* Death-
bed." The correction is well approved by a similar passage in *East-
ward Ho*, written by Jonson, Marston, and Chapman : —

      "But now he is dead, *and lain in his bed,*
      And never will come again."

ACT IV., SCENE IV.

P. 192. "Will you be ruled by me?
   Laer.   I *will*, my lord,
  So you will not o'errule me to a peace."

So Capell. Not in the folio. The quartos, except the first, read "I
my lord." *I* was commonly printed for the affirmative *ay*, as well as
for the pronoun ; and so modern editors generally print *Ay*. But this
leaves an ugly gap in the metre. The probability is, that *will* dropt
out in the printing or the transcribing.

P. 193. "Upon my life, *Lamond*."

So Pope The quartos have *Lamord;* the folio, *Lamound.*

P. 194.   " Sir, this report of his
              Did Hamlet so envenom with *your* envy," &c.

The old copies read " with *his* envy "; *his* having probably slipped
in by mistake from the line above.   At all events, as Walker observes,
the old text can hardly have any meaning but that " Hamlet did envenom this report"; which I cannot easily believe to have been the Poet's
thought.   Of course, with *your*, the meaning is, " this report did so envenom Hamlet with envy *of you*."   See foot-note 21.

P. 195.   "And then this *should* is like a *spendthrift* sigh,
              That hurts by easing."

So the quarto of 1637.   The earlier quartos have "a *spend-thrifts*
sigh."   The passage is not in the folio.

P. 197.   "How *now*, sweet Queen ! "

So the second folio.   The first omits *now;* accidentally, no doubt.
The quartos, after 1603, have " but stay, what noyse."

P. 198.   "I have a speech of fire, that fain would blaze,
              But that this folly *drowns* it."

So the quartos.   Instead of *drowns*, the folio has **doubts**, which
Knight changes to *douts*.

ACT V., SCENE I.

P. 206.   "I have been sexton here, man and boy, *thirty*
              years."

"This skull has lain in the earth *three*-and-*twenty* years."

These statements, taken together with a preceding speech, infer
Hamlet's age to be thirty years ; which cannot well be reconciled with
what Laertes and Polonius say of him in i., 3.   Mr. Halliwell substi-
tutes *dozen* for *three-and-twenty*, and quotes from the first quarto,
" Here's a skull hath bin here this dozen yeare."   But, as Mr. Furness
observes, it is by no means certain that the Clown refers to the same
skull there as here : he may have just turned up another.   I cannot
help suspecting that the Poet wrote " 20 yeares," and " 3 & 10 yeares,"

and that the 2 and 1 got corrupted into 3 and 2. It would be not unlike the Clown's manner, to put *three-and-ten* for *thirteen*. This, of
course, would make Hamlet twenty years old; which is just about the
age wanted.

P. 206. "This same skull, sir, was Yorick's skull, the King's
jester."

So the quartos, except that they have "*sir* Yorick's," *sir* being
doubtless repeated by mistake. The folio reads "This same Scull Sir,
this same Scull sir, was Yoricks Scull." What should be the use or
sense of this repetition, does not appear.

P. 208. "Yet here she is allow'd her virgin *crants*,
Her maiden strewments," &c.

So the quartos. The folio has *rites* instead of *crants*.

P. 210. "Woo't drink up *Esill?* eat a crocodile?"

So read all the quartos except the first, which has *vessels*. The
folio has *Esile*, printed in Italic, as if to mark it as a proper name.
This would naturally infer that some stream or body of water was
meant. Theobald, and some others after him, read *eisel*, which is an
old word for *vinegar*. With that word, we must take *drink up* as
simply equivalent to *drink*: and would Hamlet in such a case be likely
to mention such a thing as drinking vinegar? Surely not much of a
feat to be coupled with eating a crocodile. So that I cannot reconcile
myself to the reading *eisel*. See foot-note 29.

ACT V., SCENE II.

P. 212. "Our indiscretion sometimes serves us well,
When our deep plots do *pall*."

So the second quarto. The other quartos have *fall* instead of *pall*.
The folio has *paule*, which is probably but another spelling of *pall*.
Pope substituted *fail*, and some editors have followed him. But what
need of change? See foot-note 4.

P. 213. " Being thus be-netted round with *villainies*," &c.

The old copies have *villaines*.   Corrected by Capell.

P. 214. " And stand a *cement* 'tween their amities."

Instead of *cement*, which is Hanmer's reading, the old copies have *comma*.   The image of peace standing as a comma between two persons, to hold them friends, goes rather hard.   In *Antony and Cleopatra*. iii., 2, Cæsar speaks to Antony of Octavia, as " the piece of virtue which is set betwixt us as the *cement* of our love, to keep it builded."

P. 216. " Does it not, *think'st thou*, stand me now upon?"

The quartos have *thinke thee;* the folio, *thinkst thee*.   Rowe corrected *thee* to *thou*.

P. 217. " For by the image of my cause I see
          The portraiture of his : I'll *court* his favours."

This is not in the quartos, and the folio has *count* instead of *court*. Corrected by Rowe.

P. 219. " To divide him inventorially would dizzy the arithmetic of memory, and yet but *yaw* neither," &c.

So the quarto of 1604.   The other quartos have *raw* instead of *yaw*. The context shows *yaw* to be right.   Dyce undertakes to help the sense by substituting *it* for *yet;* which, to my thinking, just defeats the sense.   Staunton proposes to substitute *wit;* which would have the same effect.   See foot-notes 28 and 29.—The speech is not in the folio; nor has the first quarto any traces of it.

P. 222. " A kind of yesty collection, which carries them through and through the most *fond and winnowed* opinions ;" &c.

So the folio.   The second and third quartos have " most *prophane* and *trennowed* opinions ;" the later quartos the same, except that they substitute *trennowned* for *trennowed*.   Warburton changed the folio reading to " most *fanned* and winnowed opinions," which several editors have adopted.   But surely *fond* gives a natural and fitting sense,—

affected or *conceited;* while the sense of *fanned* is fully expressed by *winnowed.* See foot-note 43.

P. 223. "The readiness is all : since no man knows aught of what he leaves, what is't to leave betimes?"

So Johnson. The quartos read "The readines is all, since no man of ought he leaves, knowes what ist to leave betimes, let be." The folio reads "The readinesse is all, since no man ha's aught of what he leaves. What is't to leave betimes?" Modern editors differ a good deal in their readings of the passage. The Cambridge editors print as follows : "The readiness is all ; since no man has aught of what he leaves, what is't to leave betimes? Let be."

P. 227. "He's *hot,* and scant of breath."

Instead of *hot,* the old text has *fat;* which seems decidedly out of place here, as a word is required signifying something peculiar to Hamlet in his present situation or at the present moment. The reading in the text was lately proposed by Plehwe, a German Shakespearian, who justly quotes in support of it from iv., 4 : "When in your motion you are *hot* and dry." It has also been proposed, by "Mr. H. Wyeth, of Winchester," to read *faint,* which is perhaps better in itself, but does not infer so easy a misprint. — For this reading and reference I am indebted, immediately, to Mr. Furness's variorum edition.

P. 230. "*Hora.*   The rest is silence :
Now cracks a noble heart. — Good night, sweet Prince."

The old editions print "The rest is silence" as the close of Hamlet's preceding speech. The words are evidently quite out of place there : it is simply incredible that the dying Prince should so spend his last breath. This has, apparently, been felt by some others ; but I am not aware that any one has made the change. I saw the need of it long ago.